HISTORIC
NEW LANARK

*The Dale and Owen Industrial Community
since 1785*

Ian Donnachie and George Hewitt

'This Delightful Colony'

EDINBURGH UNIVERSITY PRESS

For Claire and Agnes

© Ian Donnachie and George Hewitt, 1993

Edinburgh University Press Ltd
22 George Square, Edinburgh

Reprinted 1999

Transferred to digital print 2006

Typeset in Lasercomp Palatino
by Alden Multimedia Ltd.

Printed and bound in Great Britain by
CPI Antony Rowe, Eastbourne, East Sussex

A CIP record for this book is available from the British Library.

ISBN 10: 0 7486 0420 0
ISBN 13: 978 0 7486 0420 3

The Publisher acknowledges subsidy from the Scottish
Arts Council, and the authors from the Scouloudi
Foundation, Institute of Historical Research, towards the
publication of this volume.

All illustrations not otherwise acknowledged
have been provided by the authors.

CONTENTS

ACKNOWLEDGEMENTS

IN LINE WITH ROBERT OWEN'S THOUGHTS on the relationship between environment and character, it will come as little surprise that we have been much inspired in writing this history by New Lanark itself. We recall it – in one instance since childhood – as a working mill village full of life and activity, remember its sad decline and near demise, and salute its period of recent revitalisation. But if the place and its associations – personal and historical – exercised considerable influence, it is above all the people there and elsewhere who have helped to make this book possible.

First and foremost we acknowledge the initial enthusiasm and encouragement of the late Martin Spencer, formerly Secretary of Edinburgh University Press. He could see clearly what we wanted to do and helped to shape the book, both in terms of content and physical appearance. We share the sadness of his colleagues and associates that he did not live to read the end product. We are grateful to the staff of the Press for their subsequent support and help.

Although this is by no means an official history of New Lanark and the restoration of the mills and village, we have, nevertheless, benefited from the friendship and advice of many people associated with this bold initiative particularly that of the New Lanark Conservation Trust Director, Jim Arnold MBE, and their

Education Officer, Lorna Davidson. Likewise, many old friends in Lanark and the neighbourhood have been helpful and supportive, notably Bill and Linda Hazel.

While we have undertaken much original research we have also drawn on the works of other scholars, notably those of Professor J. F. C. Harrison, whose book on Robert Owen and the Owenite movement is unlikely to be matched for many a generation, and of the various contributors (including one of the present authors) to the two Owen bicentennial studies published in 1971. David McLaren's short study of Dale also provided some useful leads. Anne Taylor's study of Owen's role in the community movements at New Lanark and New Harmony presents a challenging 'new view' which we have found immensely stimulating.

Inevitably we owe an enormous debt of gratitude to libraries and archives with holdings relating to New Lanark. At Glasgow University, whose Archives and Business Records Centre holds the voluminous papers of the Gourock Ropework Company, Michael Moss, Alma Topen and Vanna Skelley provided vital assistance in unearthing relevant material. In what must be one of the most congenial and supportive atmospheres in which scholars could expect to find themselves, we are also very grateful to Jim Nixon for his cheery assistance during our researches.

We also had the benefit of examining archival material held by the British Library; the Library of the Co-operative Union Ltd, Manchester (where we are especially grateful to Gillian Lonergan); Edinburgh University Library; the Lindsay Institute, Lanark; the Mitchell Library, Glasgow; Motherwell District Library; the National Library of Scotland; the Scottish Record Office; the Signet Library of the Court of Session; the Robert Owen Memorial Museum, Newtown; and the National Library of Wales. Our thanks go to the staff for their assistance.

In the United States we were fortunate enough to have the opportunity of examining major holdings relating to Robert Owen and his family, which have helped piece together the story of New Lanark from a very different perspective. At the Workingmen's Institute and Library in New Harmony, Indiana, special thanks are due to Rosemary Allsop, Josephine M. Elliott and all the staff for their assistance. We have to thank the Trustees of the Institute for giving permission to carry out research and quote from papers in their care.

Elsewhere in the United States kind assistance and hospitality was provided by Gina R. Walker, Archivist, Special Collections Department in the Library of the University of Southern Indiana, and Professor Donald E. Pitzer of the Department of History, who has made a detailed study of New Harmony and other communal societies in North America. The impressive archival holdings of the Indiana Division of the Indiana State Library proved another invaluable source of information and we are particularly grateful to Pamela Wasmer for her assistance. The Indiana Historical Society kindly permitted access to their holdings on Owen and Owenism. Various departments in the Library of Congress, Washington DC helped to access their voluminous holdings of material relating to Owen and New Harmony. In Washington Ian Ferguson and his wife, Caroline, provided both friendly guidance and generous hospitality.

Michael Fry has taken his usual genial interest in our project and kindly pointed out some useful references in the Melville Castle Muniments at the Scottish Record Office, which would otherwise have eluded us. Dr Christopher Whatley of the University of Dundee played a similar role and was good enough to give us an early newspaper account of New Lanark. Anthony Cooke, also of Dundee, helped us by supplying information from his own researches about Arkwright's activities in Scotland and his relationship with Dale. John Macgregor generously provided us with information about the history of transport developments in the locality. Likewise, Ron Oliver kindly supplied several useful references to New Lanark and the Falls of Clyde.

We have had considerable help with illustrations from Jean Fraser and Professor John Butt of the University of Strathclyde. John Hume of Historic Scotland, Innes Macleod of the University of Glasgow, R. J. Malden of Renfrew District Council Museums Service, the *Carluke and Lanark Gazette*, *The Scotsman*, the National Monuments Record of Scotland, the New Lanark Conservation Trust, the Fine Art Society, the National Library of Scotland and the Business Archives Centre, University Archives, University of Glasgow.

The Faculty of Arts at The Open University provided a research grant to visit archives and libraries in the United States, including that at New Harmony in Indiana. The opportunity to undertake research there, as well as develop archive-linkages with material in Britain, has, we believe, given us a fresh perspective on Owen and his work at New Lanark.

Anne Grieve of The Open University in Scotland very kindly keyed in some of our text and offered genial assistance recasting much of the book prior to publication. We are enormously grateful for her efforts on our behalf.

The publication of this history of New Lanark is assisted by the Scouloudi Foundation and both the authors and Publisher express their gratitude to the trustees of that body and to the Institute of Historical Research, University of London, for their generosity in making a grant in aid of publication.

Authorship is always a precarious and demanding business which has inevitably conflicted with domestic commitments. We are thankful for the the support of Claire and Agnes, who have lived with the project longer than either would have wished.

Ian Donnachie and George Hewitt

FOREWORD

Deserted villages have a fascination. On Easter Sunday 1974 I was in the Square at New Lanark. The village shopkeeper was sitting outside in the sunshine. She and I shared an otherwise empty village. It was idyllic, even in decay.

Much has changed, and still the village remains intact and visually stunning. With restoration and development there is now a remote car park for hundreds of vehicles. Easter Sundays are thronged with people. The buildings are vibrant with domestic and commercial occupation. Robert Owen, ever the publicist, would have been delighted to welcome so many visitors.

Later in 1974 I was employed as Village Manager by a new Trust set up to revivify New Lanark. I was acutely aware that I was following in an historic tradition. For both David Dale and Robert Owen, New Lanark was a village of dreams. This exciting new book, by Ian Donnachie and George Hewitt, records visions and achievements. By examining what was done, perhaps we shall be able to learn a little more of ourselves and our own potentialities.

New Lanark has had to find a new role for the 21st century. It operated as a cotton manufacturing village until 1968, when the closure of the mills created a crisis of survival. Such a situation had been developing since the 1950s. In the 25 years since the closure there has developed a restoration project dependent on pragmatic responses to particular challenges. In its multi-various form, the collective state in which we live has been persuaded to intervene to save the village. While the future can never be anything other than precarious, current success does allow us all the opportunity to be introduced to the dreams of our predecessors.

We owe a debt of gratitude to all those government bodies, private individuals, voluntary organisations and dedicated, enthusiastic eccentrics and visionaries, who have laboured and conspired to save New Lanark. I would like to take this opportunity to record formally my own appreciation, and the thanks of New Lanark Conservation Trust.

I hope readers enjoy this book as much as I have. I hope it inspires you to visit us, to see the dream for yourselves.

Jim Arnold, New Lanark
January 1993

Frontispiece: *William Forrest's map of the Country of Lanark, published 1816*

Chapter One

THE REVOLUTION IN SCOTTISH TEXTILES

'A New Invented Spinning Machine'

NEW LANARK, the former cotton spinning village in the valley of the River Clyde near the old town of Lanark, is of international importance as the locus of pioneering management, and social and educational experiments led by the reformer who made it famous, Robert Owen. But New Lanark is also an important industrial monument, thanks to its role as an early centre of mass production using state-of-the-art technology at the time of its construction in 1785. Built by David Dale, a resourceful textile entrepreneur and banker, New Lanark harnessed the power of the Falls of Clyde to drive its spinning machinery, and is thus identified with the early stages of the Industrial Revolution. But contrary to the impression of dramatic change suggested by the term, the transformation of production from workshop to factory was as much evolutionary as revolutionary. From the 1700s onwards technological change had begun to affect several vital industries, most notably, textiles.

In the mid-18th century the principal occupation of Scotland's population of around one and a quarter million was linen manufacturing. This industry, having survived a distinctly unstable period in the years after the Treaty of Union in 1707, began to expand steadily from the 1730s onwards. Unquestionably, credit for much of this revival must be given to the Board of

1

Figure 1·1: *David Dale, merchant-philanthropist and cotton spinner, seen in this medallion by James Tassie, 1791 (Scottish National Portrait Gallery).*

Trustees of Fisheries and Manufactures. This body was formed in 1727 following repeated representations to the government by the Convention of Royal Burghs for some initiative to assist Scottish trade and industry. The Board, while also concerned with canal building, was initially closely linked with helping linen manufacturing. This was achieved by utilising the Equivalent, a sum of money set aside by the Treaty of Union in favour of

Figure 1·2: *Sir Richard Arkwright, inventor of the water-frame. Like Dale, he was an astute businessman and joined him for a short time as a partner at New Lanark.*

certain Scottish interests, which was now to be invested in various schemes for economic improvement.

Thus, under the direction of the Trustees, Dutch and French craftsmen were brought over to this country to teach their skills in spinning and weaving. Improved flax scutching or cleaning mills of continental design – driven by water power – were introduced. Subsidies were made available in the hope of encouraging farmers to cultivate more native flax as well as to meet the cost of establishing new bleachfields at sites all over the Lowlands, such as around Loch Lomond, in the Vale of Leven, the Cart Valley in Renfrewshire and Luncarty among

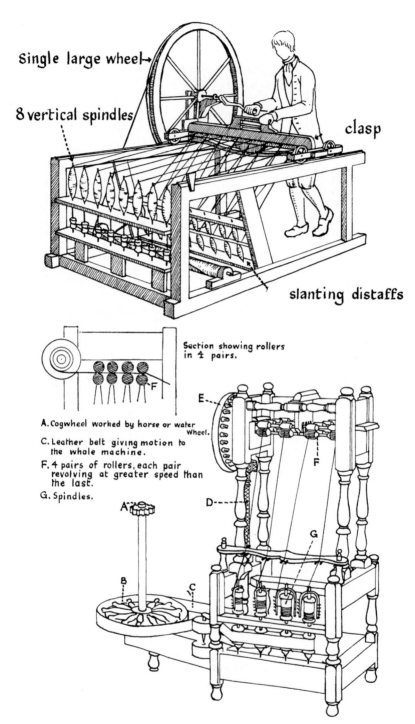

Single large wheel→

8 vertical spindles

clasp

slanting distaffs

Section showing rollers in 4 pairs.

A. Cogwheel worked by horse or water wheel.

C. Leather belt giving motion to the whole machine.

F. 4 pairs of rollers, each pair revolving at greater speed than the last.

G. Spindles.

Figure 1·3: (*Top*) *Hargreaves's first spinning jenny, 1764.* (*Bottom*) *Arkwright's first spinning frame, 1769.* (The Industrial Revolution 1760–1860, *M. E. Beggs Humphries*) other places in Perthshire. Scientific research was encouraged so that by the 1750s it had been discovered that the use of sulphuric acid reduced the souring part of bleaching from several months to a few days. A system of quality control was obtained by the formation of a linen inspectorate, the stampmasters, who affixed their seal of approval to the finished product. Finally, the government, on certain occasions, was persuaded to grant premiums for specific types of linen or to place embargoes on rival French imports.

As a result of these measures, and in conjunction with other contributory factors – such as the stimulus provided by the financial activities of the British Linen Company (later 'Bank') not to mention the fact that Scottish linen was very competitively priced compared with its main rivals – the industry continued its steady expansion during the second half of the 18th century. By the first stages of the classic Industrial Revolution it was widely dispersed; there were large areas of production in Angus, Fife and Perth making mainly coarse yarns and cloth; in counties like Ayr, Dumbarton, Lanark and Renfrew the speciality was fine threads and linen fabrics. At the centre of this activity was Glasgow, which by the 1770s was the leading linen manufacturing town in the United Kingdom.

Undoubtedly all these developments in the manufacture of linen had an important bearing on the rise of the Scottish cotton industry. For example, there was the mechanisation of the scutching process. Formerly, workers had cleaned the flax of impurities, but by 1772 there were 250 scutching, or lintmills, as they were frequently called, driven by water power and 'scutching' the flax mechanically. Moreover, on account of the capital required for the building of such mills (each one cost around £80–100 to erect) their construction encouraged the growth of what have been described as 'merchant capitalists'. Certainly this type of entrepreneur already existed, but there was an increase in the numbers of such businessmen, David Dale, for instance, being one of those who helped to swell their ranks. Indeed, it gradually became the case that virtually all the financial risks inherent in linen production were being assumed by such individuals. At the same time as greater quantities of flax became available, the workforce, especially the weavers, increasingly became full-time employees working in the various loom shops owned by the linen merchants. Lastly,

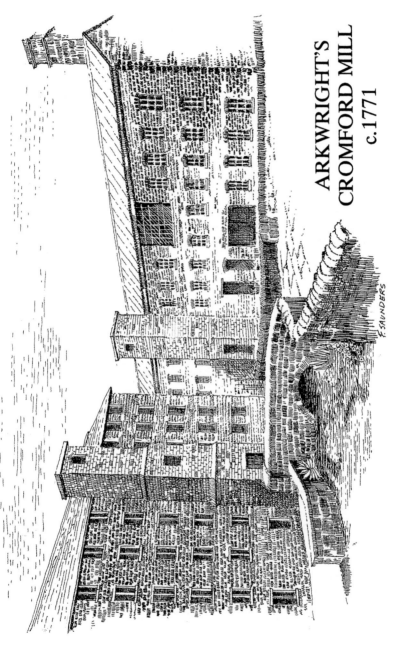

ARKWRIGHT'S CROMFORD MILL c.1771

F. SAUNDERS

Figure 1·4: *Arkwright's mills at Cromford. The first was built in 1771 and a second in 1777. The houses he built nearby for his workers are among the best examples of domestic architecture of that period* (© *Peter Pedley Postcards*).

there was the finishing sector of the industry controlled by a separate group of capitalists. It had initially been revitalised, as has been seen, by the use of sulphuric acid as a bleaching agent. Following the discovery in the 1770s that chlorine could be used instead, Charles Tennant's experiments ultimately resulted in the production of a bleaching powder although this was not in production at his St Rollox works in Glasgow until 1799. Simultaneously, there were important innovations in the printing side of the industry culminating by the 1780s with the vastly quicker cylinder printing process replacing the use of mainly wooden blocks.

In short, by the late 18th century there was a highly skilled and well organised linen industry flourishing in Scotland. However, although some sections of the finishing end had abandoned the domestic system and entered what historians now call the 'proto-industrial' stage, its main areas, spinning and weaving, were both still basically dependent on workers labouring in their own homes, mainly under an agency system operated by entrepreneurial middlemen. Admittedly, by 1787–8 a mechanical linen mill was operating at Brigton (Angus). But this was a decade after the earliest cotton factory and, because of various technical difficulties, was not followed by many other such mills. Consequently, linen manufacturing provided much of the organisational structure for the cotton industry but it was to be the latter which found itself in a position to take advantage of new developments which had been taking place in textile technology. In other words, these new inventions were quickly discovered to be more suitable for the production of cotton than either woollen or linen goods.

In 1764 James Hargreaves invented his spinning jenny, the earliest model consisting of a long wooden frame with a single large wheel and equipped with eight vertical spindles. Thus eight threads could be spun at once and by quite an unskilled person – even a child. Soon improvements made it possible to increase the number of spindles to a frame, but the frames grew larger, heavier and more costly. The biggest disadvantage was that jenny thread could only be used as weft (the short thread carried by the shuttle) on the weaver's loom because it was not strong enough to be used as warp (the thread stretched lengthwise on the loom). What was needed next was a machine to spin strong firm thread, a breakthrough made possible in 1769

Figure 1·5: *Sir William Douglas, another wealthy merchant turned cotton spinner, who was Dale's partner in the Newton Stewart (or Douglas) venture of Douglas, Dale and McCaul.*

when Richard Arkwright patented his water-frame. The first frame incorporated two sets of rollers, the second revolving faster than the first and so drawing out the carded fibre to the required thickness or 'count' before the twist was imparted. Ten years or so later, Samuel Crompton devised his mule, which, as the name suggests, combined the methods of the two previous inventions to give a yarn which was both finer and stronger than anything produced so far. As in Arkwright's frame, rollers were used to draw out the cotton rovings to greater length and to twist the thread. In common with Hargreaves' jenny, there was a moving carriage, but now it was the spindles which were mounted on the wheels. When the carriage moved away from the rollers it stretched and twisted the thread, and as it moved in again it wound the thread on to the spindles. Thus the rollers of the mule did not stretch the roving as much or as roughly as did Arkwright's frame. It was these machines, particularly the water-frame and the mule, which were soon found to be better at spinning cotton than either wool or flax. Thus, with the earlier processes of scutching and carding already mechanised, the stage was set for the import of this new technology and the 'take-off' period in the cotton industry in Scotland.

Initially this occurred in various parts of the country in locations as far apart as Galloway and Sutherland but very soon Glasgow and its neighbouring counties became the centre of the new industry. This was understandable since in the west of Scotland, like Derbyshire and Lancashire, were to be found the factors necessary for the expansion of cotton manufacturing. In the first place numerous fast-flowing rivers and streams, such as the Rivers Clyde, Cart and Ayr, could provide the water power which was an essential requirement before the advent of steam power. At the same time, raw cotton was readily available. This had been imported in considerable quantities, for combining with linen yarn in the weaving of fustian, since the mid-18th century and could be conveniently shipped from the West Indies or the plantations of the southern United States once trade links with the former colonial states were re-established. While a few of the former 'tobacco lords' seem to have transferred their assets into the cotton trade most of the capital which was required seems to have come from the existing linen industry. Thus, although there was a considerable involvement from

Figure 1·6: Apart from the new spinning technology, water power held the key to the development of the Scottish cotton industry, as here at Gatehouse-of-Fleet in Galloway, where the mills were built at the same time as New Lanark.

gentlemen with landed interests such as Claud Alexander of Ballochmyle, George Dempster of Dunnichen or Sir William Douglas, it was linen manufacturing families like the Buchanans, the Findlays and the Monteiths who played a major role in developments. Pre-eminent among all these was David Dale who from the outset was in partnership with many of the other leading figures. This involvement of Dale and the rest was hardly surprising considering their earlier background in the linen industry particularly when we note Professor Slaven's observation in *The Development of the West of Scotland, 1750–1960* that 'cotton was based on imported technology and local skills employed within the framework of the linen trade'. Finally, when the growth in population in these years and the gradual progress in improving communications are taken into account, the preconditions for the rapid expansion of the cotton industry especially around Glasgow and its environs had largely been established.

All that remains is to identify the exact moment when cotton achieved its breakthrough. This is obviously a crucial point in the development of the industry and appears to have taken place between 1775 and 1780 through the combination of three separate factors. There was, firstly, the entry of Holland and France on the side of the American colonists in the War of Independence; there was also a serious depression in the Paisley silk gauze trade, apparently the result of changing fashions; and finally the impact of the Arkwright and Crompton inventions began to have a serious effect north of the Border.

Although the first cotton mill was actually built at Penicuik in Midlothian in 1778 and there were to be other important developments in east and central Scotland, the cotton industry, as has already been noted, gradually became concentrated around Glasgow. There had been a strong English presence at Penicuik which was designed for an Edinburgh partnership by John Hacket, a former employee of Arkwright's, and it was a similar story at Rothesay where the first mill in the west of Scotland was erected in 1779. Here, on the Isle of Bute, taking advantage of an abundant water supply from Loch Fad and utilising the labour supply available from the existing linen trade, John Kenyon, an English businessman, entered the cotton trade. Rothesay, besides, had other advantages, being close to Port Glasgow

Figure 1·7: *The roofless ruin of the cotton mill at Spinningdale, Sutherland, the least successful of Dale's many enterprises. Its design closely resembled that of No. 1 Mill at New Lanark and the long-demolished mill at Catrine, Ayrshire.*

where the raw cotton was landed, as well as being fairly remote from Cromford, Derbyshire, where Arkwright had his head-quarters. Consequently the latter's water-frame as well as some of his ex-workmen could be employed with comparative impunity on the island.

The Rothesay experiment was followed by a series of similar or more ambitious ventures over the next decade or so. The third mill to be built in Scotland was in 1780 beside the Levern Water, a tributary of the White Cart, at Neilston. It was to this building, in fact, that Sir John Sinclair, the prominent politician and improving landowner brought a party from the French Chamber of Commerce in 1789 to demonstrate how industry could be developed in rural surroundings. The next mill was at Johnstone in 1782 succeeded by others shortly afterwards at East Kilbride and North Woodside in Glasgow. By April 1785, as it happened, the first mill building was being constructed at New Lanark while by the following March spinning was underway on the site. Outwith the Glasgow area there were some other impressive developments especially in Ayrshire and Perthshire. In the former county a factory village was created at Catrine on the banks of the River Ayr; while in the east, Deanston and Stanley spinning mills were erected beside the rivers Teith and Tay respectively, both with impressive cotton mill villages attached to them. Finally, there was a modest off-shoot of the Lowland industry in the south-west of Scotland, where several spinning mills were built by local landowners in partnership with merchants from the north of England and Ulster. One was the mill at Newton Stewart, in which Dale played a role, another the complex in the planned village of Gatehouse-of-Fleet, both built on prime water power sites (and the latter is now an interesting social and industrial history museum).

By 1793 and the outbreak of the French Revolutionary Wars there were 39 spinning mills either in operation or being constructed in Scotland. Most of them were within a 25-mile radius of Glasgow although, as has been seen, there were some successful big units in other parts of the country as well. Simultaneously there was a switch from linen to cotton weaving throughout the textile centres of West of Scotland while imports of raw cotton rose in spectacular fashion in order to satisfy the increase in demand. Certainly the most significant feature of this expansion was the building of large mills with huge workforces in places like Blantyre, Catrine and New Lanark. However, it is worth recalling that scattered all over counties like Galloway, Ayrshire, Lanarkshire and Renfrewshire were numerous smaller factories, frequently converted from old corn mills or other buildings and employing smaller numbers of workers.

The role of David Dale in the first phase of the growth of the cotton industry was definitely a considerable one. Thus, apart from his activities at New Lanark itself, which will be discussed separately, he was involved in a variety of other projects during these early years. In 1787 for instance he established a factory at Blantyre, subsequently sold to James Monteith in 1792 and, today, the site of the David Livingstone Museum; in the same year he also went into partnership with Claud Alexander. The latter, possibly better known for being the brother of the 'Bonnie Lass o' Ballochmyle', immortalised in

Figure 1·8: *View of Bonnington Linn, the highest of the Falls of Clyde, as seen by the artist and engraver, Paul Sandby – a more accurate view than that presented by later artists.*

verse by Robert Burns, had been a paymaster in the East India Company. He had used the large fortune he had amassed over-seas to purchase the Ballochmyle estates in south Ayrshire and proved to be an extremely suitable partner for Dale. They corresponded regularly with each other over the details of their investment and the cotton mill which they built at Catrine soon prospered.

Indeed, by 1793 there was an extensive factory complex with workers' houses, a school and a community with a population of 1,350. Meanwhile, in 1791 Dale entered into another partner-ship, on this occasion, with a group which included George Macintosh with whom he was already involved in a Turkey-red dyeworks at Dalmarnock. Others in this company were George Dempster of Dunnichen and William Gillespie. This body set up a small factory village producing cotton hand-kerchiefs at the unlikely location of Spinningdale on the Dornoch Firth with the intention of relieving unemployment in this part of the Highlands. In fact it never was a flourishing con-cern, as the mill was destroyed by fire in 1806 and it was never rebuilt. Around the same period in the 1790s Dale also had con-nections with a factory near Oban and with that at Newton Stewart (or Douglas) where another dynamic merchant-capital-ist, Sir William Douglas, was one of his partners in the firm of Douglas, Dale and McCaul. Finally, in 1803, he became closely involved in the Stanley mills. Originally he had been a member of a group of several investors including Dempster, Graham of Fintry and Sir Richard Arkwright. In 1795 the Perthshire works had been assessed as second only to New Lanark in value but a fire shortly afterwards and the adverse effects of the war with France saw the mills being put up for sale. Dale, in the last commercial undertaking of his long career now joined with a Glasgow businessman, James Craig, in what was to tran-spire to be a financially disastrous venture.

By the 1790s cotton manufacturing was well on the way to challenging its older rival, the linen industry, for industrial supremacy. The former, relying as has been noted, on the manufacturing base created by the latter was able to take advan-tage of the technological innovations which appeared in the second half of the 18th century. This enabled cotton to become the first large-scale factory industry in Scotland. At Blantyre, Catrine, Deanston and Stanley hundreds of workers were employed at the mills built on these sites. But the largest and most successful of these enterprises was New Lanark and it is its construction, early history and community which we will now examine.[1]

Chapter Two

DAVID DALE AND THE BUILDING OF NEW LANARK

'No place afforded better situations or more ample streams for cotton machinery'

DAVID DALE SERVES AS A GOOD illustration of that comparatively rare figure in the Scottish Industrial Revolution, the self-made man. Born in Stewarton on 6 January 1739, he was a son of William Dale, a grocer and general dealer in that small Ayrshire town noted in the 18th century for its bonnet making. Dale first became involved in the textile industry at Paisley in the 1750s when he served an apprenticeship in that town as a weaver. Then, following a period spent in the Lanarkshire area when, according to one account, he was 'tramping the county and buying pickles from farmers' wives', Dale settled in Glasgow in the early 1760s. There, in 1763, after a short spell as clerk to a silk merchant, he formed a partnership, in a building at Hopkirk's Land in the High Street, with Archibald Paterson. The latter shared Dale's religious convictions and a few years later, in 1768, both of them were to take part in yet another schismatic movement within the Church of Scotland ultimately resulting in the establishment of a sect known as the Old Scotch Independents. However, from a business standpoint, Paterson, who was a 'tallow chandler' or candlemaker seems to have been mainly a sleeping partner whose financial backing was a crucial factor in the rise of Dale during a period of rapid expansion in the textile trade.[1]

By the 1770s Dale was in a position to afford to become a

member of the merchant guild and a burgess of the city. Meanwhile, the figures for the quantity of cambrics made and stamped for sale in Scotland began to show a dramatic increase, rising from 29,114 yards in 1775 to 83,438 yards by 1784. Undoubtedly Dale was closely involved in this expansion, being one of a number of Glasgow yarn dealers who, unable to obtain sufficient fine yarn in Scotland, was forced to import the commodity from the continent. In short, as one authority has remarked, he was fast becoming 'a typical example of a manufacturer of cambric and lawns who was rising to a position of wealth and importance'. Moreover, in 1777, Dale, like many of his business associates, enhanced his financial position through marriage, when in that year, Anne Caroline Campbell became his wife. Caroline, as she was known, was a descendant of the first earl of Breadalbane and her father, a cashier of the Royal Bank had, during the 'Forty Five rebellion, 'caused the specie of that bank to be conveyed for security to the castle of Edinburgh'. Her brother, Colin, was subsequently Lieutenant-Governor of Gibraltar. She had one other important connection, since she was a kinswoman of Archibald Campbell of Jura, a wealthy 'improving' landowner who had made a fortune from the sale of black cattle. Campbell, who was also to become the godfather of Dale's five children, was soon to forge close financial links with him as well.[2]

Dale's partnership with Archibald Paterson was dissolved in 1782 and unquestionably the next significant development in his career was his appointment the following year, as a joint agent, with Robert Scott Moncrieff, of a new branch of the Royal Bank in Glasgow. The establishment of a Glasgow office by the bank seems to have been the outcome of a campaign by certain Glasgow merchants to mount a challenge to such existing financial institutions in the city as the Arms, the Ship and the Thistle Banks. As for Dale's appointment, which was clearly a result of his marriage, he was there primarily to provide advice on commercial matters since his business acumen was obviously very useful to any bank. One of his contemporaries, for example, recalls his financial dealings with the prominent Glasgow company, William Stirling and Sons, who apparently bought cotton fabrics from him 'at the credit of twelve-month bills, which bills he discounted at his pleasure in the Royal Bank'. It comes as no surprise, therefore, to learn that 'the long credit secured a valuable customer'. At the same time, Campbell of Jura also placed his financial affairs in Dale's hands – having a special arrangement with the bank whereby, in return for depositing his money personally with him he received five per cent interest no matter the current rate.[3]

In the same year as he accepted the offer of a position with the Royal Bank, Dale took another important step when he decided to become a founding member of the Glasgow Chamber of Commerce. The formation of this body was largely a consequence of the American War of Independence which had not only caused the collapse of the trade in tobacco but severely disrupted commerce generally for the merchant fraternity in the West of Scotland. The Chamber took an active part in such matters as campaigning against unpopular government legislation which affected cotton and linen goods, attempting to raise production standards, canvassing support from interested political figures such as George Dempster MP, and establishing links with other Chambers of Commerce in Great Britain. Therefore, it would not appear to be mere coincidence that the following year, in September 1784, Richard Arkwright, the famous English inventor and businessman, arrived in Scotland to be lavishly entertained by, among others, the leading members of Glasgow's business community. For Dale and New Lanark itself, the visit by the English manufacturer was to be a particularly significant one.[4]

Arkwright, like Dale, was a self-made man who had begun life as a barber and wigmaker in Bolton. However, around 1769, his invention of the water-frame, which provided a vital solution to the bottle-neck that had arisen in the spinning phase of cotton production, signalled a dramatic change in his fortunes. In 1771 he built a water-powered mill at Cromford in Derbyshire to be followed, as his business expanded, by others in that county and further afield in Lancashire and Staffordshire. By the date of his Scottish trip, and thanks to judicious licensing of his patent over the water-frame, the Arkwright empire was approaching its zenith and, as has already been observed, his machines were beginning to be installed in factories north of the border.[5]

It was late in September 1784 when Arkwright arrived in the West of Scotland. On Wednesday, 29 September he was 'made and created a free burgess' of Paisley while two days later a

Figure 2·1: *Rear of the cut-down No. 1 Mill and adjacent workshops viewed from the dried-up bed of the Clyde in 1966.*

similar honour was bestowed on him by the magistrates of Glasgow. The next day Arkwright and George Dempster, who was accompanying him, attended a dinner at Kelvin Grove, the private residence of the Lord Provost. Dale was one of those present at this event, which was reported in some detail in the *Glasgow Mercury* of 7 October 1784:

> The manufacturers of Anderston, through which they had to pass, in order to testify their gratitude to Mr Dempster, the patron of manufacturers in Scotland, and their esteem for Mr Arkwright, assembled their workmen to receive them. On their arrival, the populace wanted to unyoke the horses from Mr Dempster's carriage, in order to draw him to Kelvin Grove. This honour he declined, as it has been his uniform wish and practice to lead his countrymen to freedom rather than put them under the yoke. Mr Arkwright however was forced to comply with their offer, and the cavalcade proceeded, in a triumphant manner, to the Lord Provost's country seat.
>
> The inhabitants of Anderston, to testify their joy still further, lighted up bonfires, and prepared flambeaux to accompany them with in the evening upon their return to this city – The procession entered about half past eight, which consisted of five carriages; in the first the Lord Provost, who was followed by Mr Dempster in the second; his carriage was preceded by a large transparent gauze-lanthorn, raised upon the top of a pole, inscribed with these words, on the front and back, The Patriot of his Country. On the sides, The Guardians of our Manufactures. The other carriages were taken up by the Lord Advocate, member of Parliament for this city, &c. Mr Arkwright, Colonel Campbell of the 9th regiment, &c. In this manner they proceeded to the Saracen's head, where they alighted, amidst the acclamations of many hundreds of the inhabitants.

Shortly afterwards Arkwright proceeded to Lanark and then on to Perth where he was apparently honoured in a similar fashion.[6]

Precisely why Arkwright should have decided to visit Scotland in 1784 is uncertain but probably the influence exerted by George Dempster played some part in his decision. Dempster, who was member of parliament for Perth burghs from 1761 to 1790, included among his interests agricultural 'improvement', the economic development of the Highlands (he was a partner of Dale's at Spinningdale in the 1790s) and encouraging the nascent Scottish cotton industry. There is an extremely interesting

NEW LANARK VILLAGE

Figure 2·2: *Diagrammatic view of New Lanark village, showing the layout and dates of the major buildings (New Lanark Conservation).*

letter of Dempster's written in January 1800 to Sir John Sinclair, the editor of the first *Statistical Account of Scotland*, wherein he recalls his initial meeting with Arkwright in Derbyshire in 1783. He also relates how, at a subsequent encounter between them in London, Arkwright offered 'to assist me in establishing a cotton mill in Scotland, by holding a share of one and instructing the people'. Significantly, in answer to his friend Sinclair's original query regarding 'the circumstances of the bringing of the spinning of cotton by mills according to Sir Richard Arkwright's method into our part of the kingdom', Dempster wrote that he believed it was because the English entrepreneur 'conceived I had been useful to him'. In other words, Arkwright valued Dempster's political influence which in fact he was subsequently to find helpful in such matters as his unsuccessful attempt at obtaining a statutory monopoly of wool spinning and, apparently, his sponsorship for a knighthood in 1786.[7]

Nevertheless, apart from Dempster's own claim that he had 'some concern in engaging Sir Richard Arkwright to instruct some of our countrymen . . . and also to take a share in the great cotton mills of Lanark and Stanley', there is the inescapable fact that Arkwright at this juncture in his career was very keen to extend his business interests outwith the north of England. The main reason behind this was that he was deeply involved in litigation with certain manufacturers in England regarding patent rights for machinery. New Lanark and Stanley with their plentiful supplies of essential water power were attractive bases from which to launch an attack on his English rivals. Hence Arkwright's comment that 'he would find a razor in Scotland to shave Manchester'.[8]

If there is some difficulty ascertaining the precise motives for Arkwright's involvement in the Scottish cotton industry, there is no such problem over the background to the formation of his partnership with David Dale at New Lanark. Thus, shortly after the reception at Kelvin Grove, and probably on Monday, 4 October 1784, when Arkwright received a burgess ticket from the burgh of Lanark, Dale took him to see the famous and romantic Falls of Clyde. Whereupon the English manufacturer 'was astonished at the advantages derivable from the Falls of Clyde and exultingly said that Lanark would probably in time become the Manchester of Scotland as no place he had ever seen afforded better situations or more ample streams for cotton machinery.' Thereabouts, and probably before he proceeded to Aberdeen and Stanley, an agreement or understanding must have been reached between Arkwright and Dale, and apparently, Dempster, concerning the establishment of a cotton factory beside the Falls of Clyde.[9]

The area adjacent to the actual site, with its several waterfalls, known locally as the Bonnington, Cora and Dundaff Linns, was undoubtedly one of great natural beauty. The author of the First (or Old) *Statistical Account* was particularly fulsome in his praises, enthusing over the Cora Linn, where 'a rainbow is perpetually forming itself upon the mists and fogs arising from the violent dashing of the waters'. Meanwhile, the Dundaff Linn was described as being 'beautiful and romantic' and a place where 'trouts have been observed to spring up and gain the top of it with ease'. However, the location actually selected by Dale and his partners was much less highly regarded, reportedly being 'a mere morass, situated in a hollow den of difficult access'. Furthermore, 'the distance from Glasgow and the badness of

Figure 2·3: *Kay's* The Morning Walk, *showing, on the left, the stout figure of David Dale, 1793.*

the roads were rather unfavourable' so transport was likely to pose something of a problem. Nonetheless the spot did have the essential prerequisites which Dale and his colleagues were seeking. In the first place there was 'the very powerful command of water' supplied by the River Clyde which would ensure a steady volume of water throughout most summers and winters. At the same time, Dale was obviously aware of the existence in Lanark itself of workmen with such useful skills as stocking manufacturing, linen weaving, stonemasonry and clockmaking. The presence in Lanark of a modest number of clockmakers is particularly significant, since these craftsmen were regularly employed by the early cotton masters to construct or repair their machinery. Arkwright, for instance, employed a clockmaker called John Kay at Cromford to develop models of his original water-frame. Finally, as far as communications were concerned, Dale was to campaign energetically for the road improvements which were necessary for the success of the enterprise.[10]

In April 1785, using locally quarried stone, work began on the first mill which by March 1786 had been erected on the northern end of the site. Most of the ground for this mill and the others belonged to Robert Macqueen, Lord Braxfield who subsequently, as Lord Justice Clerk, was to achieve a certain notoriety for his handling of the sedition trials of 1793–4. Braxfield, unlike some of his neighbours apparently had no fears that 'the privacy of his demesnes would be invaded' and feued the land to Dale for the sum of £32 10s. Another part of the site, belonging to the Incorporation of Shoemakers in Lanark was obtained for a feu duty of £17 7s. 8d. while another immediately up-river, belonging to Sir John Lockhart Ross, for £5 annual rent. This latter transaction had become necessary as a result of the need to cut 'a subterraneous passage of near 100 yards in length . . . through a rocky hill' in order to provide a mill lade. Sir John was obviously delighted with these arrangements as a letter to Dale on 15 July 1797 illustrates: 'I sincerely hope that you may long retain in your possession the works at New Lanark and reap the fruits of those exertions which have been so honourable to yourself and productive of such evident advantage to this part of the country'.[11]

Spinning commenced at New Lanark in March 1786, while in July of that year, Dale wisely took out a fire insurance policy. Accordingly, in the event of an accident of this nature, the Sun Fire Insurance Company would pay out £2,000 for the mill itself, £2,500 for the machinery and equipment and £300 for the two houses which had also been built. This soon proved to be a sound investment, since on 9 October 1788, shortly after work on a second mill had begun, the first one was completely destroyed by a fire. Such an occurrence, because of the highly inflammable condition of the raw material and wooden machinery, was a relatively frequent one in the cotton industry. Spinningdale, for example, was to go up in flames, there was to be a major fire at Catrine and, as we will see, further serious conflagrations at New Lanark in later years. However, Dale was not discouraged and a replacement for the first mill was soon being

Figure 2·4: *The handloom weaver in his workshop, a familiar scene through-out the linen and cotton manufacturing districts of the Scottish Lowlands.*

built. Thus, the second mill was completed before the end of 1788 while the replacement for 'No. 1', as the original mill was enti-tled, was finished by 1789.[12]

By the end of 1793 there were four mill buildings and housing accommodation for over 200 families. The dimensions of these mills were all slightly different; No. 1 and No. 2 were both 154 feet long, 27 feet broad and 60 feet high; No. 3 was a little smaller while No. 4, which was 156 feet long, 33 feet broad and 70 feet high was the largest. Nonetheless the mills also had certain features common to all of them; they were all five storeys high, they all possessed an attic and a basement and they all had stairbays with Palladian or neo-classical windows, resulting in 'an attractive uniformity of style'. In addition, No. 1 and No. 2 mills had three waterwheels situated in the centre of each of them providing power for Arkwright water-frames as well as various carding and roving machines. Meanwhile, the No. 3 mill, known as 'the jeanie house', contained a large number of water-powered jennies while No. 4 mill served as a store-room and workshop as well as acting as 'a boarding house for 275 children who have no parents'. Later, in Owen's era, mule spinning was carried on in this mill. By the time Dale transferred ownership to his son-in-law the insurance value of the four mills was in the region of £30,000 – representing an enormous increase in the value of the mills over a fifteen year period.[13]

During Dale's lifetime a number of other buildings were erected – although in many cases the precise date of construction is uncertain. Thus, next to the mills and close to the river bank there was a long line of low sheds which were originally used for storing the bags of cotton when they arrived at the mills. Then, at the far end of the site, there was a mechanics' shop, three storeys high, and beside it a single-storey building used for brass and iron founding. Moreover, most of the housing provided for the workers at New Lanark was built while Dale remained in charge, the only major exception being the Nursery Buildings which were part of Owen's building programme. Hence the tenement blocks known as New Buildings, Caithness Row, Braxfield Row, Double (or Broad) Row, and Long Row were all erected in these years to provide accommodation for the 1,300 or so employees who worked there in the 1790s. In addition, beside Broad Row there were two houses, one of them used by Dale and his family as a summer residence and the other occupied by the works' manager who at that time was William Kelly.[14]

Meanwhile, at an early stage in the building of New Lanark, the original partnership between Dale, Arkwright and Dempster was dissolved. Although the reason for this happening is

In the Mill ... jobs and duties

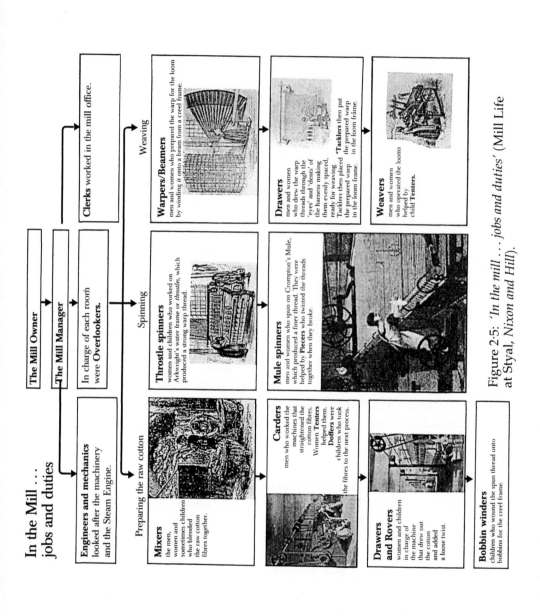

The Mill Owner

The Mill Manager

In charge of each room were **Overlookers.**

Clerks worked in the mill office.

Engineers and mechanics looked after the machinery and the Steam Engine.

Preparing the raw cotton

Mixers

the men, women and sometimes children who blended the raw cotton fibres together.

Carders

men who worked the machines that straightened the cotton fibres. Women **Tenters** helped them. **Doffers** were children who took the fibres to the next process.

Drawers and Rovers

women and children in charge of the machine that drew out the cotton and added a loose twist.

Bobbin winders

children who wound the spun thread onto bobbins for the creel frame.

Spinning

Throstle spinners

women and children who worked on Arkwright's water frame or *throstle*, which produced a strong warp thread.

Mule spinners

men and women who spun on Crompton's Mule, which produced a finer thread. They were helped by **Piecers** who twisted the threads together when they broke.

Weaving

Warpers/Beamers

men and women who prepared the warp for the loom by winding it onto a beam from a creel frame.

Drawers

men and women who drew the warp threads through the 'eyes' and 'dents' of the harness making them evenly spaced, ready for weaving. **Tacklers** then placed the prepared warp in the loom frame.

Tacklers then put the prepared warp in the loom frame.

Weavers

men and women who operated the looms helped by child **Tenters.**

Figure 2.5: *'In the mill . . . jobs and duties'* (Mill Life at Styal, *Nixon and Hill*).

not clear, there is no such uncertainty about the actual date when the agreement was ended. This occurred in December 1786 at a meeting held in Cromford at Arkwright's house. According to Dempster, who was also present and who now surrendered his share to Dale, the partnership was broken up because of a 'misunderstanding' between the two principal partners. It has been suggested that this was the outcome of a quarrel over the trivial matter of the positioning of a wooden cupola for the factory bell but it seems more likely that other considerations played a part in the break-up. For instance, it is worthwhile recalling that Arkwright, no stranger to the law courts, was deeply embroiled throughout 1785 in a contest over a patent for his machinery. Significantly, an appeal against an unfavourable decision at the Court of the King's Bench in June was rejected in November of that year. Did this verdict influence Dale's attitude towards his partner or affect Arkwright's own views about New Lanark? Certainly his connections with the cotton mill at Stanley, his other main Scottish enterprise, did not last much longer either. There again, Arkwright was growing richer and, in any case, suffered from periodic attacks of asthma. Probably he never had any serious intentions of becoming too deeply involved in Scotland where his patents did not apply or were difficult to enforce and consequently he may have welcomed the opportunity to reduce his commitments.[15]

On the other hand, it is clear that there was no permanent breach between Arkwright and his Scottish colleagues. Thus, at Catrine, where the first mill was not actually operational until 1787, it was John Low of Nottingham, a millwright employed by Arkwright, and introduced to Dale by him, who built the four water wheels required for the Ayrshire factory. Again, further evidence that Dale and Arkwright remained on good terms after 1786 is provided by the following letter of 7 April 1788 from Dale to his partner at Catrine, Claud Alexander, in which he writes, 'I have received a letter from Sir Richard Arkwright advising me that he has sent off two boxes containing plates, wheels and rollers for two spinning frames . . . directed for me at Mauchline by Dumfries'. Finally, Arkwright is supposed to have made another visit to Scotland in 1787 although there is no record of any meeting with Dale. However, if one account is to be believed, he returned to Perthshire where, as a souvenir of his trip, he bestowed his silver spectacles on Mrs Buchanan, the mother of one of his favourite apprentices, Archibald Buchanan. The latter, subsequently a prominent factory manager, was one of those sent with other workers from Stanley and New Lanark to Cromford for the purpose of being given instructions in spinning techniques.[16]

While New Lanark always figured prominently in Dale's plans, it was only one of his many business interests. Moreover, although Dale and his family sometimes spent some of the summer months at New Lanark, the family normally lived in Glasgow. His home was an opulent mansion, with an Adam fireplace as one of its central features, built in the early 1780s and situated in Charlotte Street close to the city centre. Here, Dale had as his immediate neighbour his former partner, James Paterson, now, a prosperous property developer, who had bought the land for the Charlotte Street development. Consequently, Dale's presence at New Lanark was increasingly infrequent and Owen even claims 'he was seldom there more than one day in three or four months'. This is possibly an exaggeration but certainly Dale's correspondence with Claud Alexander tends to convey a similar impression. Thus, 14 February 1787: 'I go to Lanark on Friday morning and return on Saturday forenoon'; 23 January 1792: 'I am thinking of going to Lanark on Wednesday'; 30 January 1794: 'I didn't hear from Lanark this week on account of the bad weather'. Therefore, the daily running of the mills and village until they were sold to Owen and his partners in 1799 was largely the responsibility of the two managers whom Dale appointed for this purpose. These were William Kelly, whose career will be discussed in the next chapter, and James Dale, his half-brother. This, in Owen's opinion was in some ways a sensible arrangement since 'Mr Dale knew little about cotton spinning having always left the management of his various mills, for he had other cotton mills beside New Lanark, to such managers as he could procure.'[17]

The 'other cotton mills' which Owen refers to were distributed over various parts of Scotland. One enterprise for example with which Dale was closely involved for several years was the factory at Catrine. Here, on the banks of the River Ayr, shortly after New Lanark was in operation, he formed a partnership with local landowner, Claud Alexander. Between them they established a factory village, similar to the one in Lanarkshire, eventually consisting of two cotton mills, a corn mill, a church, a brewery, a school and accommodation for a population of 1,350. As at New Lanark, Dale's role was largely to deal with the finances and proffer advice on business matters while Alexander got on with the daily running of the factory. This is borne out by their correspondence in which Dale, for instance, sends his partner lists of selling prices for cotton twist, relates the problems being experienced with Ingrams, their London agents, which might result in redundancies among their respective workforces ('I will be obliged contrary to my inclination and interest to discharge a number of workpeople as the weekly wages of Lanark and Catrine Mills is very considerable') or confides how he will try to have a word with Henry Dundas, then the Home Secretary, to see if he can persuade him to introduce some form of protection for Scottish manufacturers against imports of 'cheap Indian goods'. Sometimes, also, the advice given by Dale to Alexander was based on his own experiences at New Lanark. Thus, in January 1792, following a fire at Catrine which destroyed four houses, Dale strongly recommended in future the use of slate roofs since 'they were the best and cheapest in the end'. In addition, he warned his partner that it was highly unlikely the insurance company would make any contribution towards the purchase of a fire engine at Catrine because 'they didn't pay one shilling of the expense of the one I have at Lanark'.

Dale's links with Catrine continued until 1801 when the business was sold to the Glasgow cotton manufacturer, Kirkman Finlay. However, by the turn of the century, as his health deteriorated and he moved to a country residence at Rosebank near Cambuslang, Dale was gradually disengaging himself from most of his other business interests. Consequently, apart from the sale of New Lanark itself in 1799 and the mill at Blantyre, sold much earlier in 1792, Dale by the early 1800s had also severed his connections with other cotton mills at Oban, Rothesay and Newton Stewart. This last enterprise at Newton Stewart or Douglas, as it was then known, had come about as the result of a partnership with Sir William Douglas, one of the comparatively few 'tobacco lords' who diversified into manufacturing, as well as landowning and banking, following the collapse of the tobacco trade in the 1770s. How long Dale continued to exercise any influence over the affairs of Campbell, Dale and Company, who were inkle makers in Glasgow is not clear and it was not until 1805, that he and George Macintosh sold their dyeworks at Dalmarnock. This factory which was best known for its manufacture of Turkey-red or, as it was sometimes called, 'Dale's Red' seems to have remained a successful business being regarded, for example, by the Royal Bank in 1802 as 'a most profitable concern and easy on us'. On the other hand, the mill at Spinningdale in the Dornoch Firth, whose financial position had been causing alarm with the bank in 1803, was abandoned the following year. This meant that at his death in 1806 Dale had only one major investment outstanding – namely the cotton spinning mills at Stanley, Perthshire.[19]

During all these years Dale had also remained an active member of the Chamber of Commerce being its chairman in 1787 as well as serving regularly on its various committees. Consequently some of his time outwith New Lanark was spent on committees which were preparing reports on wages in the weaving trade, supporting cotton and muslin manufacturers during a period of recession, opposing the government's renewal of the East India Company's monopoly or investigating complaints from muslin manufacturers about 'the false count and short reeling of yarns'. His last attendance was on 2 January 1805 when he was part of a committee instructed by the Chamber to petition the government about recent legislation which was adversely affecting the price of corn.[20]

Around the same time as he was surrendering control of New Lanark to Owen and his Manchester partners, Dale's position as an agent of the Royal Bank was also undergoing a change. By 1801, for instance, he was rejecting the annual subvention which he received as an agent of the bank. Dale's role in any case had always been primarily an advisory one – 'going over the bill portfolio from time to time in the evening', is how one historian has described it – while the actual financial business was handled by his partner Robert Scott Moncrieff. In addition, Dale seems to have done a certain amount of entertaining clients or associates, hence a celebrated incident at his home in November 1795 when the General Manager of the bank and other prominent figures were his guests. This was the occasion when a section of the Monkland Canal burst its banks and engulfed Charlotte Street extinguishing the fires in Dale's kitchen and flooding his wine cellar. The situation was retrieved by having the meal cooked in neighbouring houses and getting his eldest daughter, Caroline, to perch on the shoulders of 'a seafaring man', in order to recover some of the bottles in his cellar. Thereafter 'the whole party passed the evening in mirth and jocularity, in the odd circumstances which had attended this merry meeting.'[21]

While there is disappointingly little evidence of how Dale financed his activities at New Lanark or elsewhere, there is no doubt that he and Scott Moncrieff made a highly successful partnership, ultimately handling far more business than the main office in Edinburgh and employing a staff of 13. Admittedly they went through a sticky patch during the trade depression of the mid-1790s when those at headquarters were complaining that 'we have been ruined by Scott Moncrieff and Dale who ought to have managed the Glasgow Branch with more safety and providence than they have done.' Anxious meetings were also held with their two agents. However, by the end of the decade when they were discounting bills to a value of £1 million annually they had obviously effected a substantial recovery.[22]

Aside from his banking and business interests (not to mention the constant litigation entailed by the latter) Dale was also active in a number of other different spheres. He was a town councillor and a bailie, being popularly known as 'the Benevolent Magistrate'; he was a member of the Manufacturing Committee of the Town's Hospital; he was a director of the Royal Infirmary once it was founded in 1795; he was a director of the Glasgow Humane Society dedicated to 'the rescue and recovery of drowning persons'; he was a trustee of the Anderson Institute; he regularly visited and made donations to the city's prison or Bridewell; he spent most Sundays either preaching to the members of the Old Scotch Independents at the kirk he had helped to establish, or to similar congregations throughout the West of Scotland. Little wonder, therefore, that New Lanark only occupied some of the attention of such a much-travelled and busy man.[23]

While Dale's motives for becoming involved in all these activities were not necessarily altruistic – for instance, some of the pauper children from the Town's Hospital were recruited as part of his workforce at New Lanark – there is, nonetheless, an underlying impression of a person who possessed a genuinely philanthropic nature. Certainly, Dale was noted among his contemporaries for his generosity and kindness, numerous examples of which have been recorded. Thus, apart from the assistance given to the Royal Infirmary, the city prison and the

Baptist Missionary society, he was probably best known for 'the several occasions' on which he procured large quantities of cheap food for the poor and destitute of Glasgow and by so doing 'mitigated the local effects of dearth'. In December 1791 an anonymous Glasgow donor provided the wherewithal for the purchase of a weekly waggonload of coal to improve conditions for the prisoners in the Tolbooth during winter. Described only as 'a gentleman of the city justly distinguished for his benevolence', there can be little doubt that the benefactor in question was David Dale.[24]

Enough time has been spent discussing Dale's interests and pre-occupations outwith New Lanark. What must be examined in the next chapter is how he recruited his workforce, the régime under which it laboured, the housing conditions which prevailed, the system of education which existed and, generally, the administration of the factory and the village while it remained under the control of the philanthropic David Dale.

Chapter Three

NEW LANARK AT WORK, 1785–1800

'Mr Dale's artists and young children'

LIKE MANY EARLY FACTORY MASTERS, one of the first major problems which Dale encountered at New Lanark was the acquisition of an adequate labour supply. Thus, although the neighbouring royal burgh of Lanark could provide some of the workforce which was required, the town's actual contribution only amounted to about 15 per cent of the total number of 1,334 employees working there when the first *Statistical Account* was compiled in 1793. However, Lanark, as has already been observed, did have some sort of reputation for its clockmaking as well as certain linen-weaving and building skills. Dale, operating in an industry where a system of 'build it yourself' machinery prevailed, especially in the case of Arkwright's inventions, employed 87 assorted smiths, clockmakers, millwrights, joiners and other craftsmen in his machine workshop. Certainly, several of these key workmen were recruited locally and probably some of them formed part of the group of 11 men and 15 boys, kitted out, according to one source, 'in complete dresses of brown cloth, with red collars to their coats', which was in 1785 sent to be trained at Arkwright's headquarters at Cromford in Derbyshire. A similar if somewhat larger squad of trainees sent in May 1785 from Stanley, Perthshire certainly made, as the *Derby Mercury* of 12 May reported, a considerable impression:

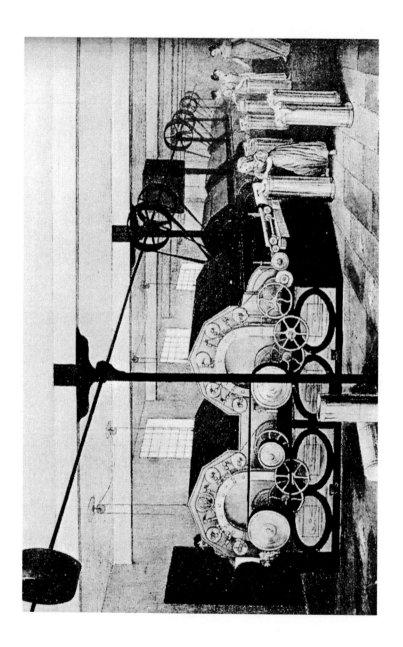

Figure 3·1: *In the carding room, showing the machines that straightened the cotton fibres.*

A few days since, between 40 and 50 North Britons, with Bagpipes and other Music playing, arrived at Cromford, near Matlock-Bath from Perth, in Scotland: These industrious Fellows left the Place on account of the Scarcity of Work, were taken into the Service of Richard Arkwright, Esq; in his Cotton Mills and other extensive Works, entered into present Pay, and provided with good Quarters. They appeared highly pleased with the Reception they met with, and had a Dance in the Evening to congratulate each other on the Performance of so long a Journey.

Whether the arrival of 'Mr Dale's artists and young children' made the same impact has not been recorded, although we do know that one of those who went on this trip was Archibald Davidson, a skilled mechanic and father of Hugh Davidson, subsequently a lawyer and local historian. Moreover, Davidson's indenture between 'David Dale, merchant in Glasgow, and Archibald Davidson, journey-man wright in Glasgow', was still in existence early this century. Therein, the latter 'binds himself to the service of the former for ten years, for six days per week and twelve hours per day, and to keep secret, under penalty of £5,000, the form, construction, use or manner of working of any machines or engines lately invented by Richard Arkwright, Esq. of Cromford'[1]

Nonetheless while it should also be remembered that 'the proprietor likewise employed in the parish and neighbourhood 324 persons in weaving and winding' the bulk of Dale's workforce had obviously to be persuaded to come to New Lanark from outwith the county. This was no easy task especially when contemporary opinion of textile factories is considered. Here, the prevalent view was that such institutions with their overseers, strict discipline and long shifts were decidedly unattractive places in which to work. To others, they also resembled rather too closely the charity workhouses existing in some Scottish cities and towns or the conditions to be found in the collieries or saltworks. Undoubtedly, as places of employment, the consensus of opinion was that they should be avoided if at all possible.[2]

With so many of the local population 'averse to indoor labour', Dale had no alternative but to enlist the majority of his workforce from further afield. Consequently, apart from a few Irish immigrants, the Highlands became the main recruiting ground for New Lanark's workforce. For many years large numbers of Highlanders had been trekking annually to the Lowlands

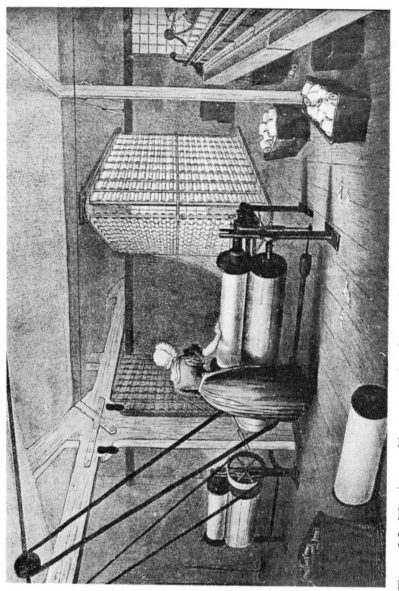

Figure 3.2: *Warping machinery, preparing the warp for the loom. To the right is a row of spinning frames.*

seeking seasonal work, notably as shearers or casual labourers in bleach-fields. Clearly it made sense for some of them, attracted by the better financial rewards, to accept the offer of permanent employment in factories such as those operating at Deanston, Stanley or New Lanark. Moreover, Dale and other factory owners, realising that potential recruits were available, made strenuous efforts to tap a reservoir of labour which extended from southern Argyll, through Perthshire and as far north as Sutherland. Accordingly, advertisements were placed in certain newspapers, while ministers in Highland parishes were also contacted. The latter were asked to use their influence in persuading those members of their flock who were contemplating emigration to consider instead the opportunities for employment available in the West of Scotland. At the same time, Dale, in order to be in the position by 1793 where 'a great proportion of the inhabitants are Highlanders mostly from Caithness, Inverness and Argyllshire' had to offer another incentive, namely adequate accommodation. Hence, Caithness Row and the other early tenement blocks providing housing for up to 200 families. We might just note that Dale rejected a proposal for establishing the weaving industry on Mull about this time because, as he said, 'I never advance any money to build houses for manufacturers, having need for all the money I can command for carrying on the works, which I am engaged in on this account'.[3]

Meanwhile, in 1791, the population of New Lanark had been increased, somewhat fortuitously, by a separate influx of workers. In that year the badly overcrowded emigrant ship, *Fortune*, bound for North Carolina with 400 passengers from the Isle of Skye, was forced, on account of bad weather, to call in at Greenock for repairs. Whereupon, Dale had astutely gone there and convinced most of those who did not have indenture agreements, about a quarter of the total complement of prospective emigrants, that they would be better working for him than seeking their fortunes in North America. 'Could the people find employment in the Highlands', as he wrote in a letter published in the *Scots Magazine* of October 1791, 'it would be much better for them to remain there; but as this is not the case the best thing that can be done for them and for this country is to invite all that cannot find employment to come here and they will be provided for'.[4]

If he ultimately acquired part of his workforce from the Highlands there is little doubt that by the time the first mill was operating at New Lanark in 1786 Dale had been 'subject to
considerable difficulties in obtaining a population'. This situation arose because, while the various mules and jennies which
were installed generally required men to be in charge of them,
the water-frames which were the machines most commonly in
use could be operated by women and children. Thus, as the first
Statistical Account states, 'widows with large families are much
wanted here' and 34 of them in fact were residing in New
Lanark by 1793. Nonetheless this was not the complete answer
to the labour shortage; the solution lay in adopting a practice
fairly common in some English establishments (but apparently
not at Cromford) of recruiting 'pauper apprentices'. These
were orphaned boys and girls 'generally from the age of five
or six to seven and eight' some of whom Dale obtained by nego-
tiating with the manager of the Town's Hospital in Glasgow of
which he was a director from 1787, although the majority of
them came from the Charity Workhouse in Edinburgh. Initially
there were about 80 of these children but the figure rose steadily
in the 1790s as the factory expanded. Thus, the number in 1793
was 275, by 1790 it was 396 and finally, when Owen took over
in 1800, there were somewhere between '400 and 500 pauper
children procured from parishes whose ages appeared to be
from five to ten'. This meant that out of Dale's employees
whom Owen claims totalled 1,700 or 1,800 on his arrival, which
was easily the largest factory population in the United Kingdom,
approximately two-thirds of them were women and children
with many of the latter, the so-called 'barrack children', from
the city orphanages.[5]

Inevitably both during Dale's own lifetime and thereafter it
has been his treatment of these pauper apprentices which,
understandably, has attracted the greatest attention. One of the
earliest descriptions of them is to be found in the *Statistical
Account* which in 1793 reported Mill No. 4 serving not only as
a store room and workshop, but also as lodgings for 275
children 'who have no parents here and who get their maintenance, education and clothing for their work'. The same
source also commented very favourably on the remarkably
low mortality rate of only five deaths in seven years, attributing
this to the hygienic accommodation and healthy diet provided

Figure 3·3: *Buttons bearing the arms of 'Lanark Cotton Mills' worn on clothes issued to child boarders under Dale's management.*

by the proprietor. The inmates, according to the *Statistical Account*, were given:

> oatmeal porridge, with milk in summer or sowens, i.e. oatmeal flummery, with milk in winter twice a day, as much as they can take, barley broth for dinner made with good fresh beef every day; and as much beef is boiled as will allow 7 ounces English a piece each day to one half of the children, the other half get cheese and bread after their broth, so that they dine alternately upon cheese and butchermeat, with barley bread or potatoes; and now and then in the proper season they have a dinner of herrings and potatoes.[6]

While the *Statistical Account* also gave brief details of the hours of work, living conditions and education of these young people, a much more comprehensive coverage of these aspects appeared in an issue of the *London Magazine* in July 1796 where an exchange of correspondence between Dale and Thomas Bayley, the president of the Manchester Board of Health, was featured. The latter, the first incumbent of such an office in Manchester, was a local Justice of the Peace, well known as a keen exponent of both prison and health reform. Moreover, his name must also have been familiar to Dale and other members of the Glasgow Chamber of Commerce as this body, since its establishment in 1783, had always maintained close links with its Lancashire counterpart. Indeed, one of the earliest exchanges of correspondence between the two Chambers took place in 1784 when Manchester sent Glasgow a copy of a letter written in October of that year by four Lancashire doctors. This was addressed to the Justices of the Peace of that county, one of whom was Bayley, proffering advice about the best way to combat an outbreak of 'a low putrid fever of a contagious nature that has prevailed among workers in the cotton mills and among the poor of the township of Radcliffe'. Therein, after various suggestions about ventilation and fumigation as well as a recommendation that 'great attention ought to be paid to the Privies', there followed the crucial proposals that there should be a reduction in the working hours for children under 14 and that 'the rising generation should not be debarred from all opportunities of instruction'. The sequel to all this was that shortly afterwards, Bayley and his colleagues issued a court order prohibiting local cotton mills from either working parish apprentices on nightshift or for more than ten hours per day, a remarkably progressive statement for its time. Consequently, with connections between Glasgow and Lancashire manufacturers stretching back for over a decade, Dale would have found nothing untoward about receiving a questionnaire relating to New Lanark from Bayley in 1796.[7]

In fact, Bayley and the other members of the Manchester Board of Health, particularly Dr Thomas Percival, who had been one of the signatories of the letter in 1784, and who was a leading figure in the health reform movement, were in the process of drafting a petition to parliament regarding factory conditions. Thus, in January 1796 Percival had prepared his 'Resolutions for the consideration of the Manchester Board of Health' which identified several unsatisfactory aspects of the existing factory system including overcrowding, excessive hours, and the absence of educational and religious instruction. Something was required to be done about all of these shortcomings, in his opinion, if such problems as 'the generation of diseases, the spreading of them by contagion and the shortening of the duration of those which exist' were going to be tackled effectively.[8]

Bayley presented Dale with 12 questions, the first batch seeking information about the dimensions of the rooms used for spinning, the number of spindles per room, the methods of ventilation and hygiene which prevailed, how many children were working in each room and their hours of employment. In reply, Dale stated that the rooms were all ten feet high but varied in width from 26 to 30 feet and in length from 120 to 150 feet. Each room, Dale continued, contained 2,000 spindles while ventilation was obtained 'by the rapid motion of many parts of the machinery' assisted in summer by the regular opening of the windows and small 'airholes' situated below every other window. As for 'purification', it was achieved by frequent brushing and weekly floor washing, by cleaning the machinery with hot water and, at the very least, an annual washing of the walls and ceilings 'with new flecked lime'. Finally, Dale estimates that there were around 50 to 75 children working in any one room, 'from six o'clock in the morning until seven o'clock each night with half an hour of intermission at nine o'clock for breakfast and a whole hour at two for dinner'.[9]

The second part of Bayley's questionnaire consisted of enquiries about Dale's main sources of labour, 'the mode and time of hiring' of his juvenile workforce and their subsequent employment opportunities, the educational arrangements in operation at New Lanark, including the amount of religious instruction available, and, lastly, the measures adopted against any typhus outbreaks at the factory.

To two of these queries in particular Dale submitted extensive replies. Thus, regarding the question of educational and religious instruction at New Lanark, the members of the Manchester Board of Health were given the following details:

Seven is the hour for supper; in half an hour after at most, and as much sooner as possible, the teaching commences and continues until nine o'clock. The schools at present are attended by 507 scholars in instructing whom sixteen teachers are employed – thirteen in teaching to read, two to write and one to figure besides a person who teaches sewing and another who occasionally teaches church music. The mode of teaching is as follows: the course is

Figure 3·4: *Tombstones in the old burial ground above the village serve as mute memorials to Highland migrants during the Dale era.*

divided into eight classes according to the progress of the scholars; to each of these classes one or more teachers are assigned as the numbers in that stage of advancement may require. To the teachers is specified in writing how far they are respectively to carry forward their scholars which, so soon as they have accomplished, the scholars are transferred to the next highest class and the teacher receives a premium for everyone qualified . . . On Sundays that part of the children who cannot go to church for want of accommodation are kept busy at school, and in the evenings after public worship, the usual teachers spend regularly three hours in giving religious instruction by causing the scriptures to be read, catechising etc . . . Besides the night schools there are two day schools for children too young to work which as well as the night schools (except the providing of their own books) are entirely free of expense to the scholars.

Likewise, there was a similarly expansive response to the enquiry about how those 'who get their maintenance in lieu of their wages' were accommodated and fed. 'There are six sleeping apartments', Dale told Bayley and his colleagues, 'and three children are allowed to each bed. The ceilings and walls of the apartments', he continued, 'are whitewashed twice a year with hot lime and the floors washed with scalding water and sand. The children sleep on wooden-bottomed beds and bed-ticks filled with straw which is in general changed once a month. A sheet covers the bed-ticks and above that are one or two pairs of blankets and a bed cover as the season requires. The bedrooms are carefully swept and the windows thrown open every morning in which state they remain throughout the day.'

Dale, having dealt with the accommodation he provided for his apprentices, also felt obliged to give some details of how they were dressed. 'In summer,' he explained, 'the upper body clothing in use for both boys and girls is entirely of cotton which as they have spare suits to change with are washed once a fortnight. In winter the boys are dressed in woollen cloth and they, as well as the girls, have a complete dress suit for Sundays. Their linens are changed once a week. For a few months in summer both boys and girls go without shoes and stockings.'

As for the children's diet, breakfast and supper consisted of porridge and milk 'in its season' and when the latter was in scarce supply, 'a composition of molasses fermented with some new beer'. All of them regularly got a form of barley soup for dinner as well as either a portion of beef or cheese.

'The beef itself,' so Bayley was informed, 'is divided among one half of the children in quantities of about 7 ounces English to each; the other half is served with cheese in quantities of about 5 ounces English.' In addition, 'there was a plentiful allowance of potatoes and barley bread'.

Addressing the remaining questions, Dale was in a position to state that although there had been some outbreaks of typhus in the village itself, there had not been any within the factory in recent years. Moreover if some illness or 'epidemical distemper' did break out among the apprentices they were promptly isolated in a separate section of the building and their bedroom fumigated with vinegar. Lastly, Dale intimated that his apprentices were mostly obtained from the Edinburgh workhouse between the ages of four and six years and usually remained with him until they were fifteen. Thereafter, he declared, 'they were fit for any trade'. In fact 'since the commencement of the war a great many have gone into the army and navy', while others had become apprenticed to smiths and joiners and particularly to weavers. 'The females', concluded the proprietor of New Lanark, 'generally leave the mills and go to private family service when about 16 years of age', but those who wished to remain in the factory were welcome to do so, 'since there was abundant employment for them'.

Not surprisingly, Dale's enlightened treatment of his apprentices attracted considerable attention and widespread approval. One visitor for instance, after a tour of the mills in 1798, enthused, 'If I was tempted to envy any of my fellow creatures it would be men such as . . . Mr Dale for the good they have done to mankind.' Equally enthusiastic was Sir Thomas Bernard, a prominent social reformer and philanthropist, who based his treatise, *Society for Bettering the Condition and Increasing the Comfort of the Poor*, on Dale's achievements. At the same time, during these years, various literary-minded travellers made a point of including New Lanark on their itinerary. One of these was the English diarist, Joseph Faringdon, who on 24 July 1788 recorded: 'Dale's cotton works have nothing in them offensive to the eye, not even when seen from the falls in Sir Charles Ross' grounds'. Again, whereas Robert Heron, the Galloway born biographer of Burns and author of *Observations on a Journey through the Western Counties of Scotland* (1792), only briefly referred to Dale's establishment, Charles Hatchett, a noted

Figure 3·5: *William Kelly, Dale's most inventive manager, as he appears in a medallion of enamel on glass by John Henning, 1802, about the time he quit New Lanark to establish himself as a cotton master in Glasgow (Renfrew District Council Museums Service).*

English scientist and mineralogist who wrote a diary of his visit to Scotland in 1796, commented, at some length, that on Monday, 25 July that year, 'We went to see the Cotton Mills belonging to Mr Dale . . . [these] consist of 4 immense buildings of 6 stories in which machines worked by a water wheel and attended principally by children, cotton is carded and spun into yarn. In these works above 400 children are employed'. Even Owen, although critical of certain aspects of his father-in-law's system, had to concede when addressing a Select Committee in 1816 that 'the children were extremely well fed, well clothed, well lodged and very great care taken of them when out of the mills.' Again, writing at a later date, he repeated these sentiments by observing that 'the benevolent patron spared no expense to give comfort to the children'.[10]

Moreover, as the 'Visitors Book' illustrates, with over 3,000 entries between 1795 and 1799, New Lanark began to take on all the aspects of a modern tourist attraction. In fact, there was remarkable public interest in Dale's enterprise from most sections of society. Thus, within the pages of the Visitor's Book are to be found members of the establishment like Lord Arnison, the Lord Advocate, and Campbell of Jura; English aristocrats such as Lord and Lady Clive and their family; figures from the Scottish enlightenment, Henry Brougham and Henry Cockburn; numerous doctors, clergymen, university students, military and naval officers, among them Alexander Trotter 'Paymaster of the Navy' and Dr Morelli from Siena; Thomas Gardiner from Savannah and John Watson from Virginia but two examples of a large number of American visitors; various British businessmen and manufacturers including for the third time, on 22 July 1799, Robert Owen, accompanied by two of his Manchester partners, John Atkinson and John Barton.[11]

If Dale's contemporaries held him in high regard some modern commentators have been less fulsome in their praise of the régime operating at New Lanark. A good example of this school of thought is T. C. Smout who in his *History of the Scottish People* has observed, 'It must seem extraordinary that any firm that permitted children to work a thirteen hour day should merit such extravagant praise and self evident that David Dale was not in the business just to be a disinterested philanthropist.' However, having stated his reservations about him, Smout does agree that by the standards prevailing at that time Dale was unquestionably an enlightened employer. Moreover, an examination of 'Peel's Act', the first legislation dealing with apprentices in cotton mills and passed by parliament in 1802, confirms that New Lanark satisfied all its statutory requirements – even those affecting hours of work. Here, Dale still operated within the letter of the law since his apprentices worked eleven and a half hours with breaks of one and a half hours for food while the Act restricted the working day to twelve hours 'exclusive of the Time that may be occupied by such Apprentices in eating the necessary Meals'.[12]

Before leaving Dale's apprentices it is worthwhile considering some of Owen's more critical views about them. Admittedly Dale's son-in-law had his own reasons for taking such a stance but, on occasions, he did cast serious doubt on both the quality of education provided and the health of the juvenile employees. 'Those children', Owen informed the Select Committee mentioned previously, 'looked fresh, and to a superficial observer,

healthy in their countenances; yet their limbs were very generally deformed, their growth was stunted, and although one of
the best schoolmasters upon the old plan was engaged to
instruct those children regularly every night, in general they
made but a very slow progress, even in learning the common
alphabet.' Again, elsewhere, in an essay about New Lanark,
Owen presented a much less optimistic picture of the apprentices especially their subsequent employment opportunities.
Thus, apart from frequently attempting to escape from the factory 'almost all looked forward with impatience and anxiety to
the expiration of their apprenticeship', whereupon, according
to Owen, 'they usually went to Edinburgh or Glasgow, where
boys and girls were soon assailed by the innumerable tempta-
tions which all large towns present and to which many of
them fell sacrifice'. On the other hand, Owen justified the
extremely early age the children started work on the grounds
that Dale was only acquiescing with the wishes of the parish
authorities and he would not have been given any if he had
not been prepared to take them at the age which he did.[13]

Finally, with regard to the apprentices, there is an interesting
article about them in the *Glasgow Mercury* dated 13 January 1795.
Under the heading, 'A pleasing instance of health', the newspaper describes how 307 of Dale's young employees 'distinguished from the rest by the name of Boarders, that is
provided by him with meat, clothing, schooling etc.,' went in
procession from the village to the town of Lanark on New Year's
Day, 1795. Thereupon, following toasts from a bowl of punch
donated by the local magistrates they returned to New Lanark
for dinner and to a day given over 'to dancing and con-
viviality'. The report continues, 'They made a very fine appearance, the boys dressed in blue clothes with leather caps
ornamented with fur and the girls in white muslins and black
hats. This sight never fails to excite the most agreeable sensa-
tions in all who have an opportunity of seeing so great a number
of orphans so comfortably provided for by industry . . .'. The
account ends with a brief allusion to the factory's favourable
health record – no deaths since June 1793 – allowing the author
of the article to pontificate, 'the above fact is sufficient to prove
that cotton mills are not prejudicial to health'.[14]

However, what about the other sections of Dale's workforce,
in particular those who had come from the Highlands to obtain

A.D. 1792 . . . . N° 1879.

Spinning Machines.

KELLY'S SPECIFICATION.

TO ALL TO WHOM THESE PRESENTS SHALL COME, I, WILLIAM KELLY, of Lanark, in North Britain, Cotton Spinner, send greeting.

WHEREAS His most Excellent Majesty King George the Third did, by His Letters Patent under the Great Seal of Great Britain, bearing date at
5 Westminster, the Fifteenth day of May, in the thirty-second year of His reign, give and grant unto me, the said William Kelly, His especial licence that I, the said William Kelly, during the term of years therein mentioned, should and lawfully might use, exercise, and vend, within England, Wales, and the Town of Berwick-upon-Tweed, my Invention of " CERTAIN NEW-CON-
10 STRUCTED MACHINERY, TO BE APPLIED TO SPINNING MACHINES FOR THE PURPOSE OF CONDUCTING THE PROCESS OF SPINNING IN A MUCH MORE EXPEDITIOUS AND LESS EXPENSIVE MANNER THAN BY ANY MODE HITHERTO DISCOVERED;" in which said Letters Patent there is contained a proviso obliging me, the said William Kelly, by an instrument in writing under my hand and seal, to cause a par-
15 ticular description of the nature of my said Invention, and in what manner the same is to be performed, to be inrolled in His Majesty's High Court of Chancery within six calendar months after the date of the said recited Letters Patent, as in and by the same (relation being thereunto had) will more fully and at large appear.
20 NOW KNOW YE, that in compliance with the said proviso, I, the said William Kelly, do hereby declare that my said Invention is described in the Plan and description thereof hereunto annexed, and in manner following, that is to say :—

The Inventions and improvements are of such a nature as to enable those
25 machines, commonly known by the names of roving billies and slobbing and

Figure 3·6: *Kelly's Patent (Glasgow City Council Libraries Department).*

employment and accommodation at New Lanark? In this case, despite noting a tendency among some of them 'to make free with the bottle', the opinion of the *Statistical Account*, for example, was generally favourable. 'Upon the whole,' it stated, 'they are a decent, orderly people' although it did believe they would benefit considerably if they had a church which conducted its services in Gaelic. In fact there was in the New Buildings, instantly recognisable today because of its bellcote, a religious meeting place, but it served only the needs of Dale's own sect, the Scotch Independents before whom he was sometimes wont to preach. On the other hand, Owen had a radically different opinion of Dale's workers. 'The people,' he declared in his autobiography 'had been collected hastily from any place whence they could be induced to come and the great majority of them were idle, intemperate, dishonest, devoid of truth and pretenders to religion which they supposed would cover and excuse their shortcomings and immoral proceedings.' Elsewhere, he stated, the inhabitants of New Lanark 'lived in idleness, in poverty, in almost every kind of crime . . . [and were] consequently in debt, out of health and in misery'.[15]

Certainly Owen's criticisms were repeated by some other commentators, notably William Davidson, a local historian, while in 1793 the Commissioners of Supply somewhat censoriously observed that 'owing to the influx of inhabitants in this upper part of the country the present prison has been found too small and not adequate for the purpose'. At the same time, particularly in Owen's case, these allegations must be treated cautiously since, undoubtedly, he always sought extensive publicity for his own achievements at New Lanark. This was obviously the response of William M'Gavin who in 1824 contributed to a series of letters which were addressed to Owen, entitled *The Fundamental Principles of New Lanark Exposed*. M'Gavin protested that he had taken exception to the impression which Owen had created that New Lanark 'was a pandemonium before you came to it and that it is a paradise now. 'It was impossible', the writer continued, 'that with his benevolent heart and ample means his workers could have been in such a state of wretchedness and degradation as that which you describe'. Owen was also reminded of the great emphasis his predecessor had placed on educating his workers and 'the comfort of all classes of the people'. If it had not been for Dale, the letter ended, many of the Highlanders would either have starved or been forced to emigrate. Another major critic, the Revd James Aiton of Hamilton, echoed these sentiments and cast further doubt on Owen's veracity. At the very least Owen had upset some members of the Glasgow establishment by his statements about his father-in-law![16]

Understandably, as far as individual workers employed by Dale are concerned, there are only a few names which have survived. For instance, there was John Alexander, a long-serving under-manager who in 1833 while giving an account of the origins of New Lanark to the Factory commissioners, recalled Dale preaching on certain Sundays to some of his employees; there was John Wright, whom Dale had promoted to the Glasgow headquarters of the company in 1799, and who in later life could still recollect 'the calm, unruffled way in which Mr Dale went through his very extended business'; there was George Wilson and David Kelly who, as existing records confirm, were, respectively, two of the ironfounders and brassfounders working in the factory between 1795 and 1804; there was a skilled workman called McArthur whom in September 1793 Dale told Claud Alexander, his partner at Catrine, he was losing to the Lancashire canal building industry; finally, there was James McKey, a labourer and one of Dale's first Highland immigrants, who in the graveyard above the village, erected a tombstone in memory of three of his children 'who died young in 1792'.[17]

If nothing very much is known about most of Dale's employees there were two who were somewhat less obscure. One of them, James Dale, is principally remembered as being Dale's half-brother and one of the two managers he appointed to run the factory in the 1790s. Owen regarded him as 'incompetent to comprehend my views or to assist me in my plans' and he parted company with New Lanark in 1800. The other individual was William Kelly, someone whose career has been the subject of much greater attention. Kelly was originally one of several Lanark clockmakers, skilled craftsmen whose gear cutting skills and other attributes were in great demand in the early days of the cotton industry. He shared responsibility for the management of the factory with James Dale but his main contribution was undoubtedly his outstanding inventive ability, in particular, his achievement of being 'the first to turn the mule by water power'.

Figure 3·7: *Spanish dollar, 1799, counter-marked 'Payable at Lanark Mills', and with a face value of 5s. (Glasgow University Archives).*

Initially Kelly installed water-powered mules which were not self-acting; 'I first applied water power to the common mules', he wrote at a later date, 'in the year 1790, that is we drove the mules by water but put them up (that is the carriage or spindle-frame) in the common way, by applying the hand to the fly-wheel'. His great technological feat, which he patented in 1792, was the invention of a self-acting mule. In other words, the need for a skilled adult male spinner to turn the driving wheel was eliminated as it certainly would have been if Kelly's self-acting machine had been adopted by the cotton industry. Unfortunately for Kelly it was not. His own explanation for the neglect of his discovery and for ultimately surrendering his patent for it was that 'The size of the mules rapidly increased to 300 spindles and upwards, and two such wheels being considered a sufficient task for a man to manage, the idea of saving by spinning with boys and girls was thus superseded.' Nonetheless it is quite likely that Kelly's machine simply was not sufficiently profitable. In any case, a viable self-acting mule was not to become a reality until about 30 years later when the Manchester engineer Richard Roberts invented a fully automatic one.[18]

However, this was not the sole extent of Kelly's ingenuity while employed at New Lanark since he also devised 'a new method of erecting the great gear' as well as various methods of safely heating the mills. With regard to the former, his 'large machinery of cotton mills', Kelly contacted the Board of Trustees in 1793 claiming it would result in significant savings in the amount of water power required, not to mention 'the benevolent tendency of preserving the lives of children and others that may be entangled by the drums or shafts'. Apparently, the Board of Trustees agreed to give him an annual premium of £20 provided his invention was introduced into the factory but whether it ever was remains uncertain. As for Kelly's experiments in heating the mills, although the type of cotton spun at New Lanark did not require the temperatures of 80 degrees Fahrenheit necessary in some mills, he had to devise a system which gave a suitable heat for the coarser counts spun at the factory. At the same time he had to consider the higher premiums which insurance companies insisted upon for factories which used stoves. By March 1796, after a couple of less successful experiments, Kelly had solved the problem by constructing a stove with a series of hot air ducts which, he declared, 'was sufficient to warm a mill of 150 feet by 30 or upwards.'[19]

Kelly, like his colleague James Dale, did not survive the new régime inaugurated by Owen in 1800. He moved to Glasgow, where he became a burgess of the city in 1806 and branched out into cotton broking. Here, although he experienced some initial setbacks with a partnership in a mill near Blackburn and with the Rothesay Spinning Company, he undoubtedly overcame these misfortunes and began to prosper. In Rothesay, for instance, he formed a successful partnership with Robert Thom, a civil engineer of outstanding ability. By the time Kelly retired in 1826 labour relations similar to those existing at New

Lanark had been established on the Isle of Bute. His portrait appears on one of the medallions cast by John Henning, the Paisley artist who was a protégé of David Dale and Scott-Moncrieff, and by 1818 he could afford to buy an expensive residence in Virginia Street, Glasgow. By the end of his life he had established an extremely successful business which continued to flourish under his son. Today at New Lanark the most obvious reminder of this ingenious inventor is his amazing clock, now situated at the entrance to the Visitor Centre. John Aspinall, an American who visited the village in 1795, as the inscription explains, made the following observations on the factory and its unique clock: 'This manufactory of cotton yarn employs 1,300 people. There are about 12,000 spindles going in these mills. There is a remarkable clock with a face something larger than a common clock. It has five dials, one for the hours and minutes and seconds; one for the weeks; one for the months; one for the years; one for the ten years ... and by which they regulate the mill as the same wheel turns the clock and the mill'.[20]

While William Kelly's career was unique, there were of course countless other workers and their families who were indebted to Dale. Thus, despite Owen's somewhat jaundiced views of his inheritance and without making any false claims for originality on Dale's part – the Arkwrights and Strutts for instance had undoubtedly devised the factory community some years ahead of its introduction at New Lanark – it is unquestionably a fact that he gave employment and accommodation to many people who, otherwise, would probably have lacked both. Moreover, he educated and looked after innumerable children who almost certainly, but for his intervention, would have suffered a much worse fate than befell them at New Lanark. Consequently, before undertaking an examination of the effects of the 'New Broom' which was to materialise under Owen's management, it would seem appropriate to include this remarkable, near-contemporary tribute to Dale and his achievements.[21]

> Come here ye sons of indolence! and know
> What genius and industry can bestow.
> Behold DALE'S Works! and think how ye've
>   abus'd
> The talent heaven but lent you to be us'd.
> These prove the active and persevering man,

Through every part of this extensive plan.
And tacitly reprove each little mind,
Whose aims are to its little self confin'd.
Admitting that his int'rest led him on,
Still the benevolent actions he has done
Form the true test by which the man is prov'd;
And which is priz'd wherever worth is lov'd.
Nor question ye his steady pious zeal,
It ne'er ran counter to the public weal;
And though he differ'd in religious forms,
His conduct gave his principles their charms.
In spite of that detraction which obtains,
His character for honest worth remains;
And to the world the name of DALE is dear,
And will outlive his earthly labours here.[23]

Finally, Dale's obvious worthiness and humanity is refelected in a splendid obituary notice which appeared in the *Scots Magazine* shortly after his death:

At Glasgow, in the 67th year of his age, David Dale, Esq. formerly proprietor of the Lanark Cotton Mills, and one of the Magistrates of Glasgow – generally known and admired for a noble spirit of philanthropy – in whose character were strikingly combined, successful commercial enterprize with piety, active benevolence, and public spirit. Here, if ever, a tribute of respect and admiration is due to departed worth. Originally in a low station of life, by prosperous adventures in trade, he was raised to state of affluence, which he directed on grand scale, to the encouragement and relief of the distressed. In a romantic den on the banks of the Clyde, the lofty mills of Lanark arose, under his eye and fostering hand; surprised and delighted the traveller, as with a scene of enchantment; and exhibited a pleasing picture of industry walking hand in hand with instruction and comfort. Thither were transplanted, and trained to virtuous habits, numerous orphans and outcasts of the streets who had been a prey to vice and misery. And there are many 'hapless sons of Caledonia', who were emigrating to a foreign land, found a comfortable asylum. For many years he discharged, with distinguished reputation, the office of Pastor to the Independent Congregation in Glasgow, for which he was peculiarly fitted, by a thorough knowledge of the Hebrew and Greek languages. His discourses bespoke a cultivated understanding, and liberality of sentiment. A steady friend to civil and religious liberty, he embraced men of every persuasion. Possessed of a disposition kind, hospitable and benevolent, of a heart generous, sincere, and truly philanthropic, his charities, public and private, were probably not surpassed by any individual in Scotland. As a Magistrate, he

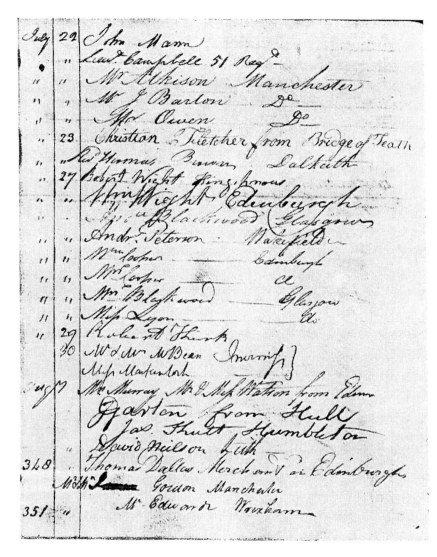

Figure 3·8: *Robert Owen's entry in the Visitors Book, 1799 (Glasgow University Archives).*

tempered justice with mercy; and, on trying occasions, he displayed
a spirit of resolution, scarcely expected by those who were familiar
with his unassuming manners in private society. In private life he
was very affectionate to his relatives and intimate friends; sometimes in a musing contemplative frame, and sometimes endearing
by a peculiar vein of cheerful pleasantry. Hence they bewail the

loss of a kind father, friend and faithful monitor. The poor will feel the want of a bountiful benefactor. Glasgow is deprived of an illustrious citizen. Public institutions have lost him who was looked up to, as the general patron of every generous and laudable undertaking. Humanity has lost a warm and steady friend.[21]

With this sort of accolade, whoever followed Dale in his role of philanthropist at New Lanark or elsewhere, had much to live up to.

Chapter Four

A NEW BROOM: NEW LANARK UNDER ROBERT OWEN, 1800–1813

*'The groundwork on which to try an
experiment long wished for'*

ROBERT OWEN WAS BORN IN NEWTOWN, Montgomeryshire in 1771. Later in life he was to lay particular stress on the importance of adolescent experience in moulding character and certainly his own early years in employment would appear to have had considerable influence upon him. Thus, even his earliest job as an apprentice draper with a Scottish family called McGuffog at Stamford in Lincolnshire taught him, to quote one eminent historian, John Butt, 'that due deference and gentility which enabled him to mix on practically equal terms with lairds of Scotland, with princes of blood-royal and with aristocratic and occasionally radical cabinet ministers'. Unquestionably, the work experience and business training which he accumulated during a fifteen-year stint in Manchester between 1785 and 1800, stood him in good stead when he eventually did move to New Lanark.[1]

In 1789 he entered into a short-lived partnership with a fellow countryman and engineer, John Jones, from whom he gained his first experience in managing a small factory building, with its own mules which produced rovings for the spinning industry. Thereupon after a brief spell running his own spinning mill there followed what was to prove the major formative influence on young Owen, namely, his association in the years 1791 to 1794 with the Manchester factory master, Peter Drinkwater, who owned Bank Top Mill. During these years with Drinkwater,

Figure 4·1: *Robert Owen of Lanark in a colour pastel drawing by Mary Ann Knight. This portrait, c. 1799, has a special interest as most other likenesses belong to his middle or old age. It catches his vitality as a young man (Scottish National Portrait Gallery).*

whose interviewing technique apparently included asking appli-
cants how often in the week they were drunk, Owen learned a
great deal which was to benefit his later career. Drinkwater,
therefore, was not the 'sleeping partner' which Owen, in his
autobiography, would like us to believe, but, in fact, a very
active and enlightened factory owner. Indeed, by his innovatory
use of Watt's governor on his rotary steam engine, the first to be
installed in a cotton mill in Manchester, he was able to obtain
particularly fine yarn counts. Owen's later reputation in this
direction was clearly a consequence of his training at Bank Top
Mill. In addition, Drinkwater took a fairly progressive stance
regarding working conditions believing, for instance, that good
ventilation and sanitation were important in factories. Doubt-
less some of these ideas also influenced Owen's later thoughts
on such matters on arrival at New Lanark.[2]

On leaving Drinkwater around 1794, Owen's next significant
step was to become a partner in a large Manchester firm, the
Chorlton Twist Company where his associates included the
Barton and Atkinson brothers. The latter had connections with
Borrodaile and Atkinson, hat manufacturers in London and Sal-
ford, who also had a wide range of trade links with Glasgow and
the West of Scotland. Henceforth, Owen became the company's
Scottish representative making twice-yearly visits to sell their
fine yarns to Scottish weavers. It was on one of these expeditions
to Glasgow that Owen had his initial encounter with Ann
Caroline Dale, David Dale's eldest daughter. At the same time
he also formed his earliest impressions of the village and had
his first meeting with its owner.[3]

Eventually Owen and Caroline wished to be married but Dale
was reluctant to agree to his daughter having as a husband
someone who not only held different opinions about religion
but who was also, for all he knew, an unscrupulous adven-
turer. Owen, however, overcame Dale's reservations and he
and Caroline were ultimately married in her father's house at
Charlotte Street in Glasgow on 30 September 1799. Moreover,
by the terms of the marriage agreement Owen was undoubtedly
placed in a very favourable financial situation. Thus, on condition that in the event of his sudden death he allotted £300
per annum to Caroline and any children, he received £3,000 as
a dowry from Dale, a sum which matched his own assets at
that juncture. As well as this, he also enjoyed the considerable

benefit of Dale's position as cashier at the Glasgow branch of the Royal Bank and his lucrative connections with the wealthy Campbell of Jura family.[4]

Meanwhile, most likely in July 1799, when as the Visitors Book indicates, John Barton and John Atkinson, two of Owen's partners, were also present at New Lanark, Dale had agreed to sell the factory to the Chorlton Twist Company for £60,000. Dale's decision to part with New Lanark was based, according to Owen, on 'his finding the management of so many concerns too heavy a burden'. Consequently, being asked to name his price Dale apparently answered, 'Mr Owen knows better than I do the value of such property at this period and I wish that he would name what he considers a fair price between honest buyers and sellers'. After some thought Owen replied, 'It appears to me that sixty thousand pounds payable at the rate of three thousand a year for twenty years would be an equitable price between both parties'. In this fashion, in the new owner's words, 'passed the establishment of New Lanark, from Mr Dale into the hands of the New Lanark Twist Company'.[5]

The Owens set off for Manchester in September 1799. Although the business headquarters of the New Lanark Twist Company were to remain in that city for another ten years, Owen and Caroline returned to Scotland in January 1800. His motives for coming back were, so he claimed, dissatisfaction with the performance of the existing managers and a desire 'to introduce principles in the conduct of the people ... and to change the conditions of the people'. Besides, he was convinced that he had 'the groundwork on which to try an experiment long wished for'. That may have been the case, but there were also sound commercial as well as philanthropic reasons for assuming personal control of New Lanark. His partners, for instance, undoubtedly wished him to be close at hand to keep a watchful eye on their investment; they also hoped this would make it easier to supply their Scottish customers and possibly offer them a wider range of yarns. There was also the attraction, once the war with France was over, of opening up trade links in the Baltic and with Russia, by utilising the Forth and Clyde Canal.[6]

Owen, as will shortly be shown, spent much of these early years attending to matters at New Lanark. The rest of his time was either taken up attempting to win the acceptance of the

Glasgow business establishment or creating a favourable impression with his father-in-law. In both objectives he was eminently successful. Thus, his rapport with the city's banking fraternity was noted by the Leeds manufacturer, John Marshall, who on one of his visits observed that Owen 'had the management of the Bank of Scotland at Glasgow, where he spends half his time'. Again, about 18 months after his arrival, Dale's partner at the Royal Bank, Scott-Moncrieff, was commenting that Dale's son-in-law 'was a clever lad, far from being sanguine or speculative'.[7] In 1806 these activities and other endeavours involving the Chamber of Commerce and the cotton industry were duly recognised when he became a burgess of the city. As for his relationship with Dale, Owen would appear to have rapidly won his confidence. Consequently within a short period Dale was taking heed of his advice to end his various partnerships at Newton Stewart, Catrine, Stanley and Spinningdale. 'I advised him to dispose of them as soon as he could meet with purchasers for them', Owen was later to write and, with the exception of Stanley, Dale parted company with the others in the early 1800s.[8]

However, before Spinningdale was sold off, Owen went there himself accompanied by George Macintosh, one of Dale's main business associates and the father of the inventor of the famous water proofing process. This 'formidable undertaking' had its serious and lighter aspects. For Owen, the expedition to Sutherland gave him his first opportunity to put forward his 'New Views of Society' to 'the several respectable highland families' with whom he and Macintosh lodged. It also enabled him to make the welcome discovery that 'such was the keenness and purity of the air, with all the exercise we took, that contrary to my former habit, I could take the spirit manufactured there so pure in the Highlands without suffering any inconvenience but which practice I never could adopt in the Lowlands'.[9]

At New Lanark itself Owen soon made his presence felt. He began by introducing a series of measures affecting both the mills and the village, which were designed, so he said, 'to bring the greatest comfort and improvement to the numerous population to whom it afforded employment'. However, as he admitted himself, his reforms were also introduced 'to produce the greatest ultimate profit to the proprietors'. One of his first actions was to dismiss the two managers, William Kelly and

LANARK COTTON MILLS the property of ROBERT OWEN Esqr &c.

Figure 4·2: *The earliest illustrations of New Lanark are the engravings by Robert Scott, 1799. This one from the west bank of the Clyde shows the mills and village as they would have appeared towards the end of Dale's régime. Notice the gap in the tenement range – later filled by Owen's only exercise in new housing (Royal Commission on the Ancient and Historical Monuments of Scotland).*

James Dale on the grounds that, in his opinion, 'they were incompetent to comprehend my views or to assist me in my plans'. Robert Humphreys whom he knew from his years at Bank Top Mill, took over as his second in command. Since, 'for new measures it was necessary to have new men', there was, as well, a general reorganisation of the rest of the senior staff in the factory. [9]

On the factory floor, the most famous innovation undoubtedly was his 'silent monitor' or 'telegraph'. The best account of it is still to be found in his autobiography:

'This consisted of a four-sided piece of wood, about two inches long and one broad, each side coloured – one side black, another blue, the third yellow, and the fourth white, tapered at the top, and finished with wire eyes, to hang upon a hook with either side to the front. One of these was suspended in a conspicuous place near to each of the persons employed, and the colour at the front told the conduct of the individual during the preceding day, to four degrees of comparison. Bad, denoted by black and No. 4, – indifferent by blue, and No. 3, – good by yellow, and No. 2 – and excellent by white and No. 1. Then books of character were provided for each department, in which the name of each one employed in it was inserted in the front of succeeding columns, which sufficed to mark by the number the daily conduct, day by day, for two months; and these books were changed six times a year, and were preserved; by which arrangement I had the conduct of each registered to four degrees of comparison during every day of the week, Sundays excepted, for every year they remained in my employment. The superintendent of each department had the placing daily of these silent monitors, and the master of the mill regulated those of the superintendents in each mill. If any one thought that the superintendent did not do justice, he or she had a right to complain to me, or, in my absence, to the master of the mill, before the number denoting the character was entered in the register. But such complaints very rarely occurred. The act of setting down the number in the book of character, never to be blotted out, might be likened to the supposed recording angel marking the good and bad deeds of poor human nature.'

However Owen's system does not appear to have been either unique or original. For example, Joseph Lancaster, the noted Quaker educationalist, employed a similar device in his schools and there are other instances of similar methods of managerial control elsewhere. What does appear to have been a more genuine innovation was the right which the workers possessed to appeal to Owen regarding the assessments made of them by the superintendents.[10]

Apart from the silent monitor there is further evidence that discipline was rigidly enforced within the mills. Whether the statement of Duncan McKinlay to the Factory Commissioners in 1833 that 'a constant system of beatings took place, not a day without someone suffering' is reliable or not, there are other grounds for believing that a strict régime operated at New Lanark. Thus, besides random searches of workers to reduce the thieving which had become widespread by the time of Owen's takeover, regular notes were taken of any errors made by employees. Others were summarily dismissed for being absent without permission or indulging in what was described in one instance as 'a fraudulent transaction altering lines'.[11]

At the same time, output, labour costs, hours of work, stocks of yarn, types of cotton and their origin as well as every other aspect of factory production were rigorously supervised, as the superbly kept 'Produce' and 'Report Books' amply illustrate. Owen's 'Produce Books' for example contain a fortnightly abstract which provides a wealth of data for every room in the mills. Therein are itemised the number of spindles in use, the species of cotton and the quantity used, the time taken to spin the yarn with a note of any delays which occurred, the precise weight and number of hanks produced as well as the wages of all the workers. Thus between 31 December 1802 and 14 January 1803, using cotton imported from such diverse sources as Georgia, New Orleans, Trinidad, Jamaica, Granada and Gaudeloupe, Mill No. 1, with its 6,556 spindles worked for 137 hours 30 minutes, with 12 hours lost during the period. A weight of 7225 lbs or 159,394 hanks of cotton yarn were spun in this interval and the wages of the workforce were £153 10s 6d. Elsewhere, from Owen's meticulously maintained 'Report Books' there can be obtained an extremely accurate figure for the annual output of the whole factory as well as the total production costs for each year. For instance, from the Annual Report, submitted on 25 December 1806, it is possible to make the following summary as seen in Table 4·1[12]

Aside from the wages mentioned above which, like most country mills, were lower than those in the towns, much of the expense incurred, for example, in 'the store', 'the repairs' or 'the extras' was for items either purchased locally or in central

Table 4·1: *Annual Report for 1806.*

	Raw Cotton		Yarn
Mill No. 1	415,046 lbs		397,223 lbs
Mill No. 2	37,715 lbs		364,495 lbs
Mill No. 3	294,891 lbs		285,635 lbs
Expenses	*Mill No. 1*	*Mill No. 2*	*Mill No. 3*
Picking	£602	£562	£279
Preparing	£2,823	£2,205	£2,391
Spinning	£3,104	£2,793	£1,747
Reeling etc.	£799	£713	£717
Store	£1,436	£1,203	£1,108
Extras	£ 128	£123	£126
Repairs	£2,519	£1,692	£2,160
TOTAL	£11,411	£9,291	£8,528

Scotland. Thus, such things as glue, candles, coal, whale oil, soap, flour, nails, locks, hinges and tacks were all provided by Lanarkshire merchants. Fifteen trees were bought from the Braxfield estate in March 1805 (Owen did not lease Braxfield House himself until 1808) but timber was normally purchased from R. and A. Sheriff and Company, Leith. Among the vast range of other materials needed for the maintenance of the mills were iron frames and wheels from the Omoa foundry, bar iron from the Muirkirk iron works, while two Glasgow firms, H. and R. Baird and Robert Gray and Sons supplied iron castings, tin lamps and glasses.[13]

The cotton yarn produced and so methodically checked at New Lanark was destined for both home and overseas consumption. Although a few consignments were destined for outlets in Trieste and Smyrna the main foreign exports were to St Petersburg. Here, especially after the defeat of Napoleon in 1812–13, Owen, assisted by his agents Allan Stewart and Company, cornered a major share of the trade in yarn. Subsequently, he commissioned John Winning, one of the art teachers in the Institute, to design a label with an illustration of the village on it for sticking on these consignments. They became known to the Russians as 'Picture Yarn'. In the domestic trade, Owen

Figure 4·3: *Stanley Mills on the River Tay, founded the same year as New Lanark by George Dempster, Graham of Fintry, Sir Richard Arkwright, David Dale and others. Owen was involved in the management of Stanley on behalf of Dale's trustees for a period between 1806 and 1813.*

had contacts all over Britain but undoubtedly Glasgow firms like James Finlay and John Bartholomew were among some of his best customers. However, as the Sales Book reveals he was selling yarn to manufacturers over the length and breadth of Scotland, from Aberdeen to Wigtown and from Kilbirnie to Kirkcaldy. Moreover, his prompt resort to litigation to recover debts outstanding to the New Lanark Twist Company, for

Table 4·2:   *Census of the workforce for 1811 and 1815.*

	1811 Male	Female	Total	1815 Male	Female	Total
No. 1 Mill: Picking	11	108	119	12	96	108
Carding	74	116	190	78	101	179
Spinning	61	140	201	45	150	195
Reeling & Sorting	4	44	48	7	39	46
Total for No. 1 Mill	150	408	558	142	386	528
No. 2 Mill: Picking	—	29	29	—	105	105
Carding	80	103	183	76	95	171
Spinning	74	114	188	55	143	198
Reeling & Sorting	9	37	46	7	38	45
Total for No. 2 Mill	163	283	446	138	381	519
No. 3 Mill: Picking	5	32	37	3	28	31
Carding	81	101	182	58	73	131
Spinning	19	116	135	16	103	119
Reeling & Sorting	7	37	44	7	38	45
Total for No. 3 Mill	112	286	398	84	242	326
Mechanics	91	—	91	58	—	58
Labourers	50	—	50	22	—	22
Managers etc.	8	—	8	7	—	7
Schoolmasters	2	—	2	—	2	2
Storekeepers	9	—	9	8	—	8
Extras	—	—	—	7	3	10
GRAND TOTALS	585	977	1,562	466	1,014	1,480

instance against a business in Dysart in February 1808 and another in Langholm three months later emphasises his hard-headed approach to business management [14]

Throughout the years 1800 to 1814 the size of the workforce remained much the same. Occupational censuses taken in January 1811 and 1815 for example, provide the following statistical information, seen in Table 4·2.

Within the factory the one significant development, although it is not revealed by the statistics, was the gradual disappearance of the pauper apprentices. On his arrival Owen had declared himself committed to ending this system and to having no employees under the age of ten. He would appear to have been well on the way to eliminating the practice by 1807 when John Marshall, the Leeds flax spinner, paid his second visit to

New Lanark. Marshall, on his first trip in 1800, calculated that there were between 400 and 500 such apprentices. By 1802 there are known to have been 264 'boarders' living in No. 4 mill, about two thirds of them, it has been estimated, probably paupers indentured by David Dale. However, when Marshall returned in 1807 he was able to comment that Owen 'was nearly giving up the plan of having parish apprentices'. Or, in the words of one local historian 'in the course of time the system of bondage was abandoned and freedom was restored to all'.[15]

Outwith the workplace itself Owen was equally concerned about the social conditions and behaviour of a workforce which, by his account, had been 'collected hastily from any place from whence they could be induced to come, and the great majority of them were idle, intemperate, dishonest, devoid of truth and pretenders to religion which they supposed would cover and excuse their shortcomings and immoral proceedings' ... Even if, as Podmore judiciously remarks 'no man is an impartial witness to his own cause', Owen does seem to have had justifiable grounds for concern about the standards prevailing at New Lanark on his take-over. Drunkenness, for instance, was one problem. Thus, to combat the habits of workers such as the brother of one of his under managers who apparently went on a regular 'spree', he instigated evening patrols around the village streets. Those apprehended were reported to Owen, subsequently fined and if they persisted getting intoxicated were ultimately dismissed. These tactics proved reasonably effective although the celebrations on New Year's Day remained something of a problem despite the offer of a day's holiday in the summer to those prepared to work on that occasion. Another reform was the introduction of a factory owned store or truck shop. Located at the far end of the Nursery Buildings, Owen's main architectural contribution in these years, it was partly designed to counter the rapacious activities of the retail traders within the village. Its prices were approximately 25 per cent lower than its rivals, but it was still able to make an annual profit of around £700 which was eventually used to support the school. Adjacent to the store, at one end of Caithness Row, was the Counting House where earnings were paid out in cash or in the form of a wages ticket. Hence the 'Ticket for Wages' whereby a worker either presented the ticket and received goods at the store or exchanged it for money from the cashier in the Counting House. Employees who ran short of cash which many apparently did, since they were only paid monthly, could obtain credit through a system of tin tokens. Twelve of these were equivalent to one shilling and the amount borrowed was deducted from their next wages. Counter-marked foreign currency, such as Spanish dollars, was also sometimes used by both Dale and Owen for this purpose.[16]

While Owen also introduced a Sick Fund to which his workers contributed one sixtieth of their pay, as well as a Savings Bank which in 1818 had deposits amounting to £3,000, Owen's most contentious measure was undoubtedly his campaign to improve housing and sanitation in the village. On arriving he had encountered a depressing state of affairs – dirty unswept streets and every house with rubbish heaps and dunghills outside it. The dwellings themselves were in a bad state of repair and, after carrying out various renovations Owen drafted a set of regulations for all the residents of New Lanark. Accordingly, each house must be cleaned weekly and whitewashed annually; there was to be a rota for the cleaning of the stairs and the area outside each home; no ashes or dirty water were to be thrown in the streets and no cattle, pigs, poultry or dogs were to be kept within the premises; during winter there was to be a curfew at 10.30 p.m. and nobody was allowed abroad after that time without the manager's permission.[17]

Unquestionably Owen's 'New Broom' was unpopular. A good eye-witness account of his reforms, and some of the reaction to them, is to be found in the remarks of one of his ex-teachers. Writing in 1839 he recollected that Owen 'advised that they should appoint a committee from amongst themselves, every week, to inspect the houses in the village and to insert in a book, to be given for that purpose, a faithful report of the state of each house as they might happen to find it. This recommendation', the author continued, 'was upon the whole acceded to by the male part of the population but the rage and opposition it met from the women was unbounded'. The upshot was that the female occupants refused to open their door to what they derisively termed the 'Bug Hunters'. Nonetheless the tenants had reluctantly to conform and agree to be supervised by what were described as Owen's 'military police'. Failure to do so would lead to banishment to an insalubrious part of the village, known, appropriately, as 'Botany Bay'.[18]

Figure 4·4: *Owen's 'Silent Monitor' or 'Telegraph' as used in the New Lanark Mills to signal performance and behaviour.*

Owen was well aware that these changes, not to mention an increase of one hour in the working day as well, were widely disliked in New Lanark. However, in his autobiography he claims that the turning point in his relations with his workforce came in 1807 following his generous behaviour during the crisis in the cotton industry. This was occasioned by a United States government embargo on exporting cotton to Britain, American retaliation for the British government's Orders in Council. The latter banned all trade with France, including neutrals like the U.S.A., who could only do so if they were selling British goods or if their vessels first touched at a British port, declared, unloaded and reloaded their cargoes, and paid a duty. The consequence of this economic warfare was, as Owen stated, that 'the prices of all kinds of cotton immediately advanced so rapidly and so high that the manufacturers of the article were placed in a dilemma'. Owen's solution was to halt the production temporarily but meanwhile to continue paying wages to his workers, an action very much in the tradition of David Dale who had acted similarly following the fire in 1788 which had destroyed Mill No. 1.[19]

Owen's benevolent action in 1807 assuredly converted many of his employees and evidence of their loyalty to him was soon to be forthcoming in the dispute which arose shortly afterwards between him and a neighbouring family. The latter, the Edmondstones of Corehouse, were two sisters who owned the property on the opposite banks of the Clyde. In 1804 they had reached an agreement with the New Lanark Twist Company regarding the construction of a dam across the river which would give the factory a greater supply of water, especially during dry spells. Under the terms of the contract there were various safeguards to placate the Edmondstones. The dam, for instance, would be as 'impassable' as possible in order to prevent workers crossing it 'during the hours they are unemployed' while the sluices would be closed at 8 p.m. and would not be opened until 5 a.m. 'unless when it was necessary to keep the works going during any part of the night'.

By 1809 relations between Owen and the Edmondstones had deteriorated and both sides became involved in legal action against each other. Owen, in his defence, stressed the fact that 'the undertaking was encouraged by the approbation of all the neighbouring proprietors'. Furthermore it occurred to them that the projected cotton mills would not only be productive of general utility but 'would lead to the increase of the value of all properties in the neighbourhood'. Lord Braxfield, he reminded his neighbours, had feued the ground to Dale because 'he had a quick and comprehensive view of all these advantages'. The sisters were not impressed. Miss Ann Edmondstone observed in reply that 'A boll of oats or potatoes sells no higher in Lanark than it does at Hamilton nor are greater rents paid for an estate than for lands of the same quality at 50 miles distant'. In any case as far as she was concerned the mills were a nuisance 'for the people employed there, notwithstanding the vigilance of the manager, are perpetually committing trespasses on her garden and her woods to a very great extent'.[20]

The quarrel was resolved at some juncture in 1810, the Company agreeing to pay the Edmondstones a new annual water rent of £200. Meanwhile during the whole altercation Owen's workers had manifested, to quote, again the former New Lanark teacher, 'a general feeling of sympathy'. Indeed the whole episode was quite a lively affair. On one occasion, for example, when the Edmondstones were on the opposite side of the river a disabled worker apparently still on the Company pay roll had suggested that the sluice gates should be raised in order to swamp those on the other bank. Owen, however, sternly rebuked him declaring: 'If the workers of New Lanark could not be saved without the loss of life, to let them go'. On another occasion, in similar circumstances, a party from Corehouse was pelted with missiles by the irate inhabitants of the village. [21]

Between 1800 and 1814 New Lanark continued to attract the attention of the outside world even if there was nothing like the influx of nearly 20,000 visitors which took place in the subsequent decade when Owen's Institute, School and educational methods attracted international interest. Thus, if there were no Russian Grand Dukes or Austrian Princes, a number of prominent individuals either inspected the mills or at the very least saw them from afar. In the latter category the most celebrated observers were William and Dorothy Wordsworth who in 1803, accompanied by Samuel Coleridge, undertook a tour of Scotland. Inevitably the Falls of Clyde featured on their itinerary and although they only caught a glimpse of 'a long range of cotton mills' they did actually meet some of the New Lanark workforce as well. This encounter occurred on the evening of 23 August outside the New Inn at Lanark when, having consumed 'a boiled sheep's head with the hair singed off' – and enjoyed it – Dorothy Wordsworth recorded the following incident:

> A party of boys, dressed all alike in blue, very neat, were standing at the chaise-door; we conjectured they were charity scholars; but found on inquiry that they were apprentices to the cotton factory; we were told that they were well instructed in reading and writing. We had seen in the morning a flock of girls dressed in grey coming out of the factory, probably apprentices also.[22]

Apart from the artist, William Turner, who visited and painted the Falls in the early 1800s but unfortunately left no account of New Lanark, another person who did comment on the village was Johanna Schopenhauer, friend of Goethe and mother of the famous philosopher. This lady was an intrepid traveller who visited this country between 1803 and 1805. Again her real objective was the Falls but she did make this brief description of Owen's establishment in her *Diary*:

> A small town lay in the middle of the valley and we saw two or three spinning mills which, as in Perth, were driven by water. We could see the wheels turning rapidly and the little cascades of water caused by their motion glinted like silver in the sun. Yet they were so far below us we could hear no sound.[23]

Finally, there was a different type of visitor namely Eric T. Svedenstierna, a self-styled 'industrial spy'. Svedenstierna, a leading Swedish metallurgist was, with his industrial compatriots, concerned about the decline of his country's iron industry. In 1802 he had come to Britain as he admitted in his account of his visit 'to get to know methods of iron working there'. Having been to certain sites in England he proceeded to Scotland where, following a tour of the nearby Wilsontown Iron Works he arrived at New Lanark. He left behind a lengthy and most interesting description of the factory as seen through the eyes of a highly intelligent foreign scientist:

> A few English miles from Wilsontown, at [New] Lanark, we looked at a large cotton spinning mill, which had been founded a few years before by a business man in Glasgow, but which had now been sold to a London company for £84,000 sterling. It consisted of four buildings several storeys high merely for carding or combing and spinning the cotton, as well as a number of workshops and small houses for the workers. Because the place was almost uninhabited at the foundation of the works, they had here been able without particular expense to observe a certain symmetry, and to give the buildings an appearance which is usually missing from English factories. This, and the fine situation on the bank of the River Clyde below the famous waterfall, made the place into one of the most beautiful and interesting of the whole district.
>
> At each of the above-mentioned four spinning mills was a low overshot water wheel a few feet wide, which drove the whole of the machinery, which was made entirely of cast iron, from the largest to the smallest hand-wheels. The head for the wheel was obtained from the River Clyde by means of a waterway which went for almost an English mile, partially underground. In one of the large halls, where the spinning was completed, 2,060 threads were spun at once. In each hall they reckon in general on four hundredweights per week of moderately fine cotton yarn, and less of the finest. A part of the works was now being overhauled, and it was said that the weekly production did not exceed nine hundredweights in total. If one assumes that normally this is only ten hundredweights, and reckons 50 working weeks to the year, there

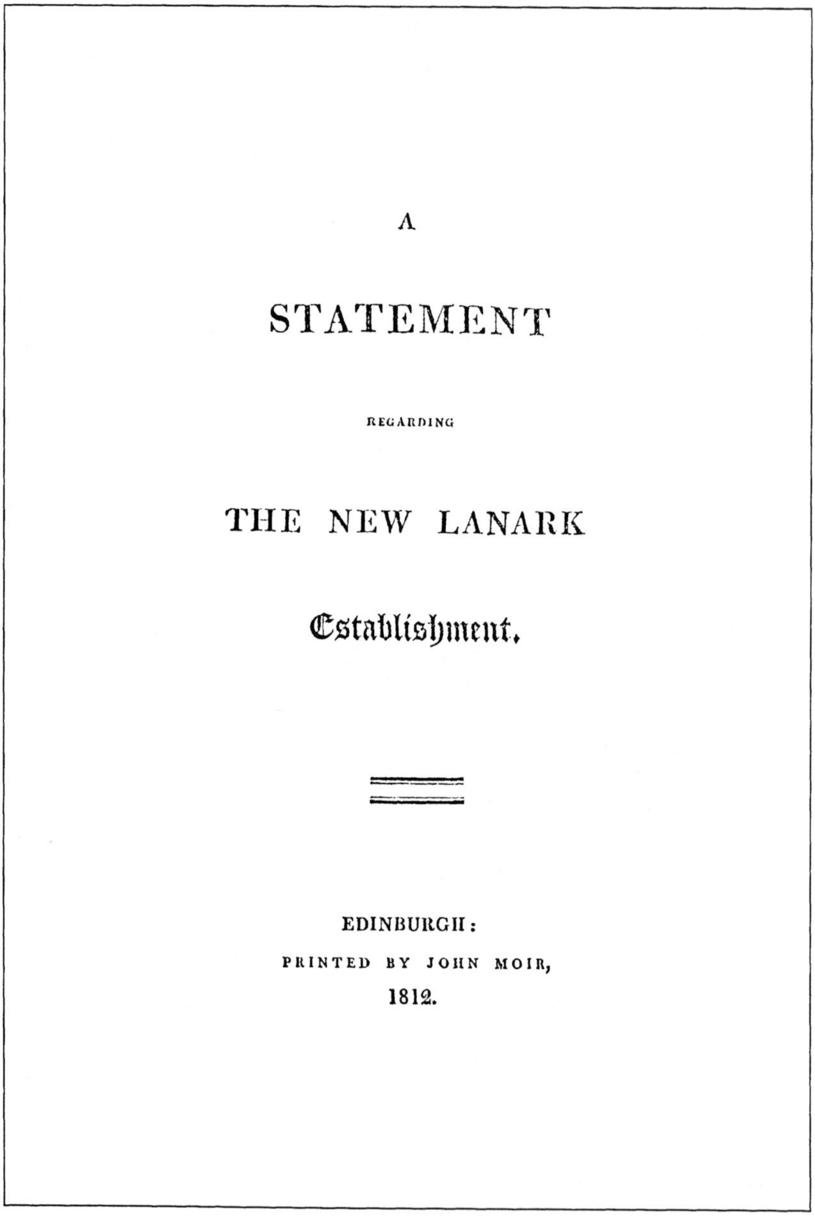

A

STATEMENT

REGARDING

THE NEW LANARK

Establishment.

═══════

EDINBURGH:

PRINTED BY JOHN MOIR,

1812.

Figure 4·5: *'A statement regarding the New Lanark Establishment' – the title page from Owen's first publication, 1812.*

nevertheless results a production of 500 hundredweights annually. The cotton worked here therefore amounts to nearly one-sixth of the bar iron which is forged at a two-hearth hammer in Sweden. I should remark in this connection that although this mill is one of the largest in the Kingdom, there are proportionally many more smaller ones, especially around Glasgow, Liverpool, and in Manchester, and I should imagine that the output of cotton yarn in the neighbourhood of these towns almost equals the weight of copper production at Fahlun.[24]

Svedenstierna's visit had taken place at a time when Owen was in the midst of his reform programme at New Lanark but by 1809 he felt he was in a position 'to clear the foundation for the infant and other schools, to form the new character of the rising population'. However his suggestions, not surprisingly, received an unenthusiastic response from his partners when they came north to study his proposals.

Consequently, although they presented him with a silver salver, the partnership was clearly under some strain. The precise date of its actual dissolution is uncertain but the contract of co-partners for the new business, to be known as the New Lanark Company, was dated 5 October 1810.

In fact, John Atkinson, one of Owen's original partners, remained with him. He was joined by Robert Dennistoun and Alexander Campbell of Hallyards, sons-in-law of Campbell of Jura and prominent Glasgow merchants, and the final member was Colin Campbell, a business colleague, but no relation, of Alexander Campbell. The partnership, according to Owen, operated amicably enough at first but, like the previous one, as soon as he became involved in his school building projects, he sensed 'a strong spirit of dissatisfaction in the two sons-in-law of Campbell of Jura'. This animosity, so Owen would have us believe, was entirely based on his partners' conviction that 'they were commercial men carrying on business for profit and had nothing to do with educating children; nobody did it in the manufactories: and they set their faces against it and against all my measures for the improvement of the condition of the work people'.[26]

Certainly there is every likelihood that Owen's colleagues disapproved of his enlightened plans for New Lanark but they had another reason for opposing him which he largely ignored in his version of events. Thus in his *Life*, where he refers to a sum of

£20,000 lent to him by Campbell of Jura saying that this transaction caused his sons-in-law 'to have been filled with the spark
of undying revenge', Owen fails to mention some of the other
aspects of this financial arrangement.

The complex details of Owen's business activities have been
meticulously unravelled by John Butt and others, but what follows is essentially what happened. Shortly before Dale's death
Owen assumed responsibility for Campbell of Jura's investments on the understanding that this money would be transferred to the New Lanark Twist Company. However, Owen
failed to do this and, instead, retained Campbell's money for
the next six years in his own partnership account. By 1812
Owen owed Campbell of Jura over £25,000, a fact which began
to give the latter increasing cause for concern since the war
with France and the quarrel that year with the United States
had plunged the cotton industry into a deep recession. Consequently, in July, Campbell endeavoured to recover £6,000 from
Owen and at the same time tried to obtain some form of guarantee about the remainder of his money. He was assisted in his
efforts by his two sons-in-law. The latter, although they might
also have been discomfited, as Owen alleges, over their father-
in-law's clandestine dealings with him, were more likely to
have been seriously concerned about the poor profit figures for
1811–12 and Owen's basic inability to repay his debts. Accordingly, for the next 12 months a legal battle took place between
the two sides with Owen finally being rescued from bankruptcy
proceedings by the intervention of David Dale's daughters.
Thus, by a settlement reached on 15 July 1813 with the Misses
Dale as guarantors, it was agreed that commencing from
November 1818 the capital sum owing to Campbell of Jura
would be repaid in five equal instalments of £4,000.[27]

As it transpired, Owen's financial worries were only temporarily allayed by this arrangement since in September 1816
investigations were begun into the affairs of John More,
Dale's successor at the Royal Bank. These enquiries had
almost immediate repercussions particularly when it was
revealed that the Dale Trustees not only owed the Royal
Bank over £33,000 plus interest but, since the bills concerned
related to the Stanley Mills between 1806 and 1813, that
Owen was also deeply implicated. Such revelations
prompted Campbell of Jura to consider further action and

by 10 October 1816 he was writing to one of his sons:

It having lately come to my knowledge that the affairs of Mr More of the Royal Bank are in a deranged state, and that it is given out, that the Trustees appointed by the late David Dale owe a good deal of money to the Royal Bank, I desire therefore that you will lose no time in enquiring into this matter, as I am at a loss to conceive how it can be ...

For the next two years Owen's financial affairs were precarious but he survived this crisis and others, his debt to Campbell of Jura being ultimately discharged in November 1822.[28]

Meanwhile, during the course of 1812 Owen's differences with his partners led to the disintegration of the partnership. In June of that year he lost his post as manager of the factory when his partners dismissed him. Their motive was his secret dealings with Robert Humphreys, the under-manager, with whom, contrary to the co-partner agreement, Owen had arranged a deal whereby he took Humphrey's share of the profits and the latter received instead an additional £350 per annum. This action was followed six months later by a proposal from John Atkinson supported by the others that New Lanark should be put up for sale. Owen, however, had taken good care to prepare himself for such an eventuality and during that year had drafted, and then engaged an Edinburgh printer, John Moir, to publish *A Statement Regarding the New Lanark Establishment*. This pamphlet has aptly been described as a 'refined company prospectus' containing, as it does, the information that Owen 'had resigned the management' and that 'the other proprietors are willing to dispose of it on the same terms as they purchased about two years ago'. Moreover, as he went on to explain, by ensuring that the profits had been ploughed back into the business and by following enlightened management principles there had been created an establishment which was more like 'a national benevolent institution than a manufacturing works founded by an individual'. Consequently, so Owen concluded, the opportunities presented at New Lanark were immense 'and so soon as peace shall again take place very abundant profits may be reasonably expected'.[29]

Nonetheless, despite circulating his *Statement* 'among the best circles of the wealthy benevolent, and of those who desired with sincerity to commence active measures for the improvement of

Figure 4·6: *New Buildings photographed from the roof of No. 2 Mill in 1967.*

the condition of the poor and working classes', Owen's initial attempts at recruiting new partners were unsuccessful. Moreover, at a meeting with the old ones in February 1813 the dispute became more rancorous when he accused them of undervaluing the partnership shares for their own benefit. This may well have been the case since his partners probably feared that Owen would be declared bankrupt at any moment and that under the terms of the partnership they would be legally bound to buy him out. At the same time, it was also normal commercial practice to act in this fashion in such a situation in order to make allowance for the unpredictability of the markets.[30]

The partnership was formally dissolved on 30 June 1813 by which date Owen was making further strenuous efforts to find a replacement. On this occasion he went armed not only with his *Statement* but with the first of his *Essays on the Formation of Character*, written by him in 1812, published early in 1813, and eventually part of *A New View of Society*. This time he was successful, forming a partnership which has been fittingly described as 'a mixture of pietistic philanthropy and shrewd, rational calculating Quaker acquisitiveness'. The justification for this description was the presence of four members of the Society of Friends, John Walker, Joseph Fox, Joseph Foster and William Allen. The last was undoubtedly the most prominent member of the group, being the owner of a large chemical works, a Fellow of the Royal Society, a part-time lecturer at Guy's Hospital and a religious zealot who, as we will see, was soon to become disenchanted with Owen's 'infidelity'. Of the others, Michael Gibbs subsequently became Lord Mayor of London, but by far the most renowned was the final member, Jeremy Bentham. At this stage in his long career the utilitarian philosopher had recently become converted to political radicalism, largely through the influence of another notable political theorist, James Mill. It was the latter who played a major role in arousing Bentham's interest in New Lanark as the following correspondence between the two of them clearly indicates:

> Newington Green 3d. Decr. 1813
> Yesterday I complied with an entreaty of Wm. Allen to dine at his house, *in order to meet with Owen*, who is just come up from the Lanark Mills.
> I took occasion to put to Mr Allen the questions respecting the mines which you had directed me to put, and the answer was

such as, I think, I had better send you. As soon as the questions were out of my mouth, he began – 'Do entreat Friend Bentham, to have nothing to do with mines' – he added, 'or at any rate to wait till I can write to Cornwal, where I have friends upon the spot, and can get him accurate information'. He said that he himself had embarked several years ago about £700 in a Cornwall mine, and that it had never produced any thing. He said, that as far as his information or experience went, more had been lost by the Cornwal mines than had been gained. Hearing all this, Owen then spoke, and said, *if Mr Bentham wants to lay out a sum of money, to greater advantage, than on any opportunity that almost ever occurs, he should buy a share of the Lanark Mills, which are to be sold at the end of this month.*

The price Owen says, will not exceed £100,000 for the whole – and that he himself will buy one half – that the raw produce, and the goods which they have on hand, with the materials of the buildings, would sell for nearly the whole sum which the concern is likely to fetch – that he has now brought the manufactory to so great perfection particularly the rational machinery, that even last year, when other manufactories of the sort could make little or nothing, they have cleared 20 per cent upon their whole capital, and that now (viz. the continent open) they will clear a great deal more – that in short he knows not of any occasion within his memory, when so profitable a speculation can be made. An obvious question was, why then on the present profile, so willing to get out of it? To this the answer was, that they had in general got soured with him on account of his perseverance in his endeavours (to which they were averse) to improve the population of the mills; and that even now, though they felt the advantage of his proceedings, they would not acknowledge them – that they were also in some measure bound by their repeated declarations to him, of a readiness to quit the concern, upon even the purchase money of their shares being made good to them – and that it was now his earnest desire to get such partners, as would go along with him, in his efforts to shew what can be done to make a manufacturing population, virtuous, and happy, and far more productive than they have yet been.[31]

The scene was now set for a dramatic showdown between Owen and his former partners. The latter had acquired a replacement for him, namely Colin Campbell, a wealthy business associate of Alexander Campbell of Hallyards and they had also persuaded Robert Humphreys, the under-manager, to take over Owen's position at the factory. Accordingly, the 'well known and extensive cotton mills beautifully and advantageously situated on the river Clyde' were advertised for sale with Owen's rivals obviously convinced they could purchase them for a knock-down price. However, Owen, strengthened by the support of his new partners, three of whom, Allen, Foster and Gibbs, accompanied him to Glasgow, undoubtedly had other ideas. Thus, the auction of the New Lanark mills held at the Tontine Rooms, Glasgow on 31 December 1813 was to result in a triumphant victory for him over his opponents.

At first, his old partners suggested an upset price of £40,000 but when they rejected a private offer of £60,000 by Owen he persisted on this figure being the starting price. Meanwhile he had given instructions to his solicitor, Alexander Macgregor, 'never to bid at any time more than one hundred pounds and to follow up the bidding to one hundred and twenty thousand pounds'. The bidding rose to £84,000 at which point his ex-partners paused for further consultations with each other. It resumed once more rising to £110,000 before there was another delay. At this point, at least according to Owen, Kirkman Finlay, one of Glasgow's leading merchants, a customer of Owen's and a prominent figure in the city, was heard to forecast that Owen would triumph. If he did, he was certainly correct with his prophecy since, when the bidding reached £114,000 and Macgregor topped it with another £100, his ex-partners conceded defeat. 'Confound that Owen', John Atkinson reputedly said to Finlay. 'He has bought it, and twenty thousand pounds too cheap!'[32]

Owen returned to New Lanark where he and his party were given a rapturous welcome by the inhabitants. A letter to the *Glasgow Herald* published on 10 January 1814 gave a graphic description of the reception which they received:

There were great rejoicings here yesterday on account of Mr Owen's return, after his purchase of New Lanark. The Society of Free Masons at this place, with colours flying and a band of music, accompanied by almost the whole of the inhabitants, met Mr Owen, immediately before his entrance into the burgh of Lanark, and hailed him with the loudest acclamations of joy; his people took the horses from his carriage and, a flag being placed in front, drew him and his friends along, amid the plaudits of the surrounding multitudes, until they reached Braxfield, where his Lady and two of her sisters being prevailed upon to enter the carriage, which was then uncovered, the people with the most rapturous exultation proceeded to draw them through all the streets of New Lanark, where all were eager to testify their joy at his return. On being set down at his own house, Mr Owen, in a very appropriate speech,

expressed his acknowledgements to his people for the warmth of
their attachment, when the air was again rent with the most enthusiastic bursts of applause. Mr Owen is so justly beloved by all the
inhabitants employed at New Lanark, and by people of all ranks
in the neighbourhood, that a general happiness has been felt since
the news arrived of his continuing a proprietor of the mills. The
houses were all illuminated at New Lanark on Friday night when
the news came, and all has been jubilee and animation with them
ever since.[33]

Unquestionably New Year's Day 1814 was a significant
watershed in Owen's career. From the day he had taken over
New Lanark in January 1800 until that date he had been strug-
gling to persuade his employees to put his principles into practice. At the same time he had also been fighting a losing battle
with his partners regarding their acceptance of his increasingly
grandiose plans for the village and its workers. Now, at long
last, all this was behind him and, as the next two chapters will
show, he was in a position to press ahead with all those ideas
which constitute what was soon to become known to the world
at large as 'Owenism'.

Chapter Five

FORMING A NEW SOCIETY: NEW LANARK 1814–1824

'Humanity to the laborers'

THE SALE OF THE MILLS AND VILLAGE at the close of 1813 undoubtedly represented a major turning-point in Owen's development of New Lanark as a test-bed for his social psychology and economic philosophy. Reinstated as director of New Lanark and supported in capital and ideals by his philanthropic sleeping partners, who were safely located far away in London and thus unlikely to interfere much in day-to-day management, he was at last able to pursue his goals. He himself was entering what was undoubtedly the most dynamic and productive phase of his life when continuing success in business at New Lanark coincided with – and indeed made possible – his rise to national and international prominence as a social reformer and philanthropic *savant* following the publication in 1812-13 of his essays on *A New View of Society*. Our next chapter will examine the role of New Lanark in his propaganda campaign for improved social conditions and the re-ordering of society, but our immediate concerns are the further reforms and innovations he introduced to the mills and village during the period 1814 to 1824, when he left to begin his second community-building experiment at New Harmony in the United States. As Owen made clear in his writings, the prime vehicle for social reform during these years was education, which it will be remembered, figured prominently in *A Statement Regarding the*

85

New Lanark Establishment, the prospectus Owen drew up in 1812 to attract potentially sympathetic partners. However, there has hitherto been little recognition of the fact that intermittently Owen himself was effectively an absentee landlord, for much of his time was spent in London or elsewhere sowing the seeds of the New System of Society. He certainly relished the role of Laird of New Lanark and as the mills and village were increasingly bathed in the glare of publicity, becoming an essential place of resort for curious middle and upper class visitors from home and overseas, Owen, when in residence, delighted in showing them the well-ordered and productive industrial colony. But during his many absences, day-to-day supervision of the well-oiled machine and the improvement of those tending it fell to others – including the young Robert Dale Owen. Indeed most visitors, even the critics, remarked on the regularity and good order maintained by New Lanark's management – with or without Owen's presence.[1]

Underpinning everything that transpired at New Lanark during this period was the fact that as far as the evidence goes the mills remained a well-capitalised, professionally managed and (for most of the time) a highly profitable enterprise. Even for what was by contemporary standards a large production unit, generating substantial economies of scale and probably with lower overheads than similar places of its size, this was still a considerable achievement in the turbulent years which coincided with the closing stages of the Napoleonic War and its immediate aftermath. Thanks to the research of historians in the surviving business and legal records, we know more about business operations at New Lanark during this period than at any time before the Birkmyres took over in the early 1880s. Moreover, because a visit to New Lanark was high on the agenda of most luminaries of the day, we can also draw upon their travel and personal diaries for detailed and sometimes perceptive accounts of what they saw during their tours of the factory village. Providing we bear in mind the observation of the Swedish traveller Eric Svedenstierna (who, as we saw, visited New Lanark in 1802), that 'a tourist cannot expect straight answers to improper questions', the remarks of visitors provide a useful gloss both on the evidence contained in the business archives and in Owen's reports and writings.[2]

New Lanark remained in 1814 one of the largest cotton spinning mills in the country, having by Owen's estimate a capital cost of around £200,000, the equivalent of its turnover, and in consequence a huge enterprise for its time. The problem of capital provision may have been effectively solved by the creation of the new partnership but to maintain its momentum and profitability, as well as subsidise more ambitious plans for further social and educational reform, Owen insisted on greater labour efficiency and the elimination of indiscipline in the plant and its surroundings. Production problems inevitably continued and had to be minimised on a routine basis. Education was to play an important role in the furtherance of these objectives. The cotton business, as Professor Butt has shown, was always volatile, so success and profitability also necessitated close attention to raw material prices and supplies as well as vigorous marketing of yarns in an increasingly competitive environment.[3]

Apart from water power, New Lanark's prime resource was labour, hence the attention devoted to its control and improvement under the new partnership. According to the data then collected periodically by Owen's staff, the total workforce stood at 1,480 by 1815, having fallen from 1,562 four years earlier. This endorses Owen's evidence in 1816 that the number employed in the mills varied between 1,500 and 1,600. Two-thirds of the total were women, reflecting the trend towards an increase in the female component of the labour force, but shedding relatively more expensive male operatives. The latter could certainly be expected to be more mobile, especially the mechanics who numbered 58, assisted by 22 labourers. The various production processes in the plant were carried out by 244 pickers, 481 carders, 512 spinners, and 129 reelers and sorters – all under the supervision of seven managers. Additionally two schoolmistresses provided instruction and eight storekeepers had charge of the company and mill stores.[4]

Given the large number of people involved labour problems were constantly present and regulations severely enforced, particularly in relation to punctuality and conscientious performance, both being closely supervised by the manager and overseers. As far as we can tell, the 'Silent Monitor' or 'Telegraph' continued to be used as a check on performance. Good order and discipline were generally remarked upon by visitors, but it seems probable that most either took away a superficial

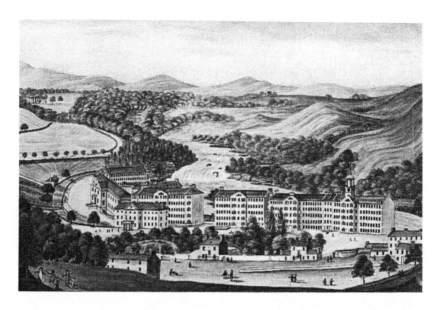

Figure 5·1: *One of a series of watercolours which Owen commissioned from John Winning, c. 1818. Winning taught painting at the Institute where his daughter, Janet, was also a teacher. This shows in remarkably accurate detail the layout of the mills – with to the left the Institute, School and workshops. Dundaff Linn can be seen in the background (Royal Commission on the Ancient and Historical Monuments of Scotland).*

impression or were dazzled by the novelty of such a regimented industrial colony, with its well-conducted workers, school-children and infants. If the entries in what is described in the Gourock Ropework papers as 'Robert Owen's Diary', but more like a rough note-book kept periodically by himself and his man-agers, are anything to go by, indiscipline in both the mills and village was still something of a problem. Stoppage through human error, absence without leave (in some cases to engage in casual harvest work, which may well have been better paid), quarrelsome behaviour and even theft in the mills were not uncommon, while drunkenness, vandalism, trespass and swearing did not go unreported in the village at various times during the period 1813–22. Masters had even to go through the spinning rooms after meals 'to prevent any running about the stairs' and general disorder among the youthful workfolk.[5]

Business efficiency as well as morality can be perceived in

Figure 5·2: *Another watercolour by Winning, c. 1818, showing the mills and village from the north-west near the entrance to Owen's estate of Braxfield. Long Row and Double Row are in the foreground, Braxfield Row can be seen through the trees (left), while beyond, Caithness Row stretches to the southern extremity of the village. One of the figures in the foreground might well have been Owen with a party of visitors (Royal Commission on the Ancient and Historical Monuments of Scotland).*

Owen's directive of 1819 relating to the employment of pregnant women. The all-male management was to enforce the rule that 'No young women who are in a state of pregnancy can be allowed to stop in the works when unable to perform their usual quantity or keep up with their work as usual' and that 'those who are unfortunate cannot be admitted until they have satisfied the church where [they] keep session' as to the origin of their condition. This was perhaps another modest effort to placate both his anxious partners and the increasingly suspicious local clergy on matters of sexual morality and religion.[6]

Though the workforce was described as 'a very temperate body of people' and their drinking as 'a fault the villagers are very seldom guilty of', inebriation certainly occurred – especially on festive occasions like New Year's Day, Lanimer Day and St James' Fair. Also in line with the aim of character formation were the directives of 1820 requesting village boys 'to

give up play at the shinty or clubs and throwing stones, as they
are by the first practice destroying the woods and by the latter
breaking windows and sometimes hurting persons', and cau-
tioning against the use of foul language to local estate and
farm workers. Trespass, as we saw in the previous chapter,
seems to have been a common problem, villagers crossing
the river to Corehouse by the dam or entering the adjacent
Bonnington and Braxfield estates. Indeed, Owen specifically
ordered that people be excluded from his estate of Braxfield,
partly because they were said to be 'conveying away waste
wood' and taking saplings. For all his pretensions to the contrary it seems Owen still regarded his operatives with some sus-
picion and even fear – members of a potentially dangerous
under-class that needed to be closely policed if its character
could not be immediately moulded to his requirements. Significantly one of New Lanark's most perceptive visitors noted that
Owen's staff were effectively operating as police officers and
'moral schoolmasters' of the colony. Another observer, John
Griscom, the American chemist and reformer, while recognising that 'humanity to the laborers' was the prevailing ethos of
the place, the community was nonetheless 'subjected to a strict
discipline'.[7]

The labour-intensive nature of cotton spinning at places like
New Lanark clearly created management problems that could
only be solved by resort to a mixture of strong discipline and
incentive. Technical and production problems were perhaps
easier to anticipate, but could just as readily affect the smooth
operation of the mills. Machinery breakdown, water supply difficulties, poor lighting, shortages of raw material, transport, and
the omnipresent danger of fire all had to be coped with to mini-
mise disruption. Cotton spinning being essentially a flow process, the breakdown of any one piece of machinery could be
highly disruptive, so routine maintenance was vital. Another difficulty faced by the mechanics was power supply, which as we
noted before, had been a major source of acrimony between
Owen and the Edmonstone sisters across the Clyde at Corehouse. Even the settlement of 1813 had imposed constraints on
working: under normal circumstances the sluice had to be
closed at 8 p.m. and not raised till 5 a.m.; and Owen had also
to agree to 'keep the said sluices down during the whole of
each Sabbath day'. Being dependent wholly on water power, a

dry summer or a cold winter could severely affect work in the mills. For example in June 1814 intermittent night work was introduced to compensate for lost production due to water shortages and the following winter of 1814–15 severe frost periodically stopped the mills. In January and February the clock was altered by 20 minutes to maximise light and in March 1816, following the introduction of a shorter working day the previous January, the dinner hour was cut by ten minutes for a similar reason. Generally, as in 1818, the clocks were put on half-an-hour in summertime – and then put back in October. The relative isolation of New Lanark meant that raw material supply and transport difficulties invariably went hand-in-hand – as they had in Dale's time and remained under Owen's various successors. High prices might cause short-term problems, but the bad roads in winter presented a constant problem every year.[8]

Finally, history repeated itself on the night of 26 November 1819 when No. 3 Mill, devoted to mule spinning, was burned to the ground 'except a few stretching frames and mules saved from the west end'. This occurred during one of Owen's frequent sojourns in London and before leaving for New Lanark he penned a note to Jeremy Bentham as follows:

1 Decr 1819

My Dear Sir
    I regret to inform you that I have received intelligence from Lanark that one of the large Mills and attendant buildings have been destroyed by fire. The loss of actual property is chiefly I hope indeed altogether covered, but the inconvenience and derangement arising from such an event cannot be insured.
    I will endeavour to see you in a few days, that is, before I return to Scotland to give you more particulars, which I expect to receive in reply to letters I have forwarded to Scotland.
With great esteem
I remain
My dear Sir
yours sincerely
Robt Owen.

Subsequently no time was lost introducing 24-hour working in No. 4 Mill from 6 December and re-deploying the workforce accordingly – an arrangement maintained throughout 1820–21.

A week later fire precautions were tightened by a directive passed on by the manager who 'told all first masters and many seconds that no person would get to inside of gates till last Bell rings in morning and all masters must be in their places 10 minutes before six am, 4, 5 or 6 minutes before home time at breakfast and dinner'. Moreover, it continued, 'A master must always be along with the person who lights Lamps or Candles, none of Little stoves shall be lighted till after the workers come in'.[9]

A high degree of labour efficiency and the minimising of production problems gave Owen a sound basis for profit-making at New Lanark, although many other factors had to be taken into account. Both the cotton-wool and yarn markets were very volatile, and transport and wage costs were other significant variables. Following the disruption caused to American and West Indian cotton supplies by the war in 1812, the trade quickly recovered. Indeed such was the increase in raw cotton cultivation and export from the plantations that prices fell continuously after 1814 and for most of the period to the mid-1820s. For example, in 1819 Owen could obtain New Orleans cotton for a third of what he paid in 1814, while Georgia, Grenada, Pernambuco and Demerara cottons also fell in price. Such price falls benefited the British industry generally but New Lanark had the advantage of flexibility in concentrating on low-to-medium quality yarns, mainly 20–30 hanks per lb on a scale from 9 to 46. The finer mule yarns could be sold to domestic buyers while the lower counts were primarily directed at European markets – although here again there was room for man-oeuvre depending on the circumstances. The bulk of New Lanark's home sales were done through the Glasgow yarn market, although the company made sales throughout Britain to places as far apart as Dublin and Norwich. During most of the period considered here European sales, especially to Holland, the Baltic and Russia, were of great importance, the majority being made through agents in Amsterdam, Elberfeld and St Petersburg. Owen's obvious business skills are clearly apparent in the way he could rapidly change production in the mills to suit demand and in the sharp marketing policies he adopted. As has been seen each 10-lb bundle of yarn had a label showing a print of the mills – and as a result the product was often recognised by foreign buyers as 'Picture Yarn'. This incidentally helped create what we would describe as a 'corporate image' not just aimed at the customer but giving the New Lanark labour force pride in their work and community.[10]

Dale had hardly chosen New Lanark for its accessibility and accordingly, as we have seen, transport was always a significant local problem. It was partly overcome by co-ordinating raw material supplies and yarn deliveries to the company's Glasgow warehouse, where a close watch was habitually kept on stocks. Foreign trade – generally via Glasgow or Leith – was also fraught with difficulties and delays, especially shipping in stormy or winter weather, customs regulations and the need to afford long-term credit to customers, which made it a very risky business. Hence the use of known and reliable agents wherever possible.

Wage costs were apparently less of a difficulty for it was widely recognised that New Lanark, in common with other Scottish country spinning mills, paid lower wages than their urban counterparts, which in turn were lower than those prevailing south of the Border. The deputation sent to New Lanark in 1819 by the Guardians of the Poor in Leeds noted specifically that 'high wages it is quite manifest are not the cause of the comfort which prevails here. Amongst us their earnings would be thought low'. At that time male operatives under 18 were paid 4s. 3d. per week for day work or 5s. 4d. for piece work; females got 3s. 5d and 4s. 7d. respectively. Average weekly wages of those over 18 were 9s. 11d. for men and 6s. for women for day work; and 14s. 10d. and 8s. for piece work. Moreover, average labour costs declined marginally after 1816, despite shorter working hours and improved yarn quality. This is confirmed by data on New Lanark's output, together with the average count of hanks per lb and corresponding labour costs which have been identified from surviving business records. The figures show that during 1814–21 production averaged 1.4 million lbs per annum, and that yarn counts gradually increased despite falling labour costs. Clearly Owen was able to effect savings on wages by other inducements, such as cheap supplies, housing, schooling and other social provisions. Even these were not enough to prevent protests in 1824 as trouble spread

Figure 5·3: *New Lanark, 1967, showing the former School (left), the Institute (right), mill lade (centre) and beyond, No. 1 Mill.*

throughout the Scottish cotton industry. More will be said in the following chapter about Owen's financial and personal relationship with his partners, but it is sufficient for the present to note that between 1814–25 Robert Owen and Company made a total profit of nearly £193,000. While this was not universally known, philanthropy could nevertheless be seen to pay handsome profits at New Lanark – hence justifying the investment made in social welfare designed to promote well-being and happiness (by which Owen really meant docility) among the workforce.[11]

The development of the mills and village under Owen had brought about an increase in population which rose – partly by migration and partly by natural increase – from 1,793 in 1806 to 2,177 at the national census in 1811 and thereafter to its probable peak of about 2,300 in 1819. We are fortunate that for some of the later years an apparently accurate record of births, marriages and deaths was maintained. For the first five years after 1818, when more detailed records began, the clerk provided a recapitulation of events, showing that in 1818 there were 29 marriages (the average age of men being 29, that of women 25), 48 births (16 male and 35 female), and 53 deaths. The population

Figure 5·4: *The School, photographed in 1971, showing the collapsed roof and general air of dereliction which prevailed in the mill compound before restoration got underway.*

that year he estimated at 2,500 – including nearby Bankhead and Kingsonsknowe on the hill above the village – giving a mortality rate of one in 47. Of the 48 births that year nearly two-thirds occurred in the spring and summer months (almost 40 per cent being in the third quarter) – statistics which at face value suggest a higher level of sexual activity during the preceding autumn and winter months than at other times of the year. For all Owen's boasts to the contrary it seems New Lanark was no more moral than elsewhere for an average of one in eight births was out of wedlock. The presence in Lanark between 1810–14 of French prisoners-of-war, one of whom taught the Owen children, had apparently contributed to the number of illegitimacies at New Lanark. Among those who escaped this stigma, and marrying earlier than most, were William Inglis, aged 26, and Eliza Richmond, 22, married on 22 January 1818, whose first child, also William, was born on 5 August 1819. While we have no way of knowing for certain, it seems likely that young female spinners were discouraged from early marriage by potential loss of earning power; and Owen's policy on the employment of younger children may also have encouraged

Table 5·1:   *Vital Statistics 1818–22.*

	1818	1819	1820	1821	1822
Marriages	29	19	16	14	27
Births (L)	48	66	57	49	49
Births (Ill.)	–	–	7	10	9
Deaths (M) ⎫	53	17	17	9	17
Deaths (F) ⎭		21	24	21	29

later and smaller families since there was no longer an immediate outlet for the labour of small hands. There was one teenage marriage, when William Rodger of Lanark married a 17-year-old spinner, Mary Wales. Sadly, despite both Owen's supposed environmental improvements and the efforts of the surgeon, infant and child mortality was high with 13 infants under two and six children under ten dying during the year. Roughly the same pattern was repeated until 1822.

There is little evidence to indicate Owen's advocacy of birth control at New Lanark, though this was rumoured to be so. He apparently gained some knowledge of the rudimentary methods of contraception that had been used in France since the previous century during his visit there in 1818 and in several works suggested birth control as one means of eliminating poverty. This particular cause was subsequently espoused at New Harmony and Robert Dale Owen achieved considerable notoriety for his views on the issue.[12]

In order to accommodate a growing population Owen continued his earlier improvements to the housing and other facilities, but the most radical innovations occurred in education. According to his autobiography he had begun 'to clear the foundation for the infant and other schools, to form the new character of the rising population' in 1809, though it is possible that his memory was defective and that work did not start until much later. Certainly *A Statement Regarding the New Lanark Establishment* described the planned 'New Institution', and provided a detailed account of Owen's ideas for its development at that point. When New Lanark was advertised for sale in the *Glasgow Herald* of 24 December 1813, a building 145 feet long by 45 feet broad 'at present unoccupied' was described as having been 'planned to admit of an extensive Store Cellar, a Public Kitchen, Eating and Exercise Room, a School, Lecture Room and Church'. Quite likely this was what ultimately became the Institute and was said by Owen in his *Statement* to have been erected at a cost of £3,000. The articles of the new partnership, by which Owen was bound, called for the establishment of a school run on the principles made fashionable by Joseph Lancaster. Teaching aids would be provided by the British and Foreign School Society, the brain-child of Owen's partners, among others, and religious instruction was to be non-sectarian, with the Bible being used only as an aid to reading. Now that Owen was in effective control of the mills and village, the long-planned building to be entirely devoted to education could be fitted out to his specifications at the cost of another £3,000. We might just add that some uncertainty surrounds the date of the building alongside the mills which was also used as a school. It was marked as 'Public Kitchen' on a plan of 1809 but if built by then was certainly never used as such. When Griscom visited New Lanark ten years later he noted that this building was 'nearly completed' and had been designed as 'a kitchen for the whole village'. At that point Owen thought this refectory could save £4–5,000 a year, 'besides the superior training and improved habits it will produce' – but it never became a reality. Unfortunately most of the descriptions leave us somewhat confused about which activities were pursued in the Institute and which in the School. To all intents and purposes they were probably interchangeable as far as the instruction of the children was concerned. William Davidson, writing in 1828 long after Owen's departure, observed dancing being taught in the school, which was also used for lectures given in rooms which still housed the 'Historical Maps and Paintings' as well as a terrestrial globe 19 feet in circumference.[13]

As events transpired, the new Institute for the Formation of Character was not formally opened until New Year's Day 1816. In a lengthy 'Address to the Inhabitants of New Lanark' – mercifully punctuated by a musical recital – Owen expounded his educational aims and explained to an audience of 1,200 villagers the main objects of the Institute. The basis of his speech was a reiteration of the central thesis underpinning *A New View of Society* in which he articulated his unfailing belief in some sort of material determinism 'that the character of man is without a single exception, always formed for him'. He stressed the importance of a proper education from early years saying that 'it must be evident to those who have been in the practice of observing children with attention, that much of good or evil is taught to or acquired by a child at a very early period of its life; that much of temper or disposition is correctly or incorrectly formed before he attains his second year; and that many durable impressions are made at the termination of the first 12 or even 6 months of his existence'. Although far from unique in this view Owen could not have anticipated modern child psychology better: his theory of character formation and general education involved the belief that social training ought to begin from the very moment a child 'can walk alone'.[14]

The Institute for the Formation of Character with its school was considered by many who visited New Lanark to be 'one of the greatest modern wonders' and Owen, revelling in the role of paternalist, obviously took great pride in showing it off. Many interesting descriptions of the Institute's arrangements are given by contemporaries, but the most helpful is that furnished by the young Robert Dale Owen, who returned to New Lanark in 1822 having spent three years (in company with his younger brother, William) at Emmanuel de Fellenberg's school at Hofwyl in Switzerland. Thereafter he occupied himself in teaching and writing a book about the school and its curriculum, which he published in 1824. According to the younger Owen:

> The principal school-room is fitted up with desks and forms on the Lancastrian plan, having a free passage down the centre of the room. It is surrounded, except at one end where a pulpit stands, with galleries, which are convenient when this room is used, as it frequently is, either as a lecture-room or place of worship.
>
> The other and smaller apartment on the second floor has the walls hung round with representations of the most striking zoological and mineralogical specimens, including quadrupeds, birds, fishes, reptiles, insects, shells, minerals etc. At one end there is a gallery, adapted for the purpose of an orchestra, and at the other end are hung very large representations of the two hemispheres; each separate country, as well as the various seas, islands etc. being differently coloured, but without any names attached to them. This room is used as a lecture- and ball-room, and it is here that the dancing and singing lessons are daily given. It is likewise occasionally used as a reading-room for some of the classes.

The lower storey is divided into three apartments, of nearly equal dimensions, 12 ft high, and supported by hollow iron pillars, serving at the same time as conductors in winter for heated air, which issues through the floor of the upper storey, and by which means the whole building may, with care, be kept at any required temperature. It is in these three apartments that the younger classes are taught reading, natural history, and geography.[15]

Dale Owen's *Outline of the System of Education at New Lanark* is perhaps the fullest description of the New Lanark schools, and is of particular value when set alongside the elder Owen's memories in *The New Existence* and his later autobiography. It is to the latter that we turn for Owen's personal recollections of the development and operation of the infant school at New Lanark. According to Owen, the school was attended by 'every child above one year old', although some observers thought the youngest were probably two or three years old. During the first few months of the nursery schools Owen 'daily watched and superintended ... knowing that if the foundation were not truly laid, it would be in vain to expect a satisfactory structure'. With his usual finesse in matters of human relations he 'acquired the most sincere affections of all the children' and apparently also won over the parents 'who were highly delighted with the improved conduct, extraordinary progress, and continually increasing happiness of their children'.

Owen was cautious about the selection of teachers in the 'new rational infant school', for 'it was in vain to look to any old teachers upon the old system of instruction by books'. He had very little belief in books – perhaps a reflection of his own education. At any rate Owen evidently parted with the old dominie at New Lanark and selected from the villagers 'two persons who had a great love for and unlimited patience with infants'. His unlikely choice was a former handloom weaver, James Buchanan, condescendingly described as a 'simple-minded, kind-hearted individual who could hardly read or write himself', but who was willing to do exactly what Owen told him. Buchanan's assistant was to be Molly Young, a 17-year old village girl.

Owen's instructions to his new infant master and assistant were simple :

... they were on no account ever to beat any one of the children or to threaten them in any word or action or to use abusive terms; but were always to speak to them with a pleasant voice and in a kind

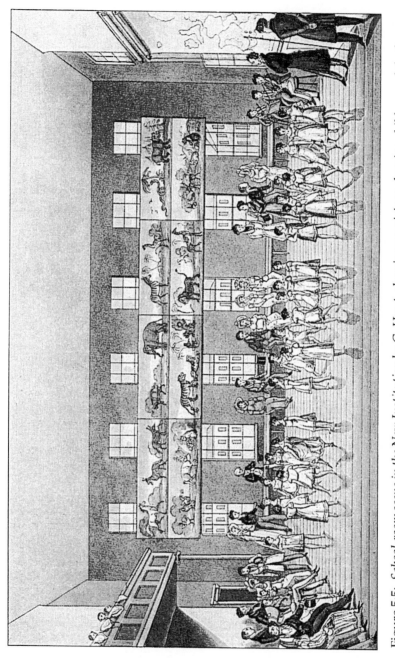

Figure 5·5: *School-room scene in the New Institution by G. Hunt, showing musicians, dancing children and the famous visual aids, c. 1825. Notice the large number of onlookers. Is one of the figures on the right that of the benevolent Mr Owen?* (*New Lanark Conservation*).

manner. They should tell the infants and children (for they had all from 1 to 6 years old under their charge) that they must on all occasions do all they could to make their playfellows happy – and that the older ones, from 4 to 6 years of age, should take especial care of younger ones, and should assist to teach them to make each other happy.

Much of this came directly from the Swiss educator, Heinrich Pestalozzi, who emphasised the importance of kindness and common sense in his teaching. It was all very Utopian and echoed the views of Jeremy Bentham, Owen's most famous partner, regarding the greatest happiness of the greatest number. But we ought to stress again that by 'happy' Owen meant 'docile' – an adjective that recurs in much of his writing at that time.

The nursery school occupied the play-ground in front of the Institute in fine weather, and on wet days the three main rooms on the ground floor. The principle on which the school was run we would call the play principle, no child being forced in any way – not even to mid-morning rest, although 'when an infant felt inclined to sleep it should be quietly allowed to do so'. Toys were rarely seen, for to Owen's mind 'thirty or fifty infants, when left to themselves, will always amuse each other without useless childish toys'. When they became bored or distracted 'a young active teacher will easily find and provide something they will be interested in seeing and hearing explained'. Owen's lengthy description of the infants' actual instruction is worth quoting in part:

'The children were not to be annoyed with books; but were to be taught the uses and nature or qualities of the common things around them, by familiar conversation when the children's curiosity was excited so as to induce them to ask questions respecting them.

The schoolroom for the infants' instruction was furnished with paintings, chiefly of animals, with maps, and often supplied with natural objects from the gardens, fields and woods – the examination and explanation of which always excited their curiosity and created an animated conversation between the children and their instructors.

The children at four and above that age showed an eager desire to understand the use of maps of the four quarters of the world upon a large scale purposely hung in the room to attract their attention. Buchanan their master, was first taught their use and then how to instruct the children for their amusement – for with these infants everything was made to be amusement.

It was most encouraging and delightful to see the progress which these infants and children made in real knowledge, without the use of books. And when the best means of instruction or forming character shall be known I doubt whether books will be ever used before children attain their thirteenth year.[16]

Again the emphasis on observation and experience was borrowed from Pestalozzi. But the infants at New Lanark were, in Owen's opinion, completely unlike others of their age – indeed 'unlike the children of any class of society'. Griscom took a more pragmatic view, probably shared by Owen, when he observed that 'this baby school is of great consequence to the establishment, for it enables mothers to shut up their houses in security, and to attend to their duties in the factory, without concern for their families'.[17]

In addition to this elementary instruction, those over two were given dancing lessons and those of four and upwards taught singing. Military-style exercises were also a major feature of both schools, and the sight of youthful marches led by fife and drum was frequently remarked upon by contemporaries – especially the upper class dignitaries who much approved of such discipline. Conformity in the children was further reinforced by a 'beautiful dress of tartan cloth, fashioned in its make after the form of a Roman toga'. However, like the kilt and plaid worn by older boys this was thought by some of Owen's partners to encourage sexual promiscuity. According to Captain Donald Macdonald of the Royal Engineers, who like Hamilton of Dalzell had become a convert to the New System and who accompanied Owen on the visit of inspection to Harmonie in 1824–25, the New Lanark dresses and plaids were part of the baggage. Owen showed them to fellow passengers and apparently had them copied in New York to be displayed there and in Washington along with his plans and models of the Village Scheme.

Dale Owen also left a detailed report of the school provided for the older children of the community. At the time of writing the Institute had been functioning for nearly eight years, and although it was in some respects a biased account, Dale Owen's *Outline* did make some attempt to assess his father's experiment. The age group concerned was that from about five to ten or twelve – the majority of youngsters being removed from school at ten by their parents to begin a full day's work in the mills. Most working children, however, continued their education at evening classes in the Institute. Attendance at the school for all ages was practically free – the payment being only 3d. per month for each child – hardly sufficient, said Owen, 'to pay for the consumption of books, ink and paper'.

The attendance at day and evening classes in the Institute during 1816 was given in evidence to a Select Committee on Education of that year, in which Owen's associate and fellow reformer, Henry Brougham, played a significant role. It is interesting to note that prior to Owen's reduction of working hours average attendance at evening schools was often less than 100 per night. After the opening of the Institute and reduction of the working day to ten and three-quarter hours (less meal-breaks) attendance rose rapidly. In January 1816 the average was 380, rising to 396 in March. According to Owen's evidence this upward trend continued, giving an average of 485 per evening session. The annual cost of running the schools in 1816 was said to be £700, £550 being for the salaries of a headmaster and ten assistants, and £150 for materials, lighting and heating.[18]

In the preparatory classes all the children learned to read, write and cipher. Owen adopted in part the methods of Joseph Lancaster, whereby certain boys and girls chosen to be monitors passed on lessons learned by rote to other children, in a sense the factory system applied to education. Great difficulty was experienced in finding suitable books for the pupils. Tales of adventure, voyages and travel were popular and, though much misrepresented on the fact, Owen consented to the use of the Bible and catechism. Children were questioned on all they read, and encouraged to look upon books as a means to an end. In writing, copy-books were abandoned as soon as possible, and the children encouraged to develop their own style. Arithmetic was at first taught 'on the plan generally adopted at that time in Scotland', but soon after Pestalozzi's system of mental arithmetic was introduced.

Proceeding alongside these elementary studies, and forming perhaps the most notable feature of Owen's educational system in the Institute, was instruction by lecture, discussion and debate, in geography, natural science, ancient and modern history, and what we might well call civics or contemporary studies – all subjects much favoured by Pestalozzi. These

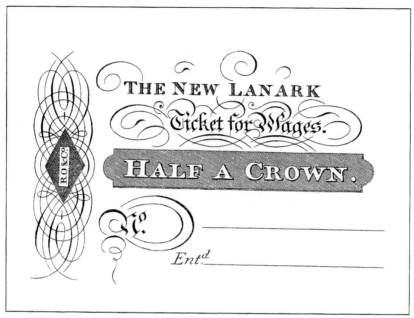

Figure 5·6: *New Lanark Ticket for Wages as issued by Robert Owen and Co.,* *c. 1815. It came in several denominations.*

lectures were a feature of both day and evening schools, and would be attended by 40 to 50 children, though possibly over 100 on some occasions. As far as the subject-matter allowed the lecture would be illustrated with maps, pictures and diagrams – aids always much favoured by Owen. The talk was usually short, so as not to lose the attention of the young listeners and time would be allowed for questions. Owen also loved plans and models and contemporary prints show the extensive use made of visual material for all age groups. Outstanding in this respect were geography and history, which both had an important place in the curriculum at New Lanark. The history time-charts or 'Streams of Time', as well as other visual aids were painted by one of the teachers, Miss Whitwell. She was a sister of the Owenite architect Stedman Whitwell and apparently an advocate of free love. Following her dismissal from New Lanark by Owen's partners, she later taught at the Orbiston Community. Her teaching aids were certainly as novel for the time as her ideas about sexual relations:

Seven large maps or tables, laid out on the principle of the Stream of Time, are hung round the spacious room. These being made of canvass, may be rolled up at pleasure. On the Streams, each of which is differently coloured, and represents a nation, are painted the principal events which occur in the history of those nations. Each century is closed by a horizontal line, drawn across the map. By means of these maps, the children are taught the outlines of Ancient and Modern History, with ease to themselves, and without being liable to confound different events, or different nations. On hearing of any two events, the child has but to recollect the situation on the tables of the paintings, by which those are represented, in order to be furnished at once with their chronological relation to each other. If the events are contemporary, he will instantly perceive it.

Many years later in 1903, when Frank Podmore, Owen's most distinguished biographer, first visited New Lanark, he was shown some of the original visual aids described in this account. Podmore's guide, John Melrose, told him that in his boyhood 30 years before he and the other village children still danced every morning from 7.15 to 8 a.m. According to Melrose the painting and maps were only taken down when the old school was replaced by the nearby Board School at Bankhead. [19]

Both Owen and his son were at pains to stress how everything was made relevant for the children, that they should understand what they were learning and why, and that they should enjoy what they were doing. Geography lessons seem to have been practical as well as relevant and also had a strong moral undertone. The children were often reminded that but for an accident of birth they might have been born into a different society with values totally unlike those of their own. They were taught to respect other people's ideas and way of life and never to be uncharitable or intolerant. Field studies were important, and youngsters were encouraged to go out into the woods and fields surrounding the village (through which Owen had cut paths and walks) collecting specimens and making observations. Owen himself painted a fascinating picture of a geography lesson during which something like 150 children vied with each other in pointing out places on large wall-maps:

This by degrees became most amusing to the children, who soon learned to ask for the least-thought-of districts and places, that they might puzzle the holder of the wand, and obtain it from him. This was at once a good lesson for 150 – keeping attention of all alive during the lesson. The lookers-on were as much amused, and many as much instructed as the children, who thus at an early age became so efficient, that one of our Admirals, who had sailed round the world, said he could not answer many of the questions which some of these children not 6 years old readily replied to, giving the places most correctly.[20]

Owen was unquestionably aiming at giving the children a good basic education – fitting the village youth for the world of work in the mills – but at the same time posing no threat to the existing order of society. Yet in spite of all this, what most impressed the 20,000-odd visitors who came to gape at New Lanark between 1815 and 1825, was the importance of dancing, music and military exercise in the school curriculum.

Dancing lessons were begun at two years of age and visitors were astonished to see how 'these children, standing up 70 couples at a time in the dancing room, and often surrounded by many strangers, would with the uttermost ease and natural grace go through all the dances of Europe, with so little direction from their master, that the strangers would be unconscious that there was a dancing-master in the room'. Dancing lessons were also given in the evening and Griscom saw 50 or 60 young people thus engaged. 'Owen', he noted, 'has discovered that dancing is one means of reforming vicious habits. He thinks it effects this by promoting cheerfulness and contentment, and thus diverting attention from things that are vile and degrading'. The children were also taught to sing in harmony in choirs of 200 or more, performing settings of Scottish and other traditional songs, to the delight of Owen and his visitors. Before the close of the evening school all the pupils would gather in one room and sing a hymn – presumably religious rather than secular. It is not without its interest that singing and music later featured prominently in the social life of New Harmony, and that much of the New Lanark repertoire was carried across the Atlantic by William Owen and others, including Joseph Applegarth, another ardent Owenite who taught at New Lanark and participated in the organisation of the schools at New Harmony and Orbiston[21]. In addition both boys and girls were regularly drilled in the playground in front of the Institute 'with precision equal, as many officers stated, to some regiments of the line'. Contemporary accounts described these military exercises in glowing detail. Owen expounded on their value at great length in *A New View of Society* – and a potentially more formidable despot, Grand Duke Nicholas (later Tzar of all the

Russias), on seeing the military drill, was evidently impressed. As we will discover Owen was not without his critics, but in concluding this brief examination of his system of education at New Lanark, we turn to perhaps the least biased contemporary description of the community by Dr Henry Macnab, who in 1819 had been sent to report on the place by Owen's most regal supporter, the Duke of Kent. 'The children and youth in this delightful colony', wrote Macnab, 'are superior in point of conduct and character to all the children and youth I have ever seen. I shall not attempt to give a faithful description of the beautiful fruits of the social affections displayed in the young, innocent and fascinating countenances of these happy children'.[22]

Owen, the brilliant man-manager turned social philosopher, seems to have evolved in *A New View of Society*, an educational system based partly on a mixed bag of contemporary social and educational thinking and partly on his own benevolent paternalism, deriving from his experience in Manchester and as Laird of New Lanark. His basic assumption was that character could be formed under favourable conditions, and if we are not to discount the multitude of evidence about the New Lanark schools, he succeeded in creating a system which was able to produce conforming and apparently happy (or docile) children equipped with basic literacy and numeracy. New Lanark was certainly not unique in this regard for Archibald Buchanan in 1816 reported a thirst for knowledge and a high level of literacy among the cotton spinners of Catrine and other mills under his management. In many other industrial parishes throughout Scotland the same observations could no doubt have been made. However, the educational venture at New Lanark certainly helped to pioneer infant schools in Britain, and many of the subjects taught there were given a place in the school curriculum a century later. Yet Owen's educational views were in reality only a single facet of a more powerful social gospel which preached community building on the New Lanark model as a solution to contemporary evils in the wider world.[23]

Another much publicised facility – perhaps mistakenly famous in the annals of consumer co-operation – was the company store, which Owen built to improve upon or replace the retailing arrangements set up under Dale's régime. Its actual

date of foundation is difficult to establish. The detailed advertisement which appeared in the *Glasgow Herald* when the mills
were up for sale in December 1813 does not mention it, though
it was almost certainly in existence by that date. Located directly
opposite the Institute, it was a three-storey building with slightly
bowed display windows on the ground floor, which has subsequently had an almost continuous existence as the village store
or shop. The upper floors (now dwellings) were used for storage
of goods, while butcher meat was supplied from a slaughter
house at the back. A bakehouse was added by the Walkers sometime after Owen quit. From the outset the store provided milk
and fresh produce (much of it from the company farm in
season) and bulk buying 'of the best quality' made possible
cheaper prices than previously prevailed – to such an extent it
was said that people from Old Lanark availed themselves of
its facilities.

During his tour of inspection Dr Macnab noticed 'a large store-
house in the very centre of the colony, in which were furnished
all the necessaries of life, and also those which labouring men
regard as the luxuries of the poor' (an oblique reference to
meat, tea, and alcohol, among other items). He estimated that
the prices were 25 per cent cheaper than elsewhere, but apparently this did not encourage over-indulgence. According to
Macnab 'one of the chief directors of [the] works is constantly
in attendance, and recollecting that the luxuries of life could
not be had without being known publicly, our reformer was
well aware, that the publicity of vice thus effected in individuals, would be one of the most powerful causes of reforma-
tion'. As in the mills, considerable moral pressure could clearly
be exercised to produce conforming characters.[24]

Owen paid his workers in both the coin of the realm and by the
remarkably simple device of the cheque. The former was often in
short supply, hence, as we saw, the widespread use, from Dale's
time of counter-marked Spanish dollars and privately circulated
copper tokens; while the latter, known as the 'Ticket for Wages'
(in various denominations) was a highly practical alternative in
the closed community of New Lanark. Interestingly it also provided Owen with a model for the 'Labour Note' introduced by
his later National Equitable Labour Exchange and also
exchangeable for goods. Indeed, from the employer's point of
view the 'Ticket for Wages' can be seen as a useful device to

avoid payment in cash, enforce the procurement of goods at the store and hence maximise its profits. This, after all, was common practice elsewhere, though much criticised. It could also, incidentally, be regarded as a useful device to prevent over-expenditure on drink, but at least the profits of the store, including those on alcohol, were used to defray the expenses of the school.

The poet, Robert Southey, a close acquaintance of Wordsworth and Coleridge, third of the 'Lake Poets' and Poet Laureate, was one of many distinguished visitors. He called at New Lanark during his tour of Scotland in 1819. While few of the Romantic poets or writers of the day were particularly sympathetic to the march of industry, Southey's description of the community is very perceptive. Southey apparently liked Owen but thought he was a bit misguided. The diary entry for New Lanark has never been quoted in full, most likely because it highlighted the manipulation of the workforce in what was for Owen and his partners essentially a remarkably efficient and productive enterprise – and indicated to its readers some of the fundamental weaknesses in Owen's social philosophy. Southey likened the buildings of New Lanark to 'a large convent', built in 'such a dingle' and reached by such a steep descent that 'you might throw a stone down the chimneys'. The rows of houses he thought were 'cleaner than the common streets of a Scotch town, and yet not quite so clean as they ought to be', giving, to his eyes the general appearance of what might be expected 'in a Moravian settlement' (no doubt much like New Harmony at the time).

As can be surmised from Southey's tone he had probably been fore-warned of Owen's flowing enthusiasm and had consequently decided to devote only a day to his tour. Nevertheless Owen 'made as full an exhibition' as time allowed, conducting Southey and his party through both the mills and Institute. The former, thought Southey, were 'perfect in their kind, according to the present state of mechanical science' and apparently well managed. Like many visitors he noted the cleanliness (essential in textile mills because of the fire risk to wooden machinery and from waste materials), the attention to ventilation (vital for the control of temperature and humidity) and the lack of any 'unpleasant smell'. According to Southey maintenance costs were £8,000 a year, a figure that must have come from Owen himself.

Southey's account of the Institute, 'a large building just completed, with ball and concert and lecture rooms, all for "the formation of character",' is highly revealing – both of Owen's
paternalism and the regimentation of his system. The party
were shown a 'plan', most likely one of the 'Streams of Time',
which, as they were designed to do, clearly caught the eye
of the youngsters in the party. Then followed the customary
exhibition of children's marching and dancing. As can be seen
in the extract from Southey's diary he thought the youngster's
'puppet-like motions' might have been produced by the water-
wheel and compared them to Dutch cows whose tails – tied to
a common string – wagged in unison. He was better pleased
with the infant school, whose inmates 'made a glorious noise,
worth all the concerts of New Lanark and London to boot'.
Here too Owen's paternalism was vividly displayed though it
seems he took genuine pleasure in his role of father-figure to
his infant charges.

Kind looks and kind words were all very well but 'Owen in
reality deceives himself', wrote Southey. Owen might as well
be director of a plantation. Though the workers were white
and could quit his service at any time, they were under the
same 'absolute management as so many negro-slaves'. Driven
by a variety of motives Owen would make his 'human
machines' as happy as he could and 'make a display of their happiness'. In all this, said Southey, Owen was jumping to the
'monstrous conclusion' that because he could manipulate 2,210
mill workers to do his will the whole of mankind could be 'gov-
erned with the same facility'. But man is not a machine and
Owen was wrong to presume that what worked in his cotton
mills had universal application 'to the whole empire'. Then
comes a statement which on the evidence of history proved
remarkably prophetic, for Southey observed that Owen 'keeps
out of sight from others, and perhaps from himself, that his
system, instead of aiming at perfect freedom, can only be kept
in play by absolute power'. Owen's problem was that he never
looked beyond one of his 'ideal square villages' – or indeed
New Lanark itself – to work out the implications of his system
for the rest of humanity. Rather than forming character,
Owen's institutions would lead to its destruction – with the
result that 'the power of human society, and the grace, would
both be annihilated'. Despite Southey's misgivings, however,

the New Lanark experiment was regarded by most onlookers as a success. It gave Owen both the means and the model he needed to further promote his programme for a New System of Society.[25]

Chapter Six

A CANDLE IN THE DARKNESS: NEW LANARK AND THE PROPAGANDA OF THE NEW SYSTEM

'It may be true but it is not new'

AT THIS POINT IT IS NECESSARY to digress from our chronological survey to review how New Lanark came to play such a vital role in Owen's ambitious plans for a New System of Society and to look at its relationship with other Owenite activities and community experiments. The influence that New Lanark exercised on both Owen the man and the movement he inspired was of such significance that even a separate chapter here can hardly do justice to the full story. After 1812, when his public career really began, a narrative history of the mills and community under his management figured prominently in practically all Owen's speeches, writings and evidence to parliamentary enquiries. His interest in reform gradually broadened from children's employment and working conditions in factories, to poor relief and education – leading ultimately to the wider social and economic concerns addressed in *A New View of Society* and later writings, such as the *Report to the County of Lanark*. As far back as Dale's time New Lanark had been an object of curiosity, for as we mentioned earlier, large factories were unusual. Hence the community attracted many visitors and was a place of note for tourists en route to the Falls of Clyde. But Owen – a skilled publicist with the means to sustain a long-term propaganda campaign – made it even more famous. In his autobiography Owen acknowledged the

113

Figure 6·1: *Robert Owen, c. 1823, from an engraving by Matilda Hemming.*

influence on his life of *Robinson Crusoe*, which he had read as a child, and with whose hero he personally identified. Indeed, New Lanark could be likened to Owen's island – a place without a history until he himself could write it, or invent it. This he did, using it as a role-model for other communities and the future organisation of society.[1]

While the pamphlet of 1812 describing his early management of New Lanark and articulating his aspirations for the future gave some indication of the way his thoughts were developing, it was not until the publication in 1813 of the first two essays on *A New View of Society* that his proposals were placed before the public.[2] The story of the background to Owen's writing of the four essays in the series has been pieced together by the historian, Anne Taylor, and provides us with another illustration if not of egotism then certainly a lack of willingness to acknowledge the achievements and help of others. When Owen arrived in London in 1812 to seek new partners he naturally sought out the company of those likely to be sympathetic to his cause and rich enough to invest in the New Lanark concern. At a dinner party given for him in January 1813 by a Scot, Daniel Stuart, a supporter of the Tory government and proprietor of the newspaper the *Courier*, he met William Godwin, the prominent social philosopher and author of *An Enquiry Concerning Political Justice*, which had been published in 1793. Godwin's work was a skilful summary of ideas generated during the Enlightenment and argued for a new social order stressing justice, freedom and equality for the individual. The entries in Godwin's diary prove that during the coming months, as Owen worked on the essays, he was frequently at Godwin's house for breakfast, tea and dinner. It comes as no surprise that Owen's work owed much to Godwin's. Not only this, Godwin introduced Owen to the great Radical, Francis Place, at whose shop and library he also seems to have spent time. Among other *savants* with whom Owen kept company was James Mill, the political economist and close associate of Bentham. Although Owen never acknowledged the fact, it was Place and Mill who edited *A New View of Society* and gave the essays the clarity that is missing from his later works. As Taylor says, even his supporters thought much of his writing was very woolly. Place was greatly offended not only by the second edition of the essays, published in 1816, which contained material he had earlier read and rejected, but also by Owen's apparent arrogance in the face of reasoned criticism. Moreover, practical politics were clearly not Owen's strong-point.[3]

The earliest essay, entitled 'On the Formation of Character', was dedicated in its first edition to William Wilberforce, the evangelical Christian MP and humanitarian, who for so long had fought for the abolition of slavery. It was prefixed by the oft quoted statement that 'Any general character, from the best to the worst, from the most ignorant to the most enlightened, may be given to any community, even to the world at large, by the application of proper means; which means are to a great extent at the command and under the control of those who have influence in the affairs of men'.[4] In Owen's view environmental planning and education held the key to the formation of character – and thus suitably moulded characters could produce a pacific and harmonious working class. The excesses of industrialisation and the Factory System must be corrected otherwise 'general disorder must ensue'. 'Happiness' could even be equated with 'pecuniary profits' – as he himself would presently demonstrate.

Little of this was new, for the influences of environment on individuals and society came from Rousseau and other thinkers of the Enlightenment era, whose ideas Owen had first read as a member of the Manchester Literary and Philosophical Society.[5] According to Owen the fundamental precept that character and environment were mutually related could readily be applied in an industrial context. There paternalistic methods might produce a humanitarian régime and generate greater productivity and profit, in which, theoretically all could share. Unity and mutual co-operation were concepts for the future. At this time too Owen's thoughts on education were still being formulated, but expanding his earlier statement of 1812, he duly acknowledged his debt to Lancaster and to Dr Andrew Bell, another reformer who had pioneered the simultaneous instruction of large numbers of children. This was likely to appeal in the first instance to other educational reformers, including his new Quaker partners who were anxious to encourage the development of schools applying Lancaster's principles.[6]

The second essay, written and published later in 1813,

described progress at New Lanark since Owen assumed management. As we have seen, he certainly exaggerated the poor state of the population before he went there, even if he told the truth about the hours worked by children. He provided a glowing picture of the numerous improvements, environmental, moral and social, which his paternalistic methods had effected – showing the 'incalculable advantages' brought to both workers and proprietors. Inevitably considerable attention was again devoted to the role of education and training, which had proved vital in removing 'unfavourable circumstances'. Owen was also able to claim that because there was constant communication between Old and New Lanark his experiment had not occurred in isolation and that his ideas had unlimited potential nationally and internationally.[7]

This was the underlying theme of the third essay, mixed with a general attack on human error and how truth could be made to prevail over it. There was further exemplification of his principles with reference to New Lanark, though more about its future rather than its past and present. He described the central educational role of the 'New Institution', also highlighting the importance of relaxation to his workforce. In this context he attacked the Scots sabbath as being a day of extremes – on the one hand 'superstitious gloom and tyranny over the mind', on the other 'of the most destructive intemperance and licentiousness'.[8] Although at first circulated privately, this essay and its successor in the series were not published until July 1816, but nevertheless this first public attack on religion set a dangerous precedent for the future – particularly in his relationship with his partners and the local presbytery. Quite why Owen maintained his subsequent campaign against religion is hard to determine, because he clearly tolerated and even encouraged church attendance, probably as another means of promoting order and morality. Indeed he made special arrangements for the Gaelic-speaking population by engaging preachers in the language. For many years the summer communion at Lanark parish church was celebrated – on the invitation of Owen's neighbour, Lady Mary Ross – by Dr John Macdonald, the 'Apostle of the North' and the most popular Gaelic preacher in the Highlands. On these occasions tables were set apart for New Lanark's Highland population and Macdonald 'gave the addresses in their own native Gaelic'.[9]

THE TOWN OF LANARK.

Figure 6·2: J. Clark's spectacular view of The Town of Lanark, 1825, showing the mills and housing viewed from the south-west. Notice the gap in the centre of the mill range caused by the destruction of Mill No. 3 in the fire of 1819 (Royal Commission on the Ancient and Historical Monuments of Scotland).

Again generalising from his experience at New Lanark and no doubt much influenced by the views of one of his new partners, Jeremy Bentham, Owen argued in his fourth essay for government intervention to develop a national system of education, to counter increasing problems of poverty and unemployment, and generate greater 'happiness'.[10] There was also a logical link between Owen's practical experience at New Lanark and his interest in three major concerns of the day – the social impact of the Factory System, poor law reform and popular education. He was not alone in realising how closely all three were related and that New Lanark might provide lessons for universal problems. He took up these issues at a crucial time. Certainly the suppression of a dangerous, poverty-stricken, under-class and the creation of a conforming and profitable workforce had an obvious appeal to the governing elite – regardless of party. Indeed for a while Owen could count on as much sympathy from the governing Tories as from the opposition Whigs and, as we will see, he took every opportunity to use his connections in high places to advance his ideas.[11]

Owen's participation in the movement for Factory Reform is universally acknowledged and has been the subject of several detailed studies.[12] Although mainly concentrated in the period 1815–19, it began in 1803 with his paper on the cotton trade addressed to the Glasgow cotton masters. This showed his renewed concern, first evidenced in Manchester, about the impact of the Factory System on society – a theme to which he consistently returned.[13] His personal record on the employment of children at New Lanark was certainly an example of good practice for the cotton trade, which in Owen's words was invariably 'destructive of health, morals, and social comforts of the mass of the people engaged in it'. His campaign for improved conditions began in 1815 with a speech to fellow cotton barons in Glasgow and the substance was subsequently elaborated into a pamphlet, *Observations on the Effects of the Manufacturing System*, which he distributed to members of both Houses of Parliament. This contained the draft of a bill calling for a limit on regular hours of labour to 12 per day including one and a half hours for meals; preventing the employment of children under ten and limiting the hours of those under 12 to six hours per day; and providing basic education for children so employed.[14]

After considerable lobbying, including discussions with Vansittart, the Chancellor of the Exchequer, Owen succeeded in persuading some members of both Houses that a bill on the lines he proposed should be introduced. Sir Robert Peel, father of the future Prime Minister, and himself a wealthy calico printer, would act as sponsor. Peel was an appropriate choice since he had been responsible for the first piece of factory legislation, to which reference has already been made, the Health and Morals of Apprentices Bill, passed in 1802. The new bill was introduced in June but, with the intervention of Waterloo and high politics in its aftermath, nothing was done until the following year when a Select Committee was appointed to take evidence. While this could be seen as a delaying tactic Owen could speak optimistically about the intentions of the country's rulers in his address during the opening of the New Institute at New Lanark that year. Before the committee met Owen and his son, Robert Dale, then just 14, set off on a tour of inspection to gather evidence. Sixty years later Robert Dale was to describe the conditions they found in many mills as 'utterly disgraceful to a civilised nation'.[15]

During several appearances before the committee in 1816 Owen was closely questioned on what he had seen and what had been enacted at New Lanark. He explained that his reduction of factory hours and other reforms were partly humanitarian and partly on the grounds of improved efficiency and thought that they had not increased costs or reduced family income. He was able to produce school registers, which as we saw, indicated increased attendance as a result of shorter working hours. The arguments of the other mill masters – supported in some cases by medical evidence – sought to prove that the measures were unnecessary because they were already being implemented, that cotton mills were perfectly healthy places, and that children would be better put to work than becoming a burden on the parish or taking to a life of crime.[16] Owen issued two further statements on the employment of children (one addressed directly to the Prime Minister, Lord Liverpool) but as things transpired the bill was shelved until 1818 and only reached the statute book in much modified form the following year.[17] Although Owen regarded it as pretty much of a dead letter it nevertheless owed much to his determination and was slowly improved upon by subsequent acts in 1825 and 1833.

Indeed, the first Factory Inspectors to visit New Lanark after the act of 1833 came into force could report that it was still a model establishment of its kind.[18]

Meantime Owen's views on the problem of poverty were also much influenced by his experience at New Lanark and had particular relevance to the difficult era that opened up after the Napoleonic Wars. Economic depression exacerbated growing problems of poverty and unemployment and the Liverpool government struggled against a rising tide of disorder, which was manifest in protests and riots. The administration of the Poor Law, which had been a problem before, became a nightmare. From a purely personal point of view Owen could see that the contribution he and other property owners had to make was becoming intolerable. Again he canvassed his views widely in letters and pamphlets, mostly published in the wake of the second edition of *A New View of Society*, which so offended Place. It was in one of the pamphlets of 1817, that Owen first proposed his village scheme – a plan that obviously drew quite specifically on arrangements at New Lanark.[19] But unlike it, the physical appearance of the proposed villages had a symmetry that more resembled military barracks built around a square located in plots of between 1,000 and 1,500 acres, which with careful husbandry would result in self-sufficiency. However, the new communities could combine both agriculture and industry so they might be said to have something in common with the numerous planned estate villages which by this time dotted the Scottish Lowlands and must have been familiar to Owen. The population was to be similar to that of New Lanark – 1,200 to 1,500 persons, who would be educated and employed according to their abilities and skills – and at a potential profit once the capital cost of building had been recovered. The reader could be excused for thinking that this much resembled a workhouse, though this was not Owen's intention. Sceptics were not long in articulating their criticism, most prominent being another famous Radical, William Cobbett, who scathingly denounced the proposed villages as 'parallelograms of paupers'.[20]

Thanks to his energy for self-promotion 'Mr Owen's Plan' received widespread publicity. In so doing he used his influence in places of power and wealth to advantage, especially among members of parliament, government ministers and wealthy

Figure 6·3: *Henry Brougham, Whig reformer, by James Lonsdale. For a while Brougham was an influential supporter of Owen's factory and educational reforms (National Galleries of Scotland).*

individuals, known to be of a humanitarian disposition, like his Quaker partners and their Utilitarian friends. Both Sidmouth and Vansittart remained sympathetic and this encouraged others to look favourably on Owen's ideas. At that time his views even attracted a measure of support from the upper levels of the British aristocracy – most notably, as we have seen, the Duke of Kent, father of the future Queen Victoria, and the Duke of Sussex. Another early recipient of Owen's plan and a visit from its author was John Quincy Adams, then US Minister to Britain. It has to be said that Owen naïvely took the politeness of such people as a commitment to action, when they were simply prepared to listen to a rich man who had some interesting solutions to the daunting social problems that threatened the established order and their own class.[21] Nevertheless, in August 1817 many of his supporters turned out to a series of public meetings held in the City of London Tavern where Owen expounded at length on his plan. But, showing an amazing lack of tact in the circumstances he complicated his campaign by declaring openly against religion – a move which in the longer-term alienated him from some potentially useful allies. William Allen, for one, was greatly disturbed for not only was he himself a pious individual but also he saw Owen's outburst posing a threat to the British and Foreign School Society, with which he was closely associated.[22]

By September of the same year a more millennialist tone expressed in the language of religion had begun to creep into the propaganda, and the communities proposed by Mr Owen's Plan had been transformed into 'Villages of Unity and Mutual Co-operation'. However, he was careful to emphasise that equality could not immediately prevail and that social class (in four divisions), sectarian or religious affiliation and appropriate skills would be important criteria in the selection of personnel. He even appended a fantastic table showing all the possible combinations of religious and political sects to which future villagers might conceivably adhere.[23] Owen claimed in a letter to *The Times* that the public campaign had produced a more favourable response than he could have anticipated – a view violently disputed by Robert Torrens, the political economist. According to Torrens Owen's report of the proceedings was 'the most barefaced and impudent thing which ever appeared in print' and he found it difficult to decide whether Owen was a knave or 'an interesting enthusiast in whose brain a copulation between vanity and benevolence has engendered madness'.[24]

Although there was no immediate prospect of the Plan being taken up officially, Owen maintained a relentless campaign in which his success at New Lanark was continuously high-lighted. The many visitors to the community had spread its fame abroad and in 1818 he himself carried his message of the New System to Europe. He was preceded by 200 'superiorly bound' copies of *A New View of Society*, which Sidmouth had sent to the governments, universities and leading *savants* on the Continent and in America, apparently inviting their com-ments. Owen later claimed that Napoleon, while exiled on Elba, had studiously read the essays and if given the oppor-tunity would have devoted the rest of his life to implementing the New System. Letters of introduction, including one from the Duke of Kent to the Duc d'Orleans (later Louis Philippe), smoothed his way into the salons of Paris. His tour, in company with his partner, John Walker, continued from France to Switzer-land and Germany where further introductions provided by the far-travelled Allen gave the party opportunities to inspect several experimental schools, including those run by Pestalozzi and de Fellenberg, whose methods were practised at New Lanark. It is not without its interest that the New York Quaker, Griscom, followed much the same road and at roughly the same time before his visit to New Lanark the following March.[25]

Despite his declaration against sectarian religion Owen's reputation as a philanthropist stood high and on his return from the Continent he spent much of the time devoted to a relentless campaign designed to progress the Village Scheme. 'Mr Owen is remarkable for one idea', wrote William Hazlitt. 'It is that of himself and the Lanark cotton mills'. Hazlitt con-tinued by saying that Owen 'carried this idea backwards and forwards with him from Glasgow to London without allowing anything for attrition, and expects to find it in the same state of purity and perfection in the latter place as in the former'.[26] Yet if Owen was obsessed by this one project he continued to use a variety of platforms to advance his proposals for the New System. As Professor Harrison has observed Owen by this time was on friendly terms with many of the country's leaders and for a while at any rate was assured of a respectful hearing for his plans of social betterment. At the other end of the social scale his *Address to the Working Classes*, published in 1819, hammered home the message that social conditions could be changed by rational behaviour rather than revolutionary action – a view that certainly was not calculated to inspire the Radicals to join his cause.[27]

As a result New Lanark attracted even more attention than before. Among the visitors were representatives of the Leeds Poor Law Guardians, who, as we noted earlier, were greatly impressed by what they saw, and the Duke of Kent's personal physician, Dr Macnab, who had been sent by the London committee attempting to gain support for Owen's ideas, and subsequently published a very favourable report on the moral condition of the inhabitants and the provision for their welfare.[28] Apart from Griscom, who was able to tell Owen much about reform in the United States, another visitor with American connections was George Courtauld, a wealthy English silk manufacturer and one of a great dynasty in the textile trade who, during a visit to a settlement called English Prairie in Illinois had also inspected the new Rappite community of Harmonie 20 miles distant on the Indiana bank of the Wabash. Courtauld was so taken by the country that he had resolved to settle there and had just written a pamphlet about an equitable association to buy and work land on the frontier. This was certainly not the first that Owen had heard about Father Rapp and the Harmony Society, for John Melish, a Scot involved in the Glasgow cotton trade, had earlier provided the public with a description of the first Rappite community in Pennsylvania which included figures demonstrating its commercial success. While this was in itself highly commendable it was the fact that both Melish and Courtauld praised the high moral character, hard work, and docile behaviour of the Harmonists which most appealed to Owen.[29] In a pamphlet comprised of three letters addressed to the political economist, David Ricardo, published in 1819, he was able to use Harmonie as an example of successful and profitable community organisation.[30]

Owen's most famous economic thesis, *Report to the County of Lanark*, further refined his plan for self-supporting communities. Again it came at an appropriate time for it was poverty, social distress and the powder-keg of Radicalism that provoked the landed gentry of Lanark into seeking Owen's help. New

Figure 6·4: *Robert Southey, one of New Lanark's many distinguished visitors during the Owen era, by Henry Edridge, 1804 (National Portrait Gallery).*

Lanark, after all, showed that philanthropy could produce docile workers and pay handsome profits into the bargain. For his part, Owen grasped the opportunity presented by the Commissioners of Supply for the County of Lanark in the hope that it might lead to an early experiment in community building. By this time Owen had embraced 'spade husbandry' or intensive agriculture and this figured prominently in the report laid before a meeting of the commissioners on 1 May 1820. Owen's presentation was received with some interest and a further explanation concluded with an enthusiastic account of his achievements at New Lanark, which 'instead of involving any pecuniary sacrafice [sic], are found to operate beneficially in a commercial point of view'. At this point 'a respectable Gentleman of the County', Archibald James Hamilton of Dalzell, a young, disillusioned army officer on half-pay who had met Owen some years before, expressed himself willing to grant a lease of land 'sufficient for the purpose of making a trial of the Plan' and 'being assisted by the Author, to superintend the whole, without charge to the County'. This development, claimed Hamilton, would obviate the need for a new Bridewell or prison. Subsequently, the first edition of the *Report*, published in 1821, incorporated a more detailed description and a map showing the proposed community by the banks of the River Calder near Motherwell.[31] Four years later, as Owen left in some haste for New Harmony, this scheme was to be revived by Hamilton and another ardent Owenite, the wealthy Edinburgh tanner, Abram Combe, as the ill-fated Orbiston Community.[32] We might just note in passing that Combe's brother, George, the famous phrenologist, examined Owen's head and pronounced himself amazed by the size of his 'bump of benevolence'.

At the same time Owen also exploited his local prestige to advance his ever widening schemes by fighting a parliamentary election for Linlithgow Burghs, a seat that combined the burghs of Lanark, Selkirk, Peebles and Linlithgow. The vacancy arose through the death of Sir John Riddell in April 1819. Riddell had reforming sympathies – supporting Catholic relief, criminal law reform – and had been chosen for the Poor Law Committee, to which he had given evidence from Scotland. In his election address Owen explained that the distress of the working classes arose from 'the rapid and extensive introduction of Machinery and other Scientific Power' which had destroyed the equlibrium between production and consumption. This could be corrected and all could derive benefit if 'new internal arrangements' were effected in the state of society. Owen claimed that the 'coming crisis' was near at hand but could readily be met by his plans. It seems that the by-election was so delayed that polling was postponed until the General Election of 1820. At any rate the voters in both Lanark and Linlithgow seemed willing to support Owen and such was his confidence that he told Robert Dundas, Viscount Melville, First Lord of the Admiralty and the government's Scottish manager, that his return was secure. He was even able to cite the unlikely support of a highly influential spirit – the ghost of Melville's father, the great Henry Dundas. Writing to say that Linlithgow had declared in his favour by 19 to 6 and that he needed only four more votes to secure his election, he recalled the fact that Dundas, when on a visit to Lady Ross of Bonnington, whose estate lay next door to New Lanark, had promised 'to aid him in his attempts to improve the condition of the lower orders'. Although Selkirk and Peebles declared for Henry Monteith, Owen's opponent, he claimed he could still have won had not four of the Lanark voters, on whom he had depended not been bribed 'by being feasted, [and] kept intoxicated' by the other candidate.[33]

There followed several years of frenzied activity calculated to make the Plan a reality during which Owen divided his time between New Lanark and London, as well as undertaking an extended tour of Ireland. Convincing the authorities to act was no easy task. A petition to parliament presented in 1821 by the County of Lanark in favour of the *Report* and Plan was rejected and in the Commons 'the quadrangular paradises' were subjected to some ridicule. The Commissioners of Supply for Lanark also turned the scheme down, but undaunted, Owen and Hamilton got together and resolved to try a model community on the Dalzell estate at Motherwell. Although funds were not immediately forthcoming Owen's scheme still proved bold enough to attract some powerful support. This led to the establishment of potentially the most influential body likely to effect progress, the British and Foreign Philanthropic Society for the Permanent Relief of the Labouring Classes. Its first meeting in London on 1 June 1822, with John Galt, the Tory novelist and parliamentary lobbyist, as Honorary Secretary, witnessed an assemblage of the great and the good to discuss 'the great distress prevailing over the country'.[34]

Lord Torrington as chairman provided his own testimonial for the scheme, telling the audience that 'no language can do justice to the excellence of the arrangements' at New Lanark. 'To *see it*', he said, 'is to be delighted with the order and regularity that prevail there'. During a visit he had attended an evening meeting of over a thousand people, 800 of them from 16 to 20 years old, 'all uniting in friendly conversation, accompanied with some instrumental music'. He left the meeting early to see if any 'irregularity' occurred among so many young people, but 'their conduct was that of friendship and brotherly regard; and in ten minutes every individual was in his house, with order and regularity'. 'In my walks about the establishment', concluded Torrington, 'I requested Mr Owen not to attend me, that I might judge for myself; and I am convinced that whoever has seen *what I have seen* can have no doubt as to the excellency of the plan'. This must have convinced any doubters and a large list of individuals promising loans and donations was drawn up. It included many prominent Owenites and other sympathetic figures like Elizabeth Fry and Henry Brougham. Another of the subscribers was an old ally, Sir William de Crespigny, an MP who had previously embraced a variety of social reforms and assisted Owen in promoting parliamentary support for his schemes. Whether these and other supporters' enthusiasm would be backed with cash was another question.[35]

Owen afterwards carried the lessons of New Lanark to Ireland, which according to his recollections was then 'in a state bordering on barbarism ... derived from religious hatreds and conflicts'. He spent some months touring places hit by famine and food riots and saw the miserable condition of the poor and unemployed. As he went round he foolishly declared that he would soon reveal a 'secret' that would put all to rights. But at the first of several meetings held in Dublin during May 1823 he showed little sympathy with the plight of Ireland and all he could come up with to save the country was the Village plan. People may have been unrealistic in their expectations but this did not prevent Owen being denounced as something of a charlatan. His account of events, as earlier in 1817, presented a much more positive outcome. Whatever the truth of the matter, as Anne Taylor has suggested, many of his supporters were still prepared to give him the benefit of the doubt. Thus he was called to give evidence before a Select Committee investigating the Irish poor in June and July 1823. More to the point, the committee would need to give due consideration to the

Figure 6·5: *Portait of William Maclure, c. 1820 (Academy of Natural Sciences, Philadelphia).*

Village Scheme, since another petition seeking support then lay before parliament.[36]

Unfortunately things did not quite go Owen's way. The committee, which had among its number Ricardo, were quite prepared to credit him with remarkable achievements at New Lanark, and he could claim, reasonably enough, that it proved that the villages *must* work. But there was a great deal more to it and the committee quizzed him closely on the fact that the villages were meant to be self-supporting and engender complete equality amongst the participants. His answers were not convincing. Surely the commercial success of his villages would be disruptive of existing settlements and how could equality – in moral as well as social terms – be justified? How would industry and skill be rewarded? And surely the examples of successful community organisation in the United States, like the Moravians, the Shakers and the Harmonists, were based on sound religious principles? He could only answer that the character of the new villagers would be reformed by becoming members of radically different communities than any that had proceeded them. He reiterated the well-worn account of how he had found New Lanark when he assumed management. 'The very dregs of the Highlands' had been raised to a higher station by 'the withdrawal of unfavourable circumstances'. It was at this point that Owen launched into yet another of his savage attacks – this time on the law and lawyers. At New Lanark he had abolished recourse to the law and for many years no disputes had come before the local magistrates, because he himself had taken charge and levied fines on recalcitrants – as he intended in the new villages. Like the earlier attack on religion this unfortunate outburst did little to improve his case – especially with those of his supporters and their friends who were members of the legal profession.[37]

Owen's high public profile and pronouncements on religion had meanwhile caused some of his partners considerable disquiet and they could also claim with some justification that his numerous absences resulted in neglect of the business at New Lanark.

The problem over religion can be seen as part of the conflict between Old and New Society and manifested itself in a long-running campaign by a few members of the Lanark presbytery against Owen's opinions and actions. Inevitably this became

internalised in an extended debate between Owen and some of
his partners concerning the role that religious instruction
should play in the school at New Lanark. Although the smear
campaign against Owen dated back to the publication of *A
New View of Society*, it was not until 1816, when he gave evidence
to the Select Committee on Children's Employment, that daggers
were really drawn in earnest. Hostile cotton masters sent Henry
Houldsworth and another of their associates 'on a mission of
scandal hunting' to New Lanark. There they bent the ear of the
parish minister, the Revd William Menzies, who felt slighted
by Owen's patronage of dissenting clergy and thought his
address at the opening of the Institute to be 'of the most treason-
able character against church and state'. The masters persuaded
Menzies to communicate this directly to Sidmouth, but on doing
so he was forced to admit that he had not actually heard the
speech and was merely recounting his wife's report. Whatever
the true nature of Owen's relationship with Sidmouth the
accusation was dismissed. The bulk of the evidence indicates
that Owen was basically tolerant of his workers' beliefs, which
were 'complied with and aided to the utmost extent' by the provision of facilities for worship and continuing to pay a minister
'for performing divine service in the Gaelic tongue to Highland
workmen'. By Macnab's account religious observance was the
rule and at Owen's own house at Braxfield daily prayers were
observed by a large and moral family.[38]

However, the recurring charges of atheism caused Owen's
partners, notably the 'busy, bustling, meddling' Allen, to inves-
tigate both the spiritual life of the community and the moral and
religious content of the school curriculum. Allen at first opined
that Owen's views referred wholly to worldly character, not
the religious, but later became increasingly alarmed by his out-
bursts against religion. In company with Foster and Gibbs,
Allen had first visited New Lanark after the new partnership
had bought the mills in 1814, and, according to Owen, the
three had returned home to London 'delighted with their mission'. Subsequent reports about increasing secularisation upset
the Quakers who hardly shared the admiration of other distinguished visitors for the sight of 400 or 500 children manoeuvr-
ing with military precision in kilts and singing secular songs.
Allen and his companions returned on several occasions and
during the visit of inspection in 1818 insisted on addressing

the community on the importance of religion and the wickedness of elevating reason above the teachings of scripture. This time Owen was ready for them and had the villagers primed up with an address of welcome extolling the praises of the New Lanark establishment and the social and educational arrangements made for themselves and their children. Allen was clearly forced to back off and while admitting that there were those in the outside world who were 'watching for evil', concluded that 'in point of moral and religious feeling, as well as in temporal comfort, no manufacturing population of equal extent can compare with New Lanark'. Allen records that he and Foster afterwards spoke to two of the ministers in Lanark and were given a good account of morals in the village. One of the ministers was urged to visit the school, keep an eye on what was taught there, and report anything 'contrary to revealed religion'.[39]

It was another injudicious move on Owen's part that again showed his lack of tact and finally brought about an impasse with the Quakers. In 1823 he suggested to the schoolteachers that instead of reading the Bible the senior classes would derive 'more real benefit' from studying geography. When news of this reached Menzies he called an emergency meeting of the presbytery, which immediately – and without proof – condemned Owen for banning the Bible at New Lanark. A delegation from the presbytery made little headway and subsequently a vitriolic campaign in the columns of the *Glasgow Chronicle* gave the affair the sort of publicity it could well have done without. The consciences of Allen and his associates were re-awoken and, determined to have their way, the Quakers drew up an agreement for new arrangements in the school. The existing schoolmaster was to be replaced with one thoroughly trained in Lancasterian principles, religious instruction was to be introduced, dancing was not to be taught at the company's expense, nor singing 'with the exception of instruction in psalmody', and 'all males as they arrive at the age of six years should wear trousers or drawers'. This agreement, signed in January 1824, led ultimately to the appointment of John Daniel, a master trained in more rigorous monitorial methods, who apparently introduced a course of science lessons in place of some of the dancing.[40]

Although they might object to the role Owen had given New Lanark in his propaganda campaign, his partners could have

Figure 6·6: New Harmony from an engraving dating from the Owen era. The Wabash River can be seen in the background. More akin to one of Owen's 'Agricultural Villages of Unity and Mutual Co-operation', New Harmony had little in common with New Lanark apart from its idyllic river-bank setting on the Indiana frontier.

little complaint about their financial returns from the enterprise. According to the figures compiled by John Wright, who kept the books in the company's Glasgow warehouse after 1810, the third partnership made a gross profit of £192,915 during the period of Owen's management from 1814 to 1825. During the early years of the partnership Allen and Bentham complained both about the delay in signing the article of co-partnership and being kept in the dark about the progress of the business. Whether this can be regarded as evasiveness on Owen's part cannot be discerned from the record for he certainly kept in touch with his partners during his regular visits to London. In any case, the partners had agreed not to draw any profits until the end of 1817, which gave an extended breathing space to the business following its restructure. When they did so – despite the bad downturn in the cotton trade during 1820–21 – they were well rewarded with an annual return on capital of over 15 per cent. Wright's figures, shown in Table A2a–d (see pp. 214–15), provide us with a useful overview of New Lanark's continuing profitability, while other data from Balance Sheets in the Gourock Ropework Company records indicate in more detail how Owen ran his profit account down, no doubt spending heavily on his propaganda campaign. Correspondingly that of John Walker, the next major share-holder, rose – giving his family the largest financial stake and making the Walkers ultimate heirs to New Lanark.[41]

The year 1824 represented a vital turning point in Owen's career and greatly influenced the future history of New Lanark. The grudging concession which he had been forced to make on the school curriculum and the use of the Bible was only the first of several major challenges to his authority and pre-sented a setback to his plans for further reform in the village. Indirectly it also damaged his efforts for a trial of the New System. There were other alarming developments in the com-munity, which caused further disquiet among some of his partners. An outbreak of typhoid fever suggested that Owen's hygiene and housing reforms were not as effective as he had claimed and at the very least was evidence of neglect. There was much ill-feeling when Owen dismissed seven of the workers for objecting to his interference in the friendly society and apparently taking over its assets. Although we do not know exactly what – if anything – happened at New Lanark, the situa-tion was not helped by unrest throughout the Scottish cotton

trade as operatives combined to fight for better wages and working conditions. Workers, evidently fed up with the régime,
including the dancing, were rumoured to have left New
Lanark for work in other mills, notably that at nearby Blantyre.
Two books attacking Owen's views – one by the Revd Aiton
and the other by William M'Gavin – reported these events.
Both publications highlighted Dale's achievements at New
Lanark, called into question some of Owen's reforms, and
claimed that the social provision in other Scottish cotton mill
villages, especially at Catrine, was just as adequate. Clearly
these rumours and attacks did little for Owen's image as a
benevolent employer.[42]

Worse was to come, for the death of John Walker in May 1824
robbed Owen of his closest colleague and staunchest ally among
the New Lanark partners. Owen's earlier appearance before the
Select Committee and his attacks on religion and the law had
prejudiced some of his most powerful allies against him. Nor
was his case for a trial of the Village Scheme much helped by
his constant stress on 'equality', when he ought to have emphasised the importance of 'co-operation'. At any rate when Owen's
petition for further consideration of his Plan finally reached parliament it was rejected. Even his old supporter, de Crespigny,
abandoned the Scheme – telling the Commons, 'I have asked
Mr Owen not to bring it before this House again'. With this
window of opportunity closed and his pride much deflated,
Owen withdrew to his 'island' at New Lanark to take stock
and await further developments.[43]

As we saw, American interest in New Lanark was considerable and from the earliest days the mills received a stream
of visitors from the United States. Partly this arose from the commercial links generated by the cotton trade, and partly from
wealthy Americans (some with Scottish roots) doing the Grand
Tour. A few, no doubt, came to have a good look at New
Lanark's spinning equipment, hoping to pirate the machinery
and emulate its scale and profitability in New England, where
some cotton mills were said to show dividends between 20
and 30 per cent. But the majority, like their European counterparts, were simply curious to see this well regulated factory village with its enlightened management set amid the romantic
scenery of the Falls of Clyde.[44] The most influential American
by far was William Maclure, a Scottish merchant who had

settled in Philadelphia. Having made his fortune he was free to indulge his interest in travel, science, education and other good works.[45]

It is surprising that William Maclure's visit to New Lanark in July 1824 was so long delayed, for like many Americans with reforming instincts he had met Owen before and clearly kept himself up-to-date with events in his native country. Given his enthusiasm for educational innovation he was familiar with Owen's views on the subject and had known about the educational and other reforms at New Lanark for some time. On an earlier European tour during 1809 Maclure had met Erik Svedenstierna, then Director of Foundries in Sweden, and it is possible that he discussed his host's visit to New Lanark seven years before – not long after Owen's arrival as Dale's manager. Maclure, in a letter to Madame Fretageot, later a leading educationist at New Harmony, described his few days at New Lanark as the most pleasant in his life. He was greatly impressed by what he saw. He was captivated by Owen's success on two counts: first, for the good it would produce; second, because it encouraged him in his own ideas for experimental schools in the United States. Maclure was also struck by the number of ladies visiting the school 'from which it would appear that women are more interested in the improvement of society than men'.[46]

Maclure was not only sympathetic to educational reform but was also familiar with community experiments of the kind Owen advocated, such as those of the Shakers, Moravians and Harmonists in the United States. Moreover in his adopted country – as Owen must have known – he was well connected with the intellectual and political elite and consequently could open doors in high places. We might just note that Owen himself knew plenty of influential Americans, notably Adams, who succeeded James Munroe as president early in 1825. Given Owen's frame of mind at the time, he probably discussed with Maclure his long-standing interest in Harmonie and the impending arrival at New Lanark of Father Rapp's agent, Richard Flower. Whether or not a prospective partnership between himself and Owen in the purchase of the Harmonie Society was considered at that stage is uncertain but it seems highly likely.

Owen had established the first direct link between New

Lanark and Harmonie in a letter written to Father Rapp in August 1820. Although no further correspondence has survived, the interest Owen had shown in the community on the Wabash was enough to guarantee that when Rapp decided to abandon Harmonie for a third settlement he informed Owen of his intention to sell. Flower reached New Lanark in August 1824. He evidently had his suspicions about Owen but kept them to himself. Flower was amazed at Owen's determination to pursue the purchase of Harmonie – regardless of existing business and domestic commitments or the difficulties of pioneering life in the American wilderness. Although Owen must have realised how different Harmonie was from a Scottish mill village he still saw New Lanark as his model. Certainly the repeal of the Combination Acts, which had hitherto prevented the emigration of skilled artisans, opened up the possibility of enticing such operatives across the Atlantic – something Owen had earlier frowned upon but could now turn to his advantage.[47]

Within weeks of Flower's visit Owen had made up his mind to inspect Harmonie and, accompanied by his second son, William, and the faithful disciple, Captain Macdonald, hastily left for Liverpool and took ship for the United States. We have explored some of the explanations for this sudden decision, the most compelling being that despite his rebuff by the British establishment he still regarded himself as something of a visionary and that the message of New Lanark had universal application. Owen undoubtedly had expectations of his ideas being embraced with greater enthusiasm in America and had been told that there were likely to be fewer legal and social restrictions in implementing his Plan. He may well have felt that he could do no more at New Lanark, especially since he had so badly alienated his partners and lost the one individual among their number who was most supportive of his schemes. Although he had spent considerable sums on his propaganda campaign he was still a rich man, and Harmonie, by all accounts, was likely to be bought cheaply by British or European standards. Like New Lanark it was a ready-made community and apparently highly profitable. Even if the experiment was a failure he was unlikely to lose out on his investment.[48]

New Lanark was a highly successful capitalist enterprise where personnel could be rigidly monitored and controlled and on whom experiment was certainly both feasible and remunerative. Paternalism and social control made possible the real achievements at New Lanark, which produced a generally docile labour force whose working and living conditions and level of social provision were better than most – but by no means unique in the context of the planned agricultural or industrial communities of the time. But New Lanark was an inappropriate model for Owen's Plan. In terms of its government democracy had no place there. Owen was an autocratic, paternalistic employer, at that time sympathetic to reform in the wider sense but certainly no democrat, as he also demonstrated later in the role of feudal superior at New Harmony. In economic terms too New Lanark was exceptional in its high levels of productivity and profitability. It was a large unit in a dynamic growth industry applying new technology to mass production for the first time on any scale. Hence it was hugely different in capital and organisation from anything proposed for the Owenite villages which were to represent much more modest investments and have very diverse (and potentially less profitable) functions. New Lanark made no pretence of self-sufficiency, indeed its life-blood was its relationship with the commercial world and Old Society; and although New Harmony had a highly productive agriculture and could readily feed itself, its great success lay in its trade in foodstuffs, other primary commodities and simple manufactures so desperately sought by settlers on the American frontier. Sadly we must pass over the fascinating story of New Harmony – and those of other Owenite communities like nearby Orbiston – to look at the much neglected history of New Lanark in the post-Owen era.

Chapter Seven

AFTERGLOW: NEW LANARK
UNDER THE WALKERS 1825–1881

'A thriving concern'

INEVITABLY PERHAPS THE STORY of New Lanark after Robert Owen's time is little known, though both the mills and village functioned as a working community for nearly 150 years after he left. New Lanark remained an object of fascination to the general public – partly because of its close associations with both Dale and Owen, and partly for the reputation the place had as a successful application of humanitarian principles which produced a docile workforce and clearly paid profits. In a period when the social problems of rapid industrialisation and urbanisation were becoming all too apparent New Lanark still seemed to hold some of the answers, particularly for a growing band of middle-class reformers. Later, as we have seen, it became identified – wrongly some might claim – with the origins of communitarianism, co-operation and socialism. Moreover its location in an area of considerable natural beauty kept it in the public eye. Lanark itself was a place of inland resort, much like Moffat with its spa and therapeutic waters, and this function was further enhanced when the railway replaced the stage-coach in the early 1850s. According to one historical guidebook published in 1855 'the manufactory of New Lanark and the schools which are there established are now interesting objects of curiosity to all tourists'. Thus New Lanark maintained its attraction for

141

visitors who continued to come in large numbers, especially in the summer season.[1]

Nor did Owen immediately disassociate himself from New Lanark – quite the contrary. For a while the firm continued to operate as Robert Owen and Company and both Owen and his sons maintained a considerable financial interest until 1828 and, it seems, a smaller one till the early 1830s. Owen and his family apparently continued to draw a modest income from the Dale Trust and indirectly from New Lanark itself until his death in 1858.[2] More significantly, as Owen moved on to the national and international stages, the community he had helped to create figured prominently in his numerous speeches and writings. New Lanark was a major, if increasingly inappropriate, element in his propaganda of the New System of Society, articulated endlessly on trade union, co-operative and political platforms during the 1830s and '40s. Although run on essentially capitalist lines with the profit motive uppermost in mind, it might be said to be his only real success story since the majority of other Owenite communities, like New Harmony or Orbiston, were either only a limited success or downright failures. Ever the optimist and egoist, Owen could rightly claim that his social experiment in man-management and environmentalism at New Lanark had been a success and might serve as an inspiration to others at home and overseas.

One thing that undoubtedly helped to maintain this image was the fact that the Walkers, who acquired a controlling interest in 1825 after Owen had effectively quit, were also humanitarian employers. Like some of his earlier partners they were members of the Society of Friends or Quakers and held to the view that decent working and social conditions were worthy of investment. John Walker, a wealthy and cultivated man, had – it will be recalled – become one of Owen's partners in 1813–14. The family régime under Charles Sr, appointed as manager in September 1825, and Henry, two of his sons, coincided with the passage and implementation of the Factory Acts and it is from the reports of the early Factory Inspectors that we learn much of the history of New Lanark under the Walkers. Sadly the business records for this period are either lost or deficient so we are unlikely ever to know much of the detailed operation, production or profits. The new management certainly had pressing problems because the profits in 1825 were less than a third of the previous year and worse was to come in the economic crisis of 1826–27.

As far as can be gathered there was only one major partnership change throughout the Walker years, which effectively transferred the bulk of the business to the family. In 1838 Charles Walker, Henry Walker, Joseph Foster, Joseph Fox, Sarah Walker, Francis Walker and Michael Gibbs, as trustees on behalf of Walker & Company, secured control of New Lanark on the disposition of Robert Owen & Company. This move had apparently been agreed in September of the previous year, but was not legally confirmed until later. William Allen, with whom Owen had so many disagreements over religion and social policy (though they apparently maintained their association), was dropped from the partnership, but Michael Gibbs, another prominent London merchant, retained his interest.[3] The record is blank as to subsequent changes, though it seems that the Walkers gradually acquired a growing stake in the concern on the demise of their associates. Quite likely they had gained sole control before 1850 – though there is little doubt that the value of the company's assets had begun to shrink before then.[4]

What can be said with certainty is that the Walkers – at least for a while – managed to maintain the business in a climate of fiercely growing competition, for after 1830 the Scottish cotton industry was increasingly challenged by Lancashire and overseas manufacturers. But New Lanark - like some other Scottish country spinning mills which dated from what one historian has described as the 'heroic age of the industry and the era of its greatest dispersal' – seemed to weather the storm. It relied on water wheels for its power supply and although the spinning equipment became increasingly antiquated there was some modest investment in new machinery and steam power to supplement the water power from the Clyde. New Lanark enjoyed the advantages of cheap overheads (although transport was always a problem), cheap machinery and moderately cheap labour (and low wages could always be compensated for by cheap rents), and, in addition, because of its good reputation and the undoubtedly sustained attention devoted to social welfare, relative immunity from prosecution under the Factory Acts, which Owen had fought so long to see reach the statute book.[5]

The Walker régime, as far as the evidence goes, has been much maligned, being described in George Blake's official history of the Gourock Ropework Company as 'sore years' of wage cuts, the introduction of the truck system of selling provisions (partly in lieu of wages), and the neglect of the school and other social provisions – all apparent misinterpretations of the true facts. Perhaps this was a deliberate slant in order to enhance the role of Henry Birkmyre, who took over after the Walkers sold out and himself emerges from the pages of New Lanark's history with a somewhat mixed record.[6] It is true, that latterly, the Walkers seem to have lost interest in the business and made several attempts to sell it, notably in 1851. Nevertheless, David Bremner, first industrial correspondent of *The Scotsman*, writing in 1869 could still describe New Lanark as 'a thriving concern'.[7] He may well have been overstating his case given the impact of the American Civil War and the 'Cotton Famine' on the industry generally and the subsequent efforts of the Walkers (especially Charles Jr) to disengage from the business. While the buoyancy of the early years was probably never restored and the population slowly declined, New Lanark was at least a viable enterprise and this it remained throughout much of its working life under the Walkers and the subsequent ownership of the Birkmyres and the Gourock Ropework Company.

The population profile shows the relative decline of the community during the 19th century – a direct reflection of the state of the Scottish cotton industry and its diminishing labour requirements. From a peak of 2,300 people at the time of the 1821 census the population of New Lanark gradually declined:

Table 7.1: *Population of New Lanark 1831–91.*

Year	Population
1831	1901
1841	1644
1851	1807
1861	1397
1871	973
1881	706
1891	672

While this sustained fall in the number of inhabitants at New Lanark and other similar communities like Catrine or Stanley mirrored the declining fortunes in the Scottish cotton trade, it also reflected important changes in technology and the work-force. The larger and heavier spinning machines with their higher levels of automation were less efficiently operated by small hands and the introduction of factory legislation and regular inspection greatly reduced the number of children employed. While there was apparently little abuse of the Factory Acts at New Lanark, risk of prosecution was always present even if the employer was blameless and the fault lay with the young worker or his or her parents. Moreover the economics of the business dictated increased efficiency and since adult male labour was expensive, increased resort was made to women workers – in any case traditionally the largest proportion of the labour force at New Lanark. In 1833 Charles Walker provided the Factory Inspectors with a list of 37 married women employed in the mills, some of whom were by then in their fifties or sixties and had worked at the place since Dale's time. Many members of their families, especially the women, had taken mill work. Nearly two decades later the census of 1851 highlights the continuing dominance of females – almost two-thirds of the total workforce – and half of them in their 'teens and 'twenties.[8]

Male employment was consequently always a problem locally. According to Thomas Mallock's evidence to the Select Committee on the handloom weavers of 1834 'a redundancy of the male population of New Lanark was thrown upon the trade of handloom weaving', which had grown into a major industry in the locality – with no fewer than 700 looms then at work. Unfortunately the development of the power loom created much unemployment and hardship as wages fell in the face of competition from the new technology. The situation was made worse if a weaver had 'five or six children who are males', for New Lanark by that time employed few boys, especially from outside the village. Some of the daughters of local weavers did work in the mills, 'but no considerable proportion'. The trend to a predominantly female labour force continued – with a small group of male employees working as supervisors, mechanics and labourers.[9]

Although we know much less than we would like about the

New Lanark.

Figure 7·1: *New Lanark from the south-west, c. 1828, as depicted in William Davidson's* History of Lanark and Guide to the Scenery. *It shows the mills in the foreground with the housing (including that built by Owen) much as it survives. The print closely resembles one used by Owen in his account of his proceedings in Dublin five years earlier in 1823.*

business history of New Lanark under the Walkers, working and social conditions – always Owen's passions – are relatively well-documented. New Lanark was among the first of several Scottish country spinning mills visited by the new Factory Inspectorate in 1833. James Stuart, the inspector covering a huge territory embracing both Scotland and Ireland, and Sir David Barry, the Inspectorate's medical officer, were suitably impressed by the arrangements they found during their tour of inspection at New Lanark – the mills being 'under the same excellent management with a view to health, education, and general comfort of the workers, which prevailed during the proprietorship of the late philanthropic Mr. Dale and his son-in-law the well known Mr Robert Owen'.[10]

They saw 930 employees (563 women and 367 men) working in 24 apartments in the three mills, with a fourth mill in the process of construction. 'The whole of the apartments, the walls, the floors, and the machinery', they observed, 'were thoroughly clean and no unpleasant smell could be detected anywhere'. The windows all opened from the top, with the south-facing ones by the river's edge equipped with linen blinds, so both ventilation and light could be readily controlled. Given the relatively coarse quality of cotton being spun no artificial heat was ever required except to keep the workers warm in winter, when stoves were lit. One disadvantage reported was that the coarseness of the cotton created a great deal of dust and refuse in the preparation and carding rooms, for which fanners of the type then employed at Deanston cotton mill, were recommended. Otherwise the machinery was safe and well guarded. Most of the spinners were women 'working light wheels containing 108 to 128 spindles each'.[11]

John Alexander, sub-manager of the mills since 1814, was able to provide more detail on working practices, informing the inspectors that the mills were being driven by seven water wheels generating around 300 horse power. The majority of the yarn was spun by women, girls and boys using throstles or mules, and in addition there were eight larger machines, each of 352 spindles, worked by men, and ten self-acting mules with a team of three women to a pair. There was a total of 40,000 spindles, manufacturing between 23 and 24 tons of cotton into yarn each week. Wages were then 16 to 20 shillings a week for male spinners, with females earning from 7s. 6d. to 9s. or

Figure 7·2: *No. 3 Mill, sometimes called the 'New Mill', as rebuilt in 1826, viewed here from the roof of No. 2 Mill in 1967. The reconstructed Caithness Row can be seen in the background.*

perhaps more. Reelers got paid much the same as women spinners and younger workers anything up to 6s. 6d. Hours of work were 6 a.m. to 7 p.m. with three quarters of an hour at nine in the morning for breakfast and an hour at 2 p.m. for dinner. No corporal punishment of any kind was permitted and the overseers were not even allowed 'to give the young workers a lick on the side of the head' for indiscipline. In Alexander's opinion, the workers both male and female were well-behaved and 'as moral in their conduct as any of the neighbouring population'. This he attributed to the strong moral tradition upheld in the community, especially to church attendance and the fact that little strong liquor was taken.[12]

The village by then housed about 2,000 people, the majority living in dwellings provided by the company. The rent was paid monthly, with direct deductions from pay: a two-roomed apartment cost £3 and more spacious accommodation anything up to £5 per annum. By 1851 the total rental was £1,400 per annum. Otherwise the social welfare, medical and educational provision remained of a high order. A sick fund, to which all workers contributed a penny out of every five shillings of their wages raised £20–£25 per month and was supplemented whenever necessary by the company. The fund was managed by five workers appointed by the labour-force and as well as taking care of the sick, provided assistance to the aged. Robert Logan, then resident medical practitioner or surgeon, was paid by the company and routine care and medicine provided free. According to his evidence, the works were generally healthy, the least so being the preparing department, which was very dusty. The dispensary was at his house 'attached to the factory'. Although there had been ten recent cases of cholera (probably in the epidemic of 1832) with six deaths resulting, according to Logan, the health of the workers was 'as good as that of other labouring classes'.[13]

The school, as in Owen's time, undoubtedly remained the show-piece, and there, the Factory Inspectors observed 'a most extraordinary degree of attention devoted to the education of the children, candidates for admission to employment in the mills'. The school itself was described as magnificent – and there two teachers, paid for by the company, provided evening classes for the workers every night except Saturday. Upwards of 450 children attended during the day, with the older two-thirds of this number paying 4d. a month towards their fees, the youngest (from three to 11 years of age) being taught free. Sir David Barry, like so many visitors before him, was struck by what he saw. The children were taught 'reading, writing, with the elements of geography, music, dancing, natural history etc in fine spacious rooms. I witnessed considerable proficiency in some of these branches, and saw eight young persons, from ten to thirteen, dance a quadrille in the very best style, under their dancing- master'.[14] Clearly the core elements of Owen's curriculum were still being maintained, though the parish minister, the Revd William Menzies, no enthusiast for Owen's views on religion (or much else, it seems), condescendingly observed in 1834 that the scholars at New Lanark were being educated in the 'ordinary branches, more suitable to their rank in life than the ornamental accomplishments to which, under a former management, an exclusive attention had been paid'.[15]

The quality of educational provision continued to be noticed by other visitors. For example, in 1851 Sub-Inspector Balfour, on one of his many visits to the mills, recorded that 'the most

Figure 7·3: *Mule spinning c. 1825, based on modifications of Crompton's mule.*

liberal provision is made at New Lanark', where an excellent school continued to be maintained at the sole expense of the owners. Under the Factory Act, the two schoolmasters, David Dunn and Thomas Best, were required to keep a detailed register of attendance, and the sole surviving register for 1852 provides a fascinating insight into school life. At that time the children attended school from Monday to Friday, the normal hours being 8 a.m. to 9.30 a.m. and 11 a.m. to 12.30. There were 28 in the First Division (or juniors) and 29 in the Second (or seniors), 23 being boys and the rest girls. For the older children part-time and seasonal work was still apparently common. In July, for example, one girl at least, Jane Wallace, was off school herding cattle (possibly at the company's farm) and there are several instances of both girls and boys being absent at weaving, quite likely assisting their fathers at the mill. In common with other rural farming areas, children were often given to leave to work at the harvest. Like other places in the Lowlands absence at the potato lifting was pretty universal and despite the back-breaking work was referred to fondly as the 'Tattie Holiday'. Most of the absences, as one would expect, were due to 'sickness', 'sore eyes' or 'sore throat'.[16]

The last surviving account of the Institute and school in the Walker period – dating from 1860 – describes it as 'having worked admirably in effects and results as regards the morality of this community'. 'The proprietors', it recorded, 'compel the inhabitants to send all children from the age of three to thirteen', there being two masters in the senior school (still Dunn and Best), an infant master, Hugh Duncan, and two mistresses Jane May and Susan Sheddon. The circulating library and museum serving the adult population were apparently still being maintained, William Cowie acting as librarian and John Stewart, secretary. 'Strangers', it was remarked, 'would deprive themselves of much gratification if they left this part of the country without paying this instructive establishment a visit'.[17] According to data gathered for a report on schools in Scotland prepared in 1867 there were 222 scholars on the roll with 166 in actual attendance. In later years, as the population of the village slowly declined, the school was eventually handed over to the Parish School Board at Bankhead in 1875. When Frank Podmore, Owen's biographer, first visited New Lanark in 1903, his guide, John Melrose, told him that in his boyhood 30 or so years before he and the other children still danced every morning from 7.15 a.m. to 8.00 a.m. Podmore was shown some of the surviving educational aids, mainly the paintings and maps, which according to Melrose were only taken down when the school was replaced by the Board School. Unfortunately all the items Podmore saw were subsequently lost.[18]

Like much of the surrounding neighbourhood New Lanark was relatively well-supplied with the material necessities of life – and the Walkers maintained both the farm and the village store, where provisions could be readily obtained. The truck system, under which workers were obliged to buy from the company store, hardly existed in Scottish cotton factories, New Lanark being one of only three in the countryside where the company actually provided its own store. The farm – again one of three maintained by cotton mill proprietors – was still the largest of its kind in the 1840s, having operated since the days of Owen's management. It allowed workers to buy produce, such as oatmeal, potatoes and milk, 'which they require for their families'. The store, according to James Stuart, writing in 1842, brought many benefits and was in 'a flourishing condition'. 'All sorts of provisions, even wine, porter, &c., butcher's meat, bread &c., and all sorts of wearing apparel, are for sale', he reported. 'The warehouses and cellars are extensive. There

Figure 7·4: *The legend lives on. Robert Owen captured in a silhouette by Auguste Edouart, 1838 (Robert Owen Museum, Newtown).*

is a butcher's shop. Thirty cows are kept to afford milk to the people. A large garden is also under crop for their supply with vegetables. The wages of the operatives are regularly paid to them in hand, but they of course, cannot fail to be aware, that it is expected, if they make their purchases at the store, they are immediately after receiving wages in hand, to discharge their debts to the store.' But, he pointed out, 'it is entirely optional to them to make their purchases at the store, or elsewhere, just as they please, but the articles are of so good quality, and so cheap, that even the workers residing at Lanark, about a mile and a half from the factory, generally make their necessary purchases at the store, although they have the trouble of conveying them to Lanark.' In Stuart's opinion 'the population would consider it a very severe privation, were the store to be discontinued'.[19]

The everyday diet in this neighbourhood during the 1830s was typically porridge for breakfast, potatoes with herrings for dinner, and again porridge or potatoes for supper. Meat remained something of a luxury, and tea, according to the parish minister, might also be taken 'whenever it can be afforded'. It is interesting to note that the returns to the Royal Commission on the Poor Law of Scotland, published in 1844, highlighted the fact that tea-drinking was always closely associated with factory women! The same commission showed that parishes in upper Clydesdale reported meal and potatoes as the common diet, four out of five eating meat sometime in the week, a third using milk and cheese, and a quarter fish (strangely for an inland district, directly comparable to Edinburgh). Prices were found to be roughly average – though an important non-consumable, coal, readily obtained locally from Douglas, Forth or Carluke, was 35 per cent cheaper.[20]

During their visits the inspectors met many of the workforce and recorded some telling personal histories of life in the mills, in a few cases even dating back to Dale's era:

> John Laidlaw, fifteen years old, solemnly sworn, depones, that he has been seven years in the preparation rooms; that he is sometimes hoarse, and to cough in order to spit it up.
>
> Jesse Canning, nineteen years old, solemnly sworn, depones that she is a piecer to the self-acting mules, and she is very tired at night, and her feet sometimes give her pain, and swell; that she was quite well when she was a mule spinner, but she has more to do now. Depones she cannot write.
>
> William Stewart, an orphan from poor's house at Edinburgh. Does not know his own age. Has been here about thirty-eight years. Thinks he was about seven years of age when he entered this factory. Felt pain in his knees in the year 1800 for the first time, and

Figure 7·5: *Box beds, photographed in 1967, at 131 Rosedale Street (Long and Double Rows), were typical of those in many village houses. The 'hurly' bed on wheels was designed for children and could be neatly stored when not in use (Royal Commission on the Ancient and Historical Monuments of Scotland).*

went to the infirmary in Edinburgh to be cured, when Dr Munro said 'that the bones were wholly out of their place, and too long gone to do anything for them'.

Archibald Turner, aged thirty-eight. Now a labourer. Has worked twenty-seven year in this factory. Both knees are now bent inwards. Height five feet eight inches and a half. States that his knees became crooked between sixteen and eighteen; suffered no pain then. Was an orphan from Glasgow. Knows nothing of his early life before entering the mill.

One of the longest serving workers was Marion Fram [sic], who in her evidence to James Stuart claimed to have worked in the mills since 1793, at which date she was thought to be eight years of age.[21]

Other observations prove that the working and social

conditions at New Lanark – while by no means exceptional – were above average for the Scottish cotton industry and still a major concern of the management. For example, when Stuart's successor, John Kincaid, visited New Lanark in 1854, he found that an apartment had been fitted out at company expense 'for the accommodation of workers during meal-hours, and provided with a comfortable fire in cold weather'. It was large enough to accommodate the 60 or 70 workers who lived at a distance from the mills, presumably those travelling from Lanark and the surrounding neighbourhood. In all of this Charles Walker had apparently picked up a corner of Owen's mantle as he was reported to 'devote the kindest attention to his people' and to be 'beloved by them all'. While the official view certainly needs to be treated with some caution, the weight of evidence, happily, is much in Walker's favour.[22]

In this connection the second *Statistical Account* has some interesting reflections – though it has to be reiterated that the Revd Menzies, with whom, it will be recalled, Owen crossed swords over religious instruction, was by no means a detached observer. Still he seems to have taken a pretty positive view of what he saw in the Walkers' New Lanark, which he described as 'a large, handsome village, low upon the river side, completely surrounded by steep and beautifully wooded hills'. There lived a population of 1,900, which represented about a quarter of the whole town and parish, and of these about 1,100 were employed in the mills, 60 being mechanics or labourers. The hours of work were $11\frac{1}{2}$ per day throughout the year 'whatever be the state of trade'. 'The people,' he wrote, 'are very comfortably supported, are in general healthy, and in comparison with other establishments of the kind, remarkably decent in behaviour'. New Lanark under the Walkers seemed to Menzies to be 'a remarkably thriving manufactory' – despite the 'very extensive notoriety' the place had previously attracted under Owen![23]

During much of the Walker period the story of New Lanark is less than complete – for the surviving archives give us merely random snapshots of working life at indeterminate points in time. While Walker Sr was clearly very actively involved in the management of the business during the 'thirties and 'forties, when he was often designated 'resident managing partner', he thereafter seems to have taken something of a back seat –

NEW LANARK

Figure 7·6: An idealised mid-Victorian view of New Lanark from the west bank of the Clyde with an early photographer at work. The old burgh of Lanark can be seen on the horizon.

perhaps through ill-health or inability to cope with the increasing problems of New Lanark's viability in less favourable economic circumstances. He may well simply have lost interest. It is also unclear when his son, also Charles, became involved in the business, and he may have done so reluctantly in the light of the family's failure to dispose of New Lanark in the early 1850s. Certainly by 1855 a great deal of the responsibility for day-to-day management seems to have rested on the shoulders of salaried staff – the works manager, John Millar, and a clutch of four male clerks, Thomas Cunningham, William Winning, Robert Sinclair and Hugh Gold. At that time management costs averaged £40 per month, Millar's salary being about half that amount. All five were regularly given a bonus for extra duties. Millar remained on the payroll until 1862 and was not immediately replaced when he quit. During the next three years day-to-day management seems to have been left in the hands of the clerks, until the arrival of William Fulton as manager in March 1865. According to the Wages Book management overheads were then averaging £50 per month.[24]

While we have relatively little to go on it is clear that the Walkers – despite increasing economic difficulties – made some effort to modernise the mills and their machinery. The major developments which occurred are poorly documented, but thanks to the efforts of the historian, John Hume, who has investigated both the industrial history and industrial archaeology of New Lanark, we have some idea of the changes made during the fifty-odd years from 1830–81. Few alterations seem to have been made to the external fabric of the mills themselves, although there is evidence of continuous internal renovation, with particular attention being paid to fire precautions and stairways. At some point before 1851 a gasworks was built near the mechanics' workshop to provide lighting for the mills and village, replacing the earlier and always potentially hazardous oil lamps. Its retort house with a neat, octagonal stone chimney can still be seen – though the equipment and gasholders were removed many years ago.[25]

Despite the problems described later in this chapter water power remained the major prime mover throughout most of the period and by 1851 there were nine waterwheels together generating 400 horse power. Even ancillary steam power was not introduced to New Lanark until 1873, in contrast to its

EXTENSIVE AND VALUABLE COTTON WORKS.

FOR SALE, BY PRIVATE BARGAIN,
THE COTTON MILLS, &c., at New Lanark. These Works, so well known to the inhabitants of Great Britain, are situated within a mile of the Town of Lanark, and in the proximity of the Station of the Caledonian Railway, and are about 25 miles distant from Glasgow.

The Mills, which are four in number, contain—
22,800 Throstle Spindles,
28,900 Mule Spindles, Self-actors, by Messrs. Sharp & Roberts,
13,000 Hand-Mule Spindles,
with all the necessary Preparation Machinery.

There is also an extensive Foundry and Mechanic Shop, containing the most modern and suitable Machinery and Tools.

There is also a large Store fitted up with everything necessary for the Sale of Grocery Goods and Cloths, and whatever is needful for the wants of the Workers.

There is also an excellent Gas Work for supplying the Works and the Village.

There is besides a large Building admirably fitted for the Educational purposes of the Village, and, in it, a commodious Hall used as a place of Worship, and capable of holding upwards of a thousand persons.

Connected with the Works, is the Village of New Lanark, capable of accommodating upwards of 2000 inhabitants, present population about 1700; and the Rental of which, with Stores and Gas, is upwards of £1400 per annum.

The Machinery of the Four Mills and Mechanic Shop is driven by Nine Water Wheels in all, equal to about 400 Horse Power, but which may be increased according to the wishes of the Proprietors.

There is, behind the main body of the Mills, the necessary Blowing Houses. Under the roof of the back Premises is a Cotton Cellar, capable of holding upwards of 800 Bales.

Adjoining the Village, is a Stone Quarry and Sand Pits, belonging to the Proprietors.

The whole Land, including the site of the Works and the Village, is about 225 Acres Imperial, of these there are about 206 Acres Arable and in Gardens and Wood.

The Feu-Duty on the whole Property is £96, and the Public Burdens are very moderate.

' In the immediate neighbourhood of the Mills is the most sublime scenery in Scotland, or even in Great Britain. It is almost needless to mention the magnificent Falls of the Clyde, and the stupendous Cartland Craigs, with the beautiful Landscape of the Vale of Clyde. In short, Cotton Works more suited to the conducting, on an extensive scale, the Cotton Spinning Business, from the immediate application of the Water Power to the Machinery, or the capability of extending the Machinery, is not to be found in any other part of the Island.

Every facility, with regard to the terms of payment of the purchase money, will be given.

The Works may be seen at any time, on application to the present Proprietors resident there.

New Lanark, 8th February, 1851.

Figure 7·7: *Advertisement for the sale of the mills and village of New Lanark, Glasgow Herald, 10 March 1851.*

much earlier use at the mills of Catrine and Blantyre in the 1800s. The first steam engine was supplied by a Glasgow firm, William Hunter & Company, at a cost of £800. The boiler and related engineering work brought the total to £1,170 – though quite where the engine was located is something of a mystery; it was not on the same spot as its replacement adjoining the Institute, installed in 1881–2.

The machinery was also gradually up-dated, though as Hume has demonstrated, Arkwright's water-frame and its more sophisticated derivatives, the mule and the throstle remained the mainstays, as they did elsewhere in Scottish cotton spin- ning. By 1851, when the mills were first advertised for sale, there were 28,900 self-acting mule spindles and 22,800 throstle spindles, which had clearly displaced the water spindles. Even at this late date, however, New Lanark still had 13,000 hand mule spindles, which, being independent of water power, could continue in operation when water was short. Like handloom weaving the hand mule operation maintained something of the traditional, domestic character of work in the village, dating back to Dale's time. By contrast, the start of conversion to more modern ring spinning – which already prevailed in the American and to a lesser extent in the Continental industries is not clearly documented. In November 1878 a new 300-spindle ring throstle frame was bought from a firm in Accrington and an existing 300-spindle throstle frame was converted to ring spinning. While the purchase of new and second-hand equip- ment (including some from other Scottish cotton mills which had fallen on bad times) slowly helped to modernise the plant, there was much mend and make. The mechanics showed considerable resourcefulness and ingenuity maintaining both the machinery and its prime movers, the latter – saving break- downs – mainly undertaken in the summer months. The foundry also seems to have diversified into small-scale engineer- ing work locally, providing customers with castings and brass- work.[26]

From later in the Walker era the works manager's report book provides us with some interesting insights into the problems related to running a water-powered country cotton mill, in which some of the machinery was becoming increasingly old- fashioned, worn out and needed to be constantly up-dated. Moreover, there were occasional discipline problems, mainly with the village youths, which surfaced from time to time. The major concern, however, was the weather and its effect on operations, notably shortage or excess of water and lighting. While shortage of water in summer drought was perfectly natural it could also be expected in winter. On 17 March 1879, for example, 'more snow and very slow speeds on the Mill' are recorded, while the winter of 1880–1 was particularly severe. The first snow fell on 1 November and a heavy frost prevailed throughout most of the following January. On the 17th of the month 'the frost was very intense being 10 degrees below zero. For want of fuel to keep up steam since Saturday the Old Mill water wheels got frozen to the rocks. By 1pm got them thawed and the steam led beneath and started. Are short of water'. The subsequent thaw brought a different problem and the manager had to order that the 'Damhead sluices be left shut lest a flood should come down in the night-time'. Heavy floods and a high river could 'backwater' the wheels, as occurred on 22 April the same year when, 'after 48 hours incessant rain, the river rose to an unusual height today. It was in the Greasers Hole 9 inches deep, the whole of the Mid Inch was covered and the mills were all stopt. No such flood has happened since 1832'. In less extreme circumstances delays and lost production were common, as during the following March when the river again rose to 'a great height, the highest since the previous April', causing some damage and stopping the mill.[27]

The human dimension is not forgotten, particularly where local festivities are concerned:

17 March 1879. St Patrick's Day. Had to banish all green ribbons out of the Mills so as to stop cheering.

12 June 1879. 'Lanimer Day'. The moulder wrought all night with assistants to recast the shaft, cope and block by 12 o'clock today – successfully.

30 April 1880. See that in future on this date notices are put up to prevent the battles with whin bushes that occur on the 1st of May.

26 February 1881. Wrote to the Police to be in readiness to prevent the usual stone battle on 1st March (Tuesday next) between the Lanark and Village boys.

This last was a reference to that strange festival held in Lanark on 1 March when children (to this day) chase each other round the Old Cross with paper balls on strings (supposedly to chase away winter and welcome spring) and then scramble for pennies thrown by local dignitaries. The much more important Riding of the Marches and Lanimer Day (the latter generally held on the second Thursday in June) was always a holiday and villagers had a tradition of enthusiastic participation in this event long before it became essentially a children's festival towards the end of the nineteenth century.[28]

The Walkers' first attempt to dispose of New Lanark in 1851–2 is shrouded in mystery and we will probably never know the exact circumstances. The proposed sale did, however, furnish a splendid account of the mills and village, published in the *Glasgow Herald* on 10 March 1851. From the advertisement we learn much about the buildings and machinery and that 'Cotton Works more suited to the conducting, on an extensive scale, the Cotton Spinning Business, from the immediate application of the Water Power to the Machinery, or the capability of extending the Machinery, is not to be found in any other part of the Island'. The owners were prepared to offer 'every facility with regard to terms of payment'.[29] But even this alluring description and tempting offer did not attract buyers, who were almost certainly intimidated by the precarious state of the Scottish cotton industry at the time. We know that one businessman, William Watson, showed serious interest in purchasing New Lanark because his name appears as a potential buyer on a map of the mills and surrounding land drawn up by Thomas Kyle for the selling agents in September 1851. As far as we are able to tell the mill was still a profitable enterprise but Watson obviously never pursued his interest any further.[30]

Charles Walker Jr tried again 30 years later and this time two rivals bid for the mills. The first, writing to Walker's Glasgow agent, J. Baird Smith of McGrigor, Donald & Company, in March 1881, plead for more time to raise both the necessary capital and establish a limited company with the aim of introducing lace-curtain manufacture to New Lanark. This seemed potentially lucrative given its recent success in Nottingham, as the plea continued:

The country as you well know is at the present time full of unemployed capital, and in another way a more favourable opportunity never occurred for taking up an investment of this nature, as any person who has recently travelled in Ayrshire, cannot but be aware, that one of the principal topics of conversation amongst all classes is the amount of profit which has been made in the Nottingham Lace Curtain Manufacture.

The writer highlighted the fact that machine-made lace production had expanded rapidly in Nottingham, with some larger works having upwards of a 100 looms, and one firm boasting profits of £150,000. Male lacemakers there were earning from £2 10s. to £3 10s. a week, compared with wages of 25–30s. in Ayrshire, where the industry was becoming slowly established, and one plant with only ten looms had made over £11,000.

Although the exact details of the offer were not specified it is indicative of how low the fortunes of both the Walkers and of New Lanark must have sunk, that the bidder was prepared to pay only £18,000 in cash plus the promise of a bond over the property for the balance (unspecified) at $4\frac{1}{2}$ per cent. At best 'Mr Walker would lose nothing and have the public estimation of the value and capabilities of the works greatly increased. He would also have the satisfaction of knowing that a very profitable business was introduced to the welfare of his present workpeople, and the general welfare of the district'.[31]

Optimistic though this might have sounded, insufficient 'unemployed capital' was attracted and this cleared the way for a rival bid by Henry Birkmyre and his brother-in-law, Provost Robert S. Somerville, of Port Glasgow. After extensive and detailed negotiation, during which the Port Glasgow men seem to have driven a hard bargain, agreement was reached giving them entry to New Lanark works and village on Whitsunday 1881. Birkmyre and Somerville, joint partners in the newly established Lanark Spinning Company, agreed in a disposition dated 16 May to pay Charles Walker, sole partner of Walker & Company, the sum of £20,000. Stocks of cotton and goods in the village store (including the spirit-store licence) were to be bought at valuation, though the sale did not include furniture apparently stored in the mills or a stock of wine. There was also much haggling over the sale of the farm at Bankhead. Walker was clearly disappointed that Birkmyre and Somerville were 'not disposed to deal with him more liberally regarding surplus stores' and perhaps in a fit of pique took personal possession of all the business books – the majority being lost to this day.[32]

The sale in 1881 – a year when the cotton market was described as being 'very dull' – raises obvious questions about how badly run-down the business had become. At this time the manager, David Dalglish, was constantly complaining to the Glasgow office and warehouse about poor cotton supplies, constant delivery delays, and general lack of quality control. In the circumstances profitability was probably highly marginal – and clearly the mills had been allowed to decline for many years and had also almost succumbed to continuous technical and economic competition since the late 1860s. In fairness to Walker and his management this was an experience New Lanark shared with much of the Scottish cotton industry, which was in big trouble after the American Civil War and to some extent it also reflected the switch from coarse cotton to fine thread production. Foreign competition, recognised even in Owen's time, was coming from the United States, Germany and other rivals, whose industrialists had embraced textile manufacture with the same enthusiasm as their earlier counterparts in the north of England and in the Scottish Lowlands. These late-starters enjoyed all the advantages of Britain's pioneering and were able to adopt the most up-to-date equipment, for example in ring spinning machinery, which was far more efficient than the older mules and jennies and could be worked by less skilled operatives. It could be that Walker and his son represented typical examples of entrepreneurial failure – the failure of business nerve or lack of dynamism regarded by some historians as characteristic of the later Victorian period in Britain. But, on the other hand, they at least managed to keep the business going in conditions that saw the demise of much of the Scottish cotton trade. No matter what one reads into the circumstances surrounding the sale, Birkmyre and Somerville certainly bought over New Lanark at a bargain basement price and added an important asset to their already considerable business empire.

Chapter Eight

THE ERA OF THE BIRKMYRES
AND 'THE GOUROCK', 1881–1968

'Machines will not be replacing men,
women and girls'

As NICHOLAS MORGAN HAS SUGGESTED, the acquisition of New
Lanark by Birkmyre and Somerville could be regarded as a
speculative venture but it was also a logical extension of their
varied personal and joint business interests. Henry Birkmyre
was principal partner in the Gourock Ropework Company,
which, dating back to the 18th century, had grown into a substantial enterprise with the rise of Clydeside shipping and shipbuilding and had an established reputation for the manufacture
of rope and sailcloth. Birkmyre himself had subsequently diversified, and in addition to his shipping interests held shares in
several fishing companies in the north-east of England, which
had also done well due to the boom in that industry. His
brother-in-law, Robert Somerville, was a partner in the prosperous timber merchants, Somerville & Company of Port
Glasgow, timber still being very important to the local economy
before the Clydeside shipbuilding industry turned entirely to
iron and steel.[1]

The new owners wasted little time ushering in changes at New
Lanark. Under Birkmyre's supervision the first patent net-looms
for the manufacture of fishing nets from cotton spun in the mills
were installed and the necessary skilled labour to teach local
workers imported from Renfrewshire, and other places where
net-making was already well established. Quite how successful

165

Figure 8·1: *Henry Birkmyre, manufacturer and industrialist, c. 1885 (Glasgow University Archives).*

Figure 8·2: *Village store and staff photographed about 1880. Notice the 'Lanark Spinning Co.' sign above the door and the barefoot children. Recent conservation work has restored the shop-front much as it appears here (Royal Commission on the Ancient and Historic Monuments of Scotland).*

this was initially is hard to determine but certainly more looms, bought from factories in Ayrshire and Caithness, were soon fitted up at New Lanark. Others were actually manufactured on site in the workshop until there was a total of 44. According to George Blake, the Lanark Spinning Company 'secured a good market for a good product' and certainly by the 1890s the Nets Account was showing a decent annual profit and had become one of the mainstays of business at the mills. More machinery was installed after 1902, when several small net factories at Peel on the Isle of Man were acquired and the looms eventually transferred to both Greenock and New Lanark. The mechanics and other workers (apparently including some fishermen) also moved with the plant, and the villagers found themselves joined by some Manx incomers, with names like Quayle and Caine! Then, recalled J. Howe, an overseer at the time, the Net Department was so busy 'it couldn't

Figure 8:3: *New Lanark, c. 1895, showing spinners with their 'flashy, dashy shawls' and other onlookers, clearly attracted by the presence of a camera. New Buildings can be seen on the left with the old Counting House and Caithness Row in the background (New Lanark Conservation).*

meet their customers' requirements'. Subsequently some of the net manufacture was transferred to Greenock, although it continued for a while to be an important subsidiary to cotton production at New Lanark.[2]

Other dramatic changes that occurred after the takeover altered both the face of the village and the way of life there. The most handsome and largest of the early buildings, No. 4 Mill, was destroyed by fire on 20 February 1883 when about noon a fire broke out in the fifth room. 'Two men were working there levelling up the New Mules, and were using a naked light, the flames were first seen inside the carriage of the mule they [were] working at and the course of the flames was away from them, not towards them, the mill was burnt to the ground', recorded the works manager.[3] The mill was never replaced, leaving a huge gap between the mill complex and the former school – which can be seen to this day. Another major change came about with the introduction of a water turbine both to power machinery via rope and belt drives and ultimately make possible electricity generation to provide lighting in the mills and village. 'The [Jonval] turbine successfully started', recorded the works manager on 7 March 1884, and although there were teething troubles, it ushered in a new era. A second was installed in 1898, the pair generating 827 horse power between them. Sometime around the turn of the century gas was dispensed with entirely – and, far in advance of general public supply from the Clyde Valley Electric Power Scheme in the 1920s – New Lanark was lit by electricity. There are many who can remember lights burning in the house windows and streets night and day, so negligible were the overheads.[4]

While some limited modernisation and diversification on the production side occurred at that time there were other aspects of the Birkmyre régime which were less positive. The exact details of the partnership between Birkmyre and Somerville are unclear, but by 1888 they had ceased their association and the former had taken over sole proprietorship of the mills and village. A new partnership was formed between Birkmyre and his sons in 1894. Although the Lanark Spinning Company continued to show a profit, the returns from the enterprise were marginal enough for one of the sons William, to complain bitterly in 1903 – three years after Birkmyre Sr's death – that 'the results of the past ten years would have been different' if

Figure 8:4: *Another fine photograph of New Lanark from the south, c. 1895, showing the mills with housing beyond. In the foreground slaters are busy on the workshops roof, while in the centre the burnt-out remains of No. 4 Mill can be seen (New Lanark Conservation).*

Figure 8·5: *Traction engine at New Lanark, c. 1905 (New Lanark Conservation).*

the company had received 'proper management'. In one sense this was a surprising observation given the success of Birkmyre's other business interests and the substantial estate he left on his demise.[5]

It was not the only complaint that could be levelled against Birkmyre, who as Morgan put it, was 'clearly unsuited to fulfil the role of philanthropist at New Lanark'. In the light of previous experience this seems like legitimate criticism, especially as regards the housing which had been allowed to deteriorate to unacceptable levels and the general neglect of education and other social provision. Although apparently trivial, the saga surrounding the church mission is illuminating of Birkmyre's character and outlook. A staunch United Presbyterian, he came into open conflict with the villagers on several occasions over the provision of the Church of Scotland mission and later the church. The Walkers had previously supported the mission by providing a meeting hall, a dwelling house for the minister and an annual grant of £50, but in 1884 these benefits were discontinued. After an appeal to management the old Gaelic

Figure 8·6: *Outside the village post office, c. 1920 (New Lanark Conservation).*

Chapel was made available but this did not satisfy the villagers who sent a petition to Birkmyre saying that if services were not conducted on a regular weekly basis, the incumbent minister, the Revd James French would lose his grant from the Mission Fund 'and be thrown in the streets penniless and in ill health'. Birkmyre later threatened to withdraw the use of the old chapel in order to establish the mission of 'another denomination', despite that fact that the majority of the community were members of the Church of Scotland. Matters were ultimately resolved by the opening of a new church in 1898, built at a cost of £1,100 – the majority raised by the village. As events had it the Rev French continued to serve as minister at New Lanark, where he was held in great affection, for many more years, retiring on the eve of the Great War in 1914.[6]

As we have seen, the partnership of Birkmyre and his three sons, William, James and John, clearly prompted changes at New Lanark and following his death in 1900 there were further moves towards integration of the Lanark Spinning Company's operation with that of the parent Gourock Ropework Company at Port Glasgow. The latter became a limited company with a nominal capital of £700,000 in 1903. This coincided with the remodelling of the mills and the renewal of much of the machinery so that New Lanark effectively became the centre of the company's cotton cloth and net manufacture. The character of the business therefore underwent something of a change. Instead of supplying yarns for the general market, a large quantity of doubling machinery was introduced to enable the mills to turn out heavier classes of yarn for the sailcloth departments of 'the Gourock' and one of its major subsidiaries, Birkmyre Brothers of India. Nevertheless trade was not without its ups and downs as the gross profit from the Yarn Account was described as having been 'fairly normal' till 1900 – with a large decrease thereafter during a downturn in 1901–4. On the other hand, the profits from the Nets Account increased 'on account of larger business being done through the introduction of more machinery'. Profits – after deduction of interest and depreciation – over the decade 1894–1903 averaged around £6,000 a year. But the fluctuating fortunes of the firm are recorded only too clearly in a peak of nearly £8,000 in 1900, and a trough of just under £3,000 the following year.[7]

This was probably typical of most surviving firms in the Scottish cotton industry, where specialisation in the face of overwhelming competition combined with relatively cheap and non-militant labour – mostly female – had saved the day but resulted in a somewhat tenuous existence. The problems that confronted the management of an old mill like New Lanark were highlighted in Stott & Sons' valuation report of 1903, which indicated machinery plant and utensils valued at £23,384; motive power, millwrights' work and heating installation, £5,856; electric generating and lighting equipment worth £3,385 – making a total of £32,635. However account had to be taken of deductions for outdated blowing machinery, the distance of the dye-house from the boiler (with resulting loss of steam through condensation), the smallness of the spinning rooms which made carrying and supervision inconvenient, the scattered nature of the premises, the large quantity of millwright work needing constant attention and repair, and finally, much wasted power.[8] Even the more modern equipment was not without its difficulties: in July 1904 a major turbine breakdown occurred and repair work had to be carried out by the

Figure 8·7: *Inspecting nets on the roof of No. 2 Mill sometime during the First World War. The mill girls are doing the work while the gaffers and a visiting officer look on (Glasgow University Archives).*

New Lanark mechanics – who thus maintained the tradition of make and mend on site that characterised the pioneering days.[9] According to another survey of the mills and village dating from 1903 New Lanark – including land, water rights, plant and housing – was valued at £63,000. This represented a three-fold enhancement on the purchase price in 20-odd years and gives some indication of the level of investment undertaken by the Birkmyres over that period. It also suggests a higher degree of optimism on their part than the actual returns on the enterprise might have justified.[10]

While modernisation of the mills was the Birkmyres' prime concern they did not entirely neglect social provision. For many years the company organised and subsidised an annual excursion for employees, one of the first being by special train and steamer 'Doon the Water' to the Kyles of Bute. The handbill for this event in August 1884 catches the spirit of another age, with an orderly procession of villagers walking to Lanark railway station, embarking on the *Lancelot* on Steamboat Quay at Greenock and thus reaching the ultimate venue at Auchenlochan for tea, sports and dancing. Fresh milk was to be supplied by a local farmer and it was hoped everyone in the party would take advantage of this facility![11] The company also supported the village contribution to the Lanark Lanimer festivities, especially when they were developed as a major children's event after 1893 – the year of the first Lanimer Queen and her Court. New Lanark always took its turn with other local schools in electing the Lanimer Queen and the procession regularly featured the New Lanark Brass Band (later pipes and drums) and a decorated float. This was usually one of the mill drays – later replaced by steam or motor lorries.[12]

In the longer term the Birkmyre brothers made up for the sins of their father by a more substantial contribution to the well-being of the community in a major programme designed to renew the fabric of the housing. Around the turn of the century all the dwelling houses were overhauled, new windows put in, and, as we have seen, everywhere fitted with electric light. A completely new drainage system was introduced, with a septic tank for purification of the sewage before discharge into the Clyde. Outside conveniences for the tenants were also erected. Again an ample domestic supply of spring water from the hillside behind was run to filters and a reservoir in the basement

Figure 8·8: *A cheery group of workers photographed in front of the office during the Second World War on the occasion of a visit by a government public relations officer, seen on the extreme right (Glasgow University Archives).*

Figure 8·9: *Barefoot spinner, c. 1956 (Glasgow University Archives).*

Figure 8·10: *One of the nylon spinning rooms at New Lanark, c. 1958, showing the machinery installed during the first major post-war modernisation programme (Glasgow University Archives).*

of the Old School and thence pumped to stand-wells in front of the houses, with internal supplies to the managers' houses. The rents – at £2 14s. for a single apartment and £4 1s. for a two apartment – were reckoned to be less than half the ordinary rate and 'much under the fair value of the houses, even when allowance is made for their situation and the fact that they are dependent upon the mill for tenants'.[13] The surviving Rent Rolls of this period are fascinating documents and when compared with earlier records show the remarkable continuity of old-established families in the community – some dating back to its very foundation in Dale's time. The Rent Roll of 1901 records 177 tenants, the bulk employed in the mills, though several houses were let to people working elsewhere as coal miners, oil work labourers and other trades. The bulk of apartments in one of the earliest tenements at the southern end of the village, Caithness Row, were still occupied, with the basements given over to weaving shops, cellars or stores, and a milkhouse. Apart from dwellings, Nursery Buildings housed the library and what was described as an 'Amusement Room', while the old chapel – probably out of use by that time – was still set aside in the adjoining New Buildings. About one in ten of the houses in the village seem to have been unoccupied, the bulk in Long Row and Double Row.[14]

The old Institute still housed a dining hall and recreation room, while the doctor had a surgery and a house in New Buildings. The sole surviving medical report of this period indicates that in 1903–4 there were 20 births and nine deaths, with no serious accidents recorded apart from poor John Christie, who died aged 80 after a fall downstairs, and the unfortunate death of young Phemie Stewart, aged 11 years, who died from sunstroke. Interestingly the resident practitioner at the time was a Dr Helen MacDonald, as far as we can tell the first female doctor at New Lanark, who provided consultation and a dispensary five days a week. Further help with the sick was given by the Lanark district nurse who came to the village when needed. Evidently the Birkmyre sons had at least made some effort to restore the tradition of social welfare at New Lanark to the extent that Dr Duncan Glen, the medical inspector, could write in 1902–3 that he was 'greatly struck by the very marked improvement of the village generally'. Although the system of sewerage disposal needed to be further up-graded the WCs

Figure 8·11: *A classic view of the mills and village seen from above the church, November 1963, prior to the demolition of the prominent factory chimney.*

were found to be in a very clean state. Wash-houses – always a source of complaint and great centres of gossip and dispute among the village housewives – were poorly lit but, as far as Dr Glen could tell, orderly enough.[15]

One of the longest serving managers at New Lanark, John Nicol, was appointed in 1911, and his earlier career before he came to the mill shows the continuing importance to the company of its traditional European markets. He began work at Port Glasgow in 1894 and nine years later was sent to the Hamburg branch as assistant manager. Following the London manager's success in raising business for fishing nets and canvas in the Netherlands it was decided to open a branch in Scheveningen, to which Nicol was appointed manager in 1907. There the famous 'Lanrick' nets were asked for specifically and when he went round with one of the travellers he was at first known as 'Mr Lanrick's son'. When Nicol arrived at New Lanark he soon realised that the job he had taken on involved not just managing the mills, but exercising something of the paternal role in the community passed on to him by Dale, Owen, the Walkers and his more immediate predecessors, as his memoirs recall:

Whoever is in charge in New Lanark has more to do than merely superintend the running of the works. He is responsible for both village and works and I have even received a letter from abroad addressed to the 'Mayor of New Lanark'. I remember one of the Sheriffs at Lanark saying he had never had a case from New Lanark and although there used to be a policeman he was removed because there was not sufficient work for him. Keeping order was looked on as the manager's job and I had very often to arbitrate in differences of opinion, mostly between women who quarrelled about wash-houses and whether stair windows should be open or shut. I was even called in one Sunday to settle a quarrel between husband and wife, the husband having been a 'bona fide' traveller that day. Some of these cases had their amusing side as when I had to visit a washhouse and lay down the law to two quarrelsome women. The husband of one, an Irishman, told me that if this had been in Ireland he would have invited the man to come out in the street and settle the difference there. Another case, with children, seemed to show that my methods were of some effect. I caught some children up to mischief behind the village stores and managed to shepherd a few of them along to the office where I proceeded to give them a word or two. Just when I had got well going the door opened and a boy, older than the others, slipped in. He said, 'I was there tae, Mr Nicol, and I thought I would come in and get the same as the rest'. Needless to say this just about floored me.'[16]

The old-fashioned paternalism which Nicol represented was not the only thing which recaptured New Lanark's past during this era, for the rise of trade unionism and the socialist movement brought the life and ideas of Owen and the community he had helped to mould to the attention of a new generation. Both organised labour and pioneer socialists in Britain and the United States were then discovering that their roots lay with the early Radicals, Owenites, Chartists and Co-operators, perhaps owing more to them than to Karl Marx who has so greatly influenced the development of Continental socialism. Owen, who until his death in 1858, had latterly been known to a declining band of loyal followers as the 'Social Father', was quickly transformed into the 'Father of Socialism', though he certainly never saw it practised successfully either at New Lanark or New Harmony. Numerous biographies of Owen written in the late 19th or early 20th centuries re-told the story of his activities at New Lanark, perpetuating some of the myths about the place which he himself had helped to create.[17] The most outstanding and thoroughly researched work on Owen by Frank Podmore was more critical, though even this had a tendency to hagiography in telling the 'Social Father's' story.[18] The same theme was taken up by some historians of early socialism, one of their number, Alexander Cullen, going so far as to describe New Lanark as the 'Fountain of Socialism'. Many socialists since Owen's era had drunk of the waters there, he claimed, and the draught had acted like a magic potion.[19] Be that as it may, New Lanark was rightly famous for its connection with both Dale and Owen, a place with a significant historical legacy and still much frequented by the enquiring visitor – both from home and overseas.

Few communities – even the smallest – were unaffected by the traumas brought by the Great War. Its most positive impact at New Lanark was the immediate if short-term increase in demand for its products, with sailcloth, canvas and netting contributing to the war effort as well as more obviously destructive weapons like guns and shells. Since the mills had a predominantly female labour force there was no great revolution in either the workplace or community of the kind that occurred in the engineering factories of nearby Clydeside – as men left their machines in droves for the front. Nevertheless some of the village men did join up, one being David Morrison, sadly killed in action in 1916. The service given and the loss of life sustained by the village during 1914–18 is commemorated in the simple memorial that can be seen near the church, unveiled in 1922. The death of the men whose names are recorded on the memorial was an irretrievable loss to such a small, close-knit community.[20]

New Lanark shared the experience of the Scottish textile industry as a whole during the 'twenties and 'thirties, though it appears that the worst impact of the depression was mitigated to some extent by its specialised products. In 1920, for example, the net side of the business performed very much better than the yarn department, the former returning a profit of £11,455, compared with the latter's £5,214. The much larger yarn department, with an annual turnover of £200,000, had a budget of £156,000 (nearly three-quarters of the total) for raw cotton, with the wage bill accounting for a further £24,000. Certainly business efficiency does not seem to have been a high priority. According to Nicol the mills experienced very mixed fortunes in the 1920s with losses being run up several years in a row.[21] Things were marginally better in the 'thirties though a report carried out for 'the Gourock' in 1935 by the National Institute of Industrial Psychology on production processes and work planning at New Lanark gave little cause for optimism and highlighted many inefficiencies that might explain its relatively poor performance. Despite a 48-hour working week overtime was often necessary 'due to lack of facilities for planning work ahead' and in the report many other related points of inefficiency were identified including continuing problems caused by the bad layout of the plant and machinery, poor cotton deliveries and excessive waste.[22] Instead of tackling these problems head on the company resorted to general piece-work. Its introduction was hardly welcomed with enthusiasm by the workforce, but generally speaking labour relations were good despite the long hours and relatively low wages. In the 1930s trainee spinners received 10s. a week rising to 35s. for fully trained men – though the low rents – then about 2s. a week for the average house – might be regarded as something of a bonus. The store was still run as a co-operative, so the villagers also benefited through regular dividends (the 'divi') on profits. In 1935 it was leased to Lanark Provident Co-operative, which continued the business against the background of a dwindling village population until 1963.[23]

If time and motion studies reflected the impact of the modern age, so too did the development of the nearby hydro-electric scheme on the River Clyde during the 1920s. The Falls of Clyde had proved attractive enough to Dale and Arkwright, but in their time the prevailing technology could only harness the lowest of the four, Dundaff Linn, just upstream of New Lanark. Now the Clyde Valley Electrical Power Company proposed to use the joint falls of Bonnington and Cora and that of the highest at Stonebyres a few miles downstream to generate power in two new plants, possibly prejudicing water supply to the mills. So in 1923 'the Gourock' petitioned the Secretary for Scotland seeking amendment to the Provisional Order for the scheme on the grounds of water loss. It was joined by Charles Cranstoun of Corehouse who protested against the loss of water rights, historically granted to the mills since Dale's time, and destruction of his own amenity on the estate opposite the proposed generating station at Bonnington. After some legal wrangling, and largely on the grounds of the inevitable unemployment that might result at New Lanark, 'the Gourock' won its case and the amended Parliamentary Act offered protection to the company's plant and long-established water rights. Water from the Clyde was to be 'returned in undiminished and uninterrupted flow' to the weir above the mills. Despite the new dams and reservoirs, spectacular engineering works in their own right, the forces of nature still asserted themselves periodically – as they did in December 1939 when severe flooding and problems with the sluice gate raised the water level in the lade to a dangerous level and damaged the basements of the mills.[24]

Although the inter-war years were an era of mixed fortunes at New Lanark most of the workers counted themselves lucky to have steady jobs and homes in a settled community. The old Institute, still doubling as the works canteen and social centre, was a hive of activity, being used each week by the Girls' Guildry, the Boys' Brigade, Church Choir, Works Choir, the village band, the Church Women's Guild and the Village Women's Guild – as well for regular dances, concerts and other meetings. Even in those difficult times New Lanark, still pretty much a self-contained village, was thought to be much better off than any other place of its size. Visitors, who still came regularly to New Lanark, including some from Scandinavia, the United States and Japan, interested in the Owenite or co-operative connection, apparently thought the same. One idealist, however, took the view that 'the happiness, the joy-of-work' he had read (or perhaps misread) about in the works of Robert Owen were all long gone!²⁵[25]

The Second World War again saw New Lanark operating in emergency conditions – with further efforts being made by 'the Gourock' to maintain productivity. Annual consumption of raw cotton during the war fell only marginally from an average of 1.7 million lbs consumed during 1937–39.[26] Nevertheless the company had a long way to go if we are to believe the findings of a report on production standards prepared by consultants in September 1942, which echoed most of the concerns of that seven years before. It reviewed all the production processes and working practices throughout the mill including the blowing and carding rooms; the drawing, slubbing, preparing and fine roving frames; No. 2 and 3 spinning mills; No. 3 net spinning; the spinning organisation overall; warping mill activities; and time recording. Many deficiencies were revealed in most departments. In the spinning rooms there were many idle spindles, with bad 'doffing', long waiting periods and failure to keeps the frames running for the full period. Of 29 frames monitored only two were found to be 100 per cent efficient. Among the workers there was much late-coming in the mornings, late starting after breaks, early stopping and much absenteeism – all going unrecorded since too much responsibility rested on the foremen, who evidently turned a blind eye to anything other than the most blatant indiscipline. The solution lay in the generation of a 'greater team spirit and coordination of tasks', with the introduction of a bonus plan. Moreover, the use of time clocks would save at least 100 hours per day and a weekly loss of £23 or £1,150 a year.[27] Not surprisingly the workers did not take kindly to the suggestions of the 'time and motion' experts and the only recorded strike during the long history of New Lanark was the outcome – though it only lasted a few days. More positively, given that more workers were travelling from a distance, the ground floor of the Old Institute was thoroughly overhauled and made into a canteen and kitchen. The upper floor continued to be used by villagers as a concert hall and badminton hall.[28]

With the return of peace New Lanark's production temporarily slumped, raw cotton consumption being reduced from 1.5 million lbs in 1945–46 to 1.2 million in 1947–48. Thereafter a modest upturn provided something of an Indian summer for 'the Gourock' and its operation at New Lanark, again thanks partly to its specialist production of sailcloth, canvas and netting. In 1948 the much diminished Scottish cotton industry still produced over 2 million yards of cotton cloth (about 1.4 per cent of total UK production), but, significantly, coarse cloth represented over 70 per cent of the total.[29] Under the post-war Labour government the newly constituted Cotton Board carried out a survey on the modernisation of the industry, as a result of which the mills were reported to have 19,300 ring spindles (mule equivalent 28,950). At that point, added the company, little re-equipment was contemplated, the only new machinery required to the end of 1952 being two ring spinning frames of 452 spindles. The correspondence with the relevant authorities gives the distinct impression that 'the Gourock''s management did not take kindly to government 'snoopers' and bureaucracy – especially the inevitable increase in paperwork generated by numerous surveys and inspections.[30]

In 1951 New Lanark had a population of some 550, the majority of the adults being employed in the mills. An excellent spirit was said to prevail, largely because of 'the real interest which the proprietors show in their dealings with their people'. Wages were then about £6 10s. for men and just over £4 for women for a 45-hour week. In addition some of the employees had virtually free housing, while the rents of the others remained modest. There were no rates, no water or other taxes and electric light was free. All of this still paid off for Charles Oakley, the widely respected economic consultant and industrial correspondent, writing in 1953 under the bye-line 'Scotland's Heavy Cotton Canvases are Used Throughout the World' could find only praise for 'the Gourock''s achievements as the largest firm in the business. At the New Lanark factory, he wrote, the raw cotton was spun into yarn and then woven up into cloth of a variety of constructions and weights. While some of the cloth was sold straight from the loom, the bulk was sent on to Port Glasgow where it was proofed by the firm's patented process, making it waterproof and rotproof and 'suitable for both tropical and arctic conditions'. New Lanark canvas had numerous uses but by far the largest quantities were for the manufacture of vehicle covers and tents – the latter ranging in size from the smallest bivouac to the largest circus tent.[31]

The same year the first formal recognition of New Lanark's historical importance was seen in the unveiling on 11 July of a plaque to Robert Owen. A large turnout of invited and uninvited guests, including Co-operative Wholesale Society executives, trade unionists and local councillors was present. At the tea afterwards, according to the general manager, Andrew Inglis, there was a surfeit of speeches about the virtues of co-operation, all claiming Owen as the originator of co-operative ideas. Inglis himself remarked that Owen was first of all in the business of making money and that now 'the Gourock' 'in its own quiet way' was doing a lot of good by supplying travel allowances, cheap meals and spending considerable sums improving property and keeping machinery up-to-date.[32] To his credit Inglis, in the age-old tradition of previous managers, did much to maintain the social fabric of the community seeing to it that the company made annual grants to both the Mission Church and the New Lanark Pipe Band – among other causes. A great enthusiast of the Lanark Lanimer Day celebrations and the village's continuing participation in the event, he was himself elected to play the distinguished role of Lord Cornet in the Riding of the Marches ceremony in 1955.

The 1950s saw the first of two major periods of modernisation undertaken by 'the Gourock' at New Lanark. The 1954 edition of the house magazine, *The Gourock*, was able to report substantial progress in the reorganisation of the card, spinning and doubling rooms. A number of specialised machines were installed, including an Ulster warp tier (which saved time and labour in tying new warp ends to old thrums), new warping mills, fully automatic winders and a new drying machine in the dyework. In addition modern weighing machines and a range of new maintenance plants were provided. The largest single scheme was the reorganisation of the weaving department which involved the replacement of older Halls looms with 54 Northrop looms of varying types, which together with new models already installed would enable the firm to balance spinning and doubling production. In all the weaving areas major structural alterations were carried out – new floors, removal of old-fashioned obstructing pillars, better lighting, and so on. 'Although Lanark has been traditionally only a cotton centre', continued *The Gourock*, 'it is now also being made to play its part in the production of yarns and material from a variety of synthetic fibres'. Much pioneering work in the production of nylon, terylene or nylon-terylene-cotton canvases was undertaken at New Lanark during this time – when, according to a company source, 'the whole realm of synthetic fibres seemed to be almost limitless'.[33] However, traditional fibres remained its bread and butter and this presented yet another dilemma in the complex issues surrounding the maintenance of modern manufacture in what were by then increasingly antiquated premises.

As late as July 1960 Inglis reported to headquarters at Port Glasgow his opinion that 'if money is available, a new factory should be built near at hand. It is only by doing this that we can get economic running conditions and a 100 per cent satisfactory layout'.[34] It would have made sense to move to a completely new green-field site, where substantial government and local authority grants would have been available to construct a brand new plant. This 'the Gourock' seriously contemplated – a move which would certainly have spelled the early demise of both the mills and community at New Lanark. But largely because of the existing skilled labour force it compromised again on another major reorganisation and re-equipment, announced in July 1961. Work was to begin in September and was estimated to cost £250,000, the aim being to make 'these famous old mills among the most up-to-date in the country and better equipped than ever to compete in the widening world markets of the highly competitive textile trade'. 'Good news, too, for the 300 workers (two-thirds female),' said the *Hamilton Advertiser*, 'is that machines will not be replacing men, women and girls.' An even more optimistic future was predicted for 'the mills, in fact, could absorb more labour and continuous employment is virtually ensured'.[35]

The planned programme of modernisation was to be completed within a year but it was not actually finished until early in 1963. By then cotton production was concentrated into a smaller number of rooms and flats to allow further development of man-made fibres. The main objective had been to concentrate each process and get some much needed sequence and flow of production – long-standing problems which had evidently defied solution beforehand. The most modern carding, ring spinning and doubling equipment, mainly of British manufacture, was installed. No. 3 Mill, in particular, was developed to make yarns and twines from synthetic fibres, and while some of the machinery employed was very old and quite a bit of improvisation needed, there was apparently no modern machinery that could produce the thickness and weight of twine needed for 'the Gourock''s markets. The five weaving sections were brought under one roof in a much enlarged weaving shed (twice its former size) and moving in all looms and cloth warehousing. A number of new looms were purchased to balance yarn and cloth production. The net looms were among the most up-to-date then available – 12 of them built by the French engineers, Zang of Paris. At the same time the power supply was upgraded, bringing the end of rope drives to the various rooms throughout the mills – the major turbine being converted to electricity generation. When the mills were idle overnight (invariably from 10 p.m. to 6 a.m.) electricity was used for heating, the machinery generating enough itself during working hours.[36] However, one traditional difficulty manifested itself in the hard winter of 1963, when major power problems arose during the long freeze-up. Some of the ice slabs on the river when the thaw set in were reported to be 20-feet square and 2-feet thick!

Prior to the modernisation programme workers' views were sought on the new proposals for shift working and a three-one vote was carried for abandoning the existing day-shift (7.45 a.m. to 5 p.m.) and going on to double shift-working. One shift of about half the workers would work from 6 a.m. to 2 p.m., and the other half from 2 p.m. to 10 p.m. Only the small weaving section of 30 men and eight women would continue to work day shift – with nightshift for male weavers only. The result was that millhands had a shorter five-day week of $37\frac{1}{2}$ hours instead of $42\frac{1}{2}$ without loss of earnings. Moreover, 'the Gourock' was quick to emphasise, 'employees earnings are amongst the highest in the district for textile work, because piecework conditions or incentive bonus schemes apply to all grades, male and female'.[37]

Labour remained essentially local, though the attraction of higher wages 'doon through' – Lanarkian for anywhere in the

Clyde Valley north of Carluke, including Wishaw, Motherwell and more distant Glasgow – meant that many spinners, the majority female, travelled from the surrounding district, especially colliery villages like Douglas, Coalburn, Forth and even further afield. Employment opportunities for women locally were usually limited to the land (especially in horticulture with its vast acres of soft fruit and then numerous, cheaply heated glass-houses) or they found work as shop assistants, secretaries or clerks. So the woollen and cotton mills of Lanark provided relatively well-paid and (in terms of the camaraderie) often quite congenial employment. The buoyancy of New Lanark's specialist production was seen as recently as 1965 when the firm advertised vacancies for spinners and net makers with 'excellent wage rates, training in the factory and allowances for travel'.[38] These incentives may have been all very well, but mill work for both women and men remained pretty noisy and sweaty, as many former spinners, weavers and other ancillary workers can still testify to this day.

Chapter Nine

RESTORING NEW LANARK: THE MAKING OF A WORLD HERITAGE VILLAGE

'A Future for New Lanark'

THE NEW LANARK THAT THE visitor sees today – visually little changed from the era of David Dale and Robert Owen nearly 200 years ago – is the outcome of one of the largest heritage conservation efforts ever undertaken in Scotland and of dogged persistence on the part of everyone involved. It has proved over a quarter of a century – and remains – a major co-operative effort, inspired by the historic, architectural and environmental importance of the place and its surroundings in the upper Clyde Valley. The huge restoration project has united enormous enthusiasm with enterprise – public and private – on a scale that would have been hard to imagine in the community's darkest hours 25 years ago.

For long before the 1960s – and while the mills continued to function as the largest satellite of 'the Gourock''s operation – the company had tried to keep the mills, community buildings and housing in some semblance of repair. But it was clearly a constant struggle fought in the increasing glare of publicity being generated about the historical importance of the place. Indeed the company and the New Lanark management were often utterly overwhelmed by some of the attention they received and Inglis in particular was subject to constant interference and harassment from headquarters and the media. Robert Owen would probably have relished the situation though the

Figure 9·1: *An Owen back in New Lanark. Kenneth Dale Owen photographed in front of Nursery Buildings, November 1966.*

problems confronting management were daunting.[1] While the mill buildings and machinery – as we saw – were continuously modernised in the 1950s and early '60s, it was the village housing that presented the company with its biggest headache.

Under a succession of Housing Acts, notably that of 1950, better standards of accommodation and hygiene were progressively enforced and properties failing to meet minimal requirements condemned as unfit for habitation. Although the extension of boundaries in 1951 incorporating New Lanark in the burgh of Lanark placed some onus on the town council throughout the 'fifties 'the Gourock' itself, as we saw in the previous chapter, made at least a token effort to maintain and upgrade the properties. Indeed the company received a Saltire Society award in 1957 for its effort in maintaining the houses as far as financial resources allowed. It was never enough and, as Andrew Inglis pointed out as late as 1960, if the provisions of the Housing Acts had been implemented more rigorously 'practically every house in New Lanark could be closed'. Many were damp, had no through ventilation, low ceilings and poor lighting. Outside toilets and wash-houses prevailed. The Scottish Office, warned Inglis, was pushing local authorities to do something about unfit properties and several basement houses in Rosedale Street and Braxfield Row had either been condemned or were under Closure Orders. From the company's viewpoint this raised another problem for it normally let houses 'to young people with a family coming on to working age so that [it] can get the benefit of the labour in a few years time'. The labour position, Inglis predicted, would soon worsen.[2]

So it was all too obvious that the houses at New Lanark would either have to be modernised or condemned as unfit for human habitation. Worse still, the whole community would eventually cease to exist if nothing was done. 'The Gourock' then offered the whole village to Lanark Town Council for the nominal sum of £250. The council – having assessed the scale of the problem – felt that it could not undertake the necessary modernisation itself but did not wish to see the decay of such an historic asset on its very doorstep. The local council estimated that upgrading would cost £250,000 and decided late in 1962, by a narrow majority, that the task was too great for them alone to tackle.[3] At this point the predicament of the company and the council began to attract both government and public attention, mainly through

Figure 9·2: *The restored School and Workshop with the rounded end of Caithness Row in the foreground and Dundaff Linn in background, 1984 (New Lanark Conservation).*

the personal intervention of John S. Maclay, the Secretary of State for Scotland and officials of the Scottish Office and the Scottish Special Housing Association. The local MP, Mrs (later Dame) Judith Hart, was also concerned because any question mark on the future of the housing clearly posed a major threat to jobs in the constituency.[4]

Meantime some interesting proposals for New Lanark's future were put forward. One of the most imaginative, suggested by a correspondent to *The Scotsman*, was for the establishment of a liberal arts college or a new university on what were described as 'do-it-yourself principles'. The housing at New Lanark could provide a nucleus of accommodation and facilities for students world-wide, particularly those likely to be engaged in voluntary service overseas. Co-operation between staff and students would be a top priority with funds coming from a variety of sources. The college would 'prepare its students for a fuller life in the rapidly changing conditions of the world and make them more fully aware of the need for active co-operation in peaceful and purposeful co-existence'. Coming at a time when university expansion in the wake of the Robbins Report still lay on the horizon this was quite a radical idea for its time.[5] Another intriguing proposal lay behind the objectives of the anonymous clients of a Glasgow solicitor who wrote to 'the Gourock' saying that they acted on behalf of individuals who were interested in developing 'any village they could obtain' to the advantage of all concerned – though quite how this was to be achieved was not specified.[6]

Following the council's decision to seek assistance the Adam Housing Society Ltd agreed to seek some way of saving the village and on 19 June 1963 a meeting of interested parties was convened at New Lanark. The major groups present on that occasion were the Scottish Office, 'the Gourock', the county and town councils and the housing association represented by its secretary, Norman Dunhill, then attached to the Department of Architecture at the University of Edinburgh, who was to become a key figure in early restoration successes. A flurry of correspondence followed including the veiled threat from Inglis who hoped that the local authorities realised that if nothing was done in the near future 'they will have to provide accommodation for about 160 families. This will cost them a lot more than any contribution they might need to make to modernise the village'. Dunhill was more sanguine when he reported that 'although it can't be said our proposals were received with any great show of enthusiasm, the meeting was sufficiently encouraging for us to proceed'. 'If we could raise the money,' Dunhill was recorded as saying, 'we could convert the houses into modern flats and so preserve this historic village'.[7] According to one newspaper report the drive to save the village would cost £340,000.[8]

Dunhill worked hard to overcome any potential ill-will and animus among the various interest groups, scoring a major coup with the return of an Owen to New Lanark on 19 November. Kenneth Dale Owen, a Texas businessman, was a direct descendant of Robert Owen and also had family connections in historic New Harmony. According to Inglis, Owen appeared 'quite enthusiastic about the project' though the questions he asked were very much to the point. Inglis revealed that the

Figure 9·3: *The Owen House under reconstruction, 1984 (New Lanark Conservation).*

company paid yearly £150,000 in wages, £3,225 in rates and had spent £26,000 – mostly tradesmen's wages – over ten years in 'keeping the village in a good state of repair and making improvements to the houses'. Owen took the view that the local authority should be encouraged to take a greater interest as nearly half the houses were rented at very low rents to people who had no connection with the mill.[9]

Two days later on 21 November at an inaugural meeting in the North British Hotel, Glasgow, the New Lanark Association was formed. Among the founder members of the association were Kenneth Dale Owen, Judith Hart MP, and Dame Margaret Cole, the distinguished historian, who had written much about the history of socialism and co-operation including a major study of Robert Owen of New Lanark.[10] The association later purchased New Lanark village from 'the Gourock' in order to modernise the houses and hopefully preserve the community. The architects, Ian G. Lindsay and partners of Edinburgh, who

had considerable experience in the restoration of historic buildings, prepared plans for a Pilot Project. This was designed to
renovate Caithness Row, acknowledged, as we saw, to be one
of the oldest housing blocks, built and named during the period
of Dale's management for the expatriate Highlanders who had
come to work at New Lanark in the late 1780s.[11]

Initial restoration work went ahead quickly, though not without numerous unforeseen difficulties, caused mainly by flooding
from a burn running off the hillside at the southern end of the
row. The whole rebuilding programme on Caithness Row
demonstrated the enormity and complexity of the task that lay
ahead. However, the first of the new flats was opened by
Kenneth Dale Owen, accompanied by his daughter, Caroline,
in November 1966. It was certainly a historic day, with an
Owen again back in New Lanark and with some imagination
on the part of the participants in the simple ceremony a vision
of what the future might hold. The changes which this first
effort at renovation highlighted are still remembered by some
and needed to be seen to be believed. Gone were the communal
closets, the old kitchen sinks, the big, open ranges and the 'hurly'
beds of the old houses. In the new flats were to be found fitted
kitchens, bathrooms and electric wall radiators. Before and after
pictures of the first flat's modern living room created from the
old-fashioned kitchen, may not accord with contemporary
taste, but certainly give a good indication of the kind of transformation that could be undertaken – given imagination and
adequate funding.[12]

Despite this initial success, and perhaps because of it, 'the
Gourock' continued to attract criticism for its apparent neglect
of the village. One report by Ann Shearer in *The Guardian* of 21
April 1966 provoked a pointed reaction from Alec Dunsmore,
the company's publicity manager, wherein he indicated that
three-quarters of the village population neither worked in the
mills nor were relatives of those who did. With house rents of
5s. to 7s. 6d. a week the company, he claimed, was subsidising
the houses to the tune of £4,000 per annum. Moreover, the board
had recently decided that machinery should come before houses
and had spent £250,000 making the mills 'one of the most
modern plants of its kind in the country'. Evidently 'the
Gourock' was losing its patience and a pessimistic report on
the valuation of its real assets at New Lanark the following

Figure 9·4: *Amelia Findlater helped the Post Office publicise a stamp spotlighting the historic village of New Lanark. The stamp was one of four depicting industrial monuments produced to celebrate Museums Year in 1989* (The Scotsman).

year was clearly the last straw. According to the survey of a total floor space of 233,000 square feet, made up of the three mills and the new weaving shed alongside No. 1 Mill only three-fifths was effectively used. If empty and available for sale the mills might fetch £25,000, while the electrical generating capacity would bring another £5,000. Even this presupposed that there might be a purchaser in the market who could be found to take over the whole premises; and factories in outlying locations fetched very modest prices. A gloomier prospect was predicted if the premises were empty and allowed to deteriorate to the point that nobody would be interested – and the plant, in any case, would be virtually worthless. New Lanark had become a mill-stone round 'the Gourock's' neck and it would be only time before the company unburdened itself. However, none of this was in the public domain at the time.[13]

As events transpired the initial scheme of restoration

represented a mere fraction of the work needed to make all the houses habitable. The association estimated in 1967 that if £200,000 could be raised privately, grants-in-aid from a variety of sources would provide the remainder – a total of around £0.5 million and a relatively modest sum by today's standards. Lord Clydesmuir, then chairman of the appeal, said at the time that 'this is expenditure on a project which all are agreed is of the highest importance – the housing of the people'. If the scheme was merely to preserve a monument the cost would probably be called unjustifiable. It was clear from that standpoint that New Lanark presented an unusual opportunity to create modern housing from traditional tenements – many of which were being torn down as slums in towns and cities throughout Scotland, the Gorbals and the East End of Glasgow being prime cases in point. But preserving the exterior of a village unique in the history of Scotland soon assumed crisis proportions with the rather unexpected rationalisation of 'the Gourock's' operation at Port Glasgow and the closure of the mills in 1968. The whole fabric of the community was threatened and the future of the restoration effort thrown into turmoil by subsequent events.[14]

When the mills closed in 1968 there had been little additional building since the early part of the 19th century and the village that survived was caught in a virtual 'time warp' as probably the most original example of an early industrial community. By the late 'sixties and early 'seventies its importance was only just beginning to be acknowledged – with all the buildings, mills and housing designated as of historic importance and a conservation area created. Some might argue that New Lanark's association with Dale and Owen was a paramount consideration, but at the same time there was a growing interest in the nation's industrial heritage and archaeology, much of which had already succumbed to demolition or redevelopment since the Second World War. But the movement to rehabilitate industrial buildings and relics of working class life was still in its infancy and this left New Lanark and places like it in virtual limbo.

Unfortunately for New Lanark the advantages that had proved attractive to late 18th and early 19th century businessmen had little real relevance to the mid-20th century. All that the place could offer was extensive floor space in a relatively inaccessible but delightful rural setting with the result that the

Figure 9·5: *The Scottish Co-operative Society Brass Band gives a musical welcome to the Rt. Hon. George Younger, former Secretary of State for Scotland, on his arrival at the official opening of the Visitor Centre on 14 November 1990. Behind him are Harry Smith, Chairman of the Trustees and Jim Arnold, Manager of New Lanark Conservation* (Lanark Gazette).

mills proved very difficult to adapt to modern industrial use. Finally in 1970 the mill buildings were sold to Metal Extractions Ltd and for a while there were some hopes that new employment opportunities would be brought to the community. But these were misplaced: in the end few local jobs were created and, worse still, the actual industrial process itself proved highly destructive to the local environment, with ugly tips of scrap metal and abandoned vehicles scattered around the works area. Many of the mill buildings began to deteriorate and the roof of the nearby Old School collapsed.[15]

The pressures which contributed to the closure of the mills had also led inevitably to the decay of the village, which shrank from a population of 300 in 1968 to 80 or so in the early 'seventies. It was by then clear that extensive renovation was required and although the association had initiated sympathetic restoration of a small part – and the nearby Nursery Buildings restoration went ahead – it was not without major financial difficulties. Soon the association's programme ground to a halt. It was obvious wrote Jim Arnold, later the Conservation Trust manager, that the whole future of the village was in jeopardy and, worse still, no single agency was prepared to undertake the apparently prohibitively expensive task of rebuilding. Demolition and site clearance, Arnold gloomily observed, loomed on the horizon.[16]

However, the more publicly raised awareness of the village's historical and architectural importance led to the convening of a meeting of interested parties by the Scottish Civic Trust and Lanark Town Council in 1972. The discussion of the working party that grew out of this meeting led to a report on *A Future for New Lanark*, produced in 1973. By 1974 a full-time manager, Jim Arnold, had been appointed, the post being funded jointly by the Historic Buildings Council for Scotland, Strathclyde Regional Council and Lanark (later Clydesdale) District Council. New Lanark Conservation and Civic Trust was established as a registered charity and amenity society. The governing committee represented the wide range of governmental and private interests involved and brought together all those bodies who would be likely to support the restoration of the village, but would clearly be unable to undertake the task on its own. As an agency the Conservation Trust was able to focus the efforts of related authorities to achieve the best possible results at any particular time. The arrangement, according to Arnold, allowed great flexibility to adjust to circumstances, and was underpinned by financial support from local and central government authorities. The logo of the trust, was, appropriately enough, the Bell Tower on the top of New Buildings – themselves a major challenge in architectural restoration.[17]

The first of numerous developments was soon underway – partly the result of changed legislation, and partly of major employment creation and training initiatives introduced by national government. While Housing Association grants for rehabilitation of tenanted properties were withdrawn for a time, the purchaser-restorer schemes were got underway,

Figure 9·6: *Restored 19th-century spinning mules can be seen working in the New Lanark Visitor Centre (New Lanark Conservation).*

when in 1975 the houses in Braxfield Row were sold to prospective restorers. In common with the National Trust for Scotland schemes, which had successfully restored some fine vernacular dwellings in places like Dunkeld, Dysart and Culross, purchasers had to adhere to strict guidelines in order to preserve the appearance of the properties. Another major input in 1976 came from the Manpower Services Commission (later the Training Agency) which funded job-creation and youth training schemes to provide labour for the restoration work to the external fabric of the houses with materials financed jointly by the Historic Buildings Council for Scotland and local authorities. With the fabric restored, internal reconstruction could be undertaken within the financial guidelines of the Housing Association. Over the next decade some 33 tenanted properties were restored and 20 purchaser-restorer schemes completed in Braxfield Row and Long Row, with further work planned. One tenement at the end of Double Row was to be faithfully restored by the Historic Buildings and Monuments Directorate of the Scottish Development Department (now Historic Scotland) as a 'museum stair'.

Meantime attention shifted from the housing to the industrial and other buildings in the mill complex all of which were deteriorating rapidly. The most depressing and worrying situation was the state of the school, with almost a third of its roof collapsed and much of the interior exposed to the elements. This building and others up-river – the old foundry and adjoining workshops – were purchased by the district council in 1974 and work was soon underway on the restoration of the school. The former Robert Owen and David Dale dwellings in the centre of the village were acquired by the Housing Association from Metal Extractions Ltd in 1978.

The mill buildings and Institute for the Formation of Character presented major problems since they lay within the complex occupied by the scrap metal business. But, as Arnold himself said, the challenge they presented 'was to prove a rallying catalyst for the various bodies involved in the regeneration of the village'. In 1979 the district council served a Repairs Notice on Metal Extractions Ltd and ultimately in 1983 compulsorily purchased the buildings – the first time such legislation had been used in Scotland to preserve a historic building. It was facilitated by the National Heritage Memorial Fund which underwrote the purchase and the New Lanark Conservation Trust subsequently acquired the buildings. The historic announcement by George Younger, Secretary of State for Scotland, was appropriately headed 'New Deal for New Lanark' – and the district council expressed the hope that, once the intention to rehabilitate the buildings was made more widely known, financial assistance might become available from sources outwith public funds.[18]

Work quickly went ahead on the huge task of restoring the mills and Institute, with a permanent visitor centre and other facilities being created in the Institute and nearby Mill No. 3. By 1985 the MSC workforce was over 200, engaged in building work, environmental restoration and research. Recognising the enormous economic, and especially the tourist potential of New Lanark, other organisations became involved at this stage of the development. The Scottish Development Agency (now Scottish Enterprise) contributed to a major environmental rehabilitation scheme by cleaning up the debris left by the scrap metal operations around the mills – as well as funding a Development Officer's appointment. The Scottish Tourist Board provided

Figure 9·7: *The 'Annie MacLeod Experience', New Lanark's exciting journey back to mill life in Robert Owen's era (New Lanark Conservation).*

funds for the opening of a large car park (since greatly expanded) with picnic facilities above the village, and the Countryside Commission for Scotland helped the Scottish Wildlife Trust to open an exhibition providing information about the local flora and fauna in part of the old workshops by the lade at the southern end of the mill complex. Woodland paths were reconstructed, trees felled and undergrowth cleared, opening up wonderful vistas of both the river and the village, which few had seen for perhaps a century and more.[19]

New Lanark, always an object of curiosity, has already become a major tourist attraction with something approaching 350,000 visitors every year at the time of writing. So catering for visitors

– including a growing number of school parties and other groups
– and providing both facilities and adequate interpretation of the
historic mills, village and surroundings – were early recognised
as vital functions. Education was increasingly seen as an important part of a museum's work – although New Lanark is clearly
much more than a museum in the conventional sense.

The Visitor Centre Development embraces three major buildings, the former Institute, the engine house and Mill No. 3. The
Institute has been designed to provide visitor reception and cafe-
teria on the ground floor, with the upper floor given over to a
community hall and meeting room. The engine house displays
a restored steam engine of the kind once used to power the
mill machinery, while a glazed bridge, a modern replica of the
original rope-drive housing, gives access across to Mill No. 3.
There the Ramp Hall in turn gives access to all levels and
because the floors have been taken out it is easy for the visitor
to appreciate the construction of the building, the use of cast
iron columns and brick arch ceilings which were essential to adequate fire-proofing in the early cotton mills. In Mill No. 3 all six
levels are used to advantage. The top floor provides office
accommodation, the fifth floor below is devoted to the audio-
visual presentation, the fourth to the textile machinery display,
the third to visitor information, a sales point and the coffee
shop, the second to the school workroom, and the ground floor
to storage.

A major development in 1990 – coinciding with the formal
opening of the centre – was the unveiling of the 'Annie McLeod
Experience', described as 'a unique magical history tour', using
multi-media facilities on much the same lines as that developed
earlier at the Jorvik Centre in York. Two-seater suspended
modules allow visitors a glimpse of New Lanark in 1820, guided
by the 'spirit' of Annie McLeod, a ten-year-old mill girl, who
appears as a stunning hologram. The latest technology has
been used to show a typical day at New Lanark under the
benevolent management of Robert Owen. Travelling in dark-
ness visitors encounter workers in the mill, two neighbouring
families at home, a class taking place in the school, villagers at
play and rest, and even Robert Owen giving a speech – all
achieved with high quality special effects! The experience lived
up to its promise of being totally different from anything else
in other industrial museums and clearly appealed to all ages.

Figure 9·8: *The annual Victorian Fair, which takes place on the first Sunday in September, is one of many attractive and lively events in the revived village's calendar (New Lanark Conservation).*

For the first time in 1991 the settings and commentary were adapted for a special Christmas presentation, which proved attractive to visitors young and old.[20]

The official opening of the Visitor Centre on 14 November 1990 by the Rt. Hon. George Younger MP, former Secretary of State for Scotland and Minister for Defence, was another important milestone in the story of New Lanark. The honour of performing the ceremony came Younger's way because, as we saw, he had been Secretary of State when it was decided to compulsorily purchase the mill buildings and hand them over to the New Lanark Conservation Trust for restoration. His arrival in the village was both traditional and historic – in an open carriage pulled by villagers, in much the same way that Robert Owen and several of his new partners were triumphantly brought home after securing ownership of the mills in 1813. There was a musical welcome from the Scottish Co-operative Society Brass Band and a formal welcome from Harry Smith, Chairman of the Trustees at New Lanark. Mr Younger declared the Visitor Centre open by unveiling a plaque to commemorate the occasion. That evening one of the splendidly restored halls in the Institute was the venue for a historic concert given by Lanark and Carluke Choral Union. Under their enthusiastic conductor, Philip Fox, and with a commentary provided by Ian Donnachie, the choir presented a programme with a distinctive Scottish flavour to a capacity audience. It was a fitting celebration since, as the historical record shows, choral music had an important and historic place in the Institute's activities.

An early recognition of the Visitor Centre's success came in a major prize for the most outstanding tourist attraction of 1990 as well as five other awards in a competition regarded as the Oscars of the tourism industry. The New Lanark centre beat 22 other British tourist attractions to win the 'Come to Britain Trophy'. The British Tourist Authority, which made the award, said the centre was very popular and it was hoped that the award would help attract more overseas visitors. 'New Lanark', said the report, 'is an excellent interpretation of high quality, providing an entertaining and educational visit for domestic and overseas visitors'. Events like the regular 'Victorian Fair' unite visitors and residents in a thoroughly enjoyable occasion for all concerned. The Centre itself has become a popular conference venue – a highly competitive market but one which brings

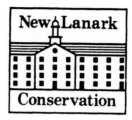

Figure 9·9: *The logo of the New Lanark Conservation Trust features the famous bell-cot, which appears on every historic view of the village.*

useful business to the community. Part of Mill No. 2 now houses 'Owen's Warehouse', a major woollen and clothes retail outlet, which has also proved a great attraction with visitors.[21]

The restoration of New Lanark has been undertaken with the assistance of numerous bodies, public and private, all of whom are acknowledged in the Visitor Centre. They include the European Economic Community's Regional Development Fund, the Council of Architectural Heritage, Strathclyde Regional Council, Clydesdale District Council, the Scottish Development Agency, the Countryside Commission for Scotland, the Scottish Development Department, the Training Agency (and its predecessor the Manpower Services Commission), the Scottish Tourist Board, the Local Museums Purchase Fund, the National Heritage Memorial Fund, the Carnegie United Kingdom Trust, the Scottish Civic Trust, the Architectural Heritage Fund, the Co-operative Wholesale Society, the Pilgrim Trust, the Royal Bank of Scotland, as well as the New Lanark Community Council and the New Lanark Village Group.[22]

The British Tourist Authority accolade was just one in a succession of awards New Lanark has received over the years. One of the first came from the Saltire Society which commended the maintenance effort undertaken by the Gourock Ropework Company in 1957. Later in 1971, with restoration work already underway, the New Lanark Association received a Civic Trust Award for making an outstanding contribution to the appearance of the local scene by its New Lanark Phase II restoration of Nursery Buildings and the shop to provide nine houses and a museum house – all designed to fit the existing fabric by the architects, Ian G. Lindsay and partners, the structural engineers being T. Harley Haddow and partners and the builders, Alexander Hall and Son Ltd.

Other major awards include the Bass Community Award, presented to the trust in 1980, the Royal Institute of Chartered Surveyors (in association with *The Times*) Conservation Award in 1981, and the Europa Nostra Medal of Honour awarded by the International Federation of Associations for the Protection of Europe's Cultural and Natural Heritage in 1987 for the restoration of the Village Square as the nucleus of the community. The same year New Lanark was selected as a special contribution to European Year of the Environment and a plaque commemorating this was unveiled by Lord James Douglas-Hamilton, a Scottish Office minister, on 2 October. With New Lanark nominated as a UNESCO World Heritage Site, another major award came from Europa Nostra in 1987–8 for the major restoration effort of an important example of Scotland's late 18th- and early 19th-century industrial heritage. Jim Arnold, the dynamic director of the project since its inception under the trust since 1974, was awarded the MBE in 1989.[23]

Both New Lanark and its original creators have, of course, been otherwise publicly recognised. The famous Tassie medallion portrait of David Dale appeared on a five pound banknote of the Royal Bank of Scotland in 1967, but unfortunately this has been superseded and is now a collectors' item. A stamp bearing the image of Robert Owen, one of a series on social reformers, was issued (strangely five years after the bicentenary celebrations) by the Post Office in 1976, while New Lanark itself featured as one of four in an Industrial Archaeology Series (including Ironbridge, the centre-piece of another major restoration project with an industrial theme in Shropshire) in 1989.

The same year, the community was seen by thousands of school students throughout Europe, thanks to a Lanark Grammar School teacher, John Goldie, and several sixth-year pupils who produced a video broadcast by the Olympus Satellite Project to schools in Europe. The project was overseen by the Scottish Council for Educational Technology and both this body and the Lanark Grammar group produced a programme of the high standard expected by professionals on Europe's first dedicated educational satellite channel. Not only was New Lanark seen by a huge audience but the students themselves gained a SCOTVEC qualification in video production. A copy of the programme was sent to the New Harmony High School in Indiana, thus maintaining the links between the two communities, which we saw earlier were established through Owen's association in the mid-1820s. Subsequently, thanks to the enthusiasm of Lorna Davidson, Education Officer at New Lanark, packages of teaching materials and resources have been exchanged between New Lanark and New Harmony. Using these 'Boxloads of Knowledge' – named after the so-called 'Boatload of Knowledge' that carried the Owenites down the Ohio to New Harmony – pupils and students have been able to gain greater knowledge of their own community and its history, as well being able to compare different lifestyles and cultures on either side of the Atlantic.[24]

At the time of writing ambitious plans for future developments are being contemplated with an £8-million package of proposals to turn New Lanark into one of the country's top tourist attractions. In 1990 government-appointed consultants revealed a master plan for the continuing restoration and future development of the village. This package had the aim of increasing the number of visitors from 100,000 per annum to four times that within the next five years and doubling the number of jobs in the village to over 300. Although the continued protection and restoration of the village's historic buildings remained a prime concern, the report dealt mainly with the economic future of New Lanark, both as a tourism centre and developing the name as a trademark for a wide range of goods and crafts. Indeed, the village is seen as an ideal environment for a major expansion of the crafts industry with a special consortium being established to market the products under the new brand name. New Lanark is certainly well known and attracts widespread media attention: it was seen by millions when it featured on the BBC's *Songs of Praise* on 13 October 1991.

In common with most museums and heritage sites these days New Lanark, said the report, needed to look closely at its business potential. The plan, also revealed in 1990, to turn Mill No. 1 into a luxury hotel would need £3 million of government aid to repair the shell of the building in preparation for its internal development as a hotel. On the tourism front the report proposed the creation of self-catering cottages, the building of a Youth Hostel, a new wildlife centre and a visitor welcoming centre (which interestingly is provided in a stunning modern building at New Harmony) to complement the existing facilities in the Institute. Another imaginative concept was the possibility of building a footbridge to link New Lanark with the leisure development proposed across the Clyde at the nearby Pleasance. All this would be likely to generate an increased volume of traffic, for long a problem in the village, and require expanded car parking and a new road leading down The Beeches from Hyndford Road to the existing car park. The whole package of proposals was estimated to cost more than £7.6 million – 'not an unrealistic sum', said the *Lanark Gazette*, 'if central and local government all took a share of the bill'.[25]

The achievements of the last quarter century have been truly remarkable and could never have been contemplated at the outset. New Lanark might well have decayed to such an extent that restoration would have proved inconceivable. As it is the enthusiasm of individuals has been harnessed to public and private enterprise to rescue one of the major international monuments of the classic Industrial Revolution era. To date over £10 million have been spent on the restoration of the mills and village. The work continues and it is likely to take millions more to complete the project. With continuing good fortune and drive New Lanark and its magnificent surroundings will remain for future generations not just a place of historic associations with David Dale's philanthropy and Robert Owen's social experiments, but a vibrant community inspiring both those who are lucky enough to live there and those who visit it in growing numbers each year.

APPENDIX

Table A1: *Production and Labour Costs 1801–21.*

Year	Yarn Output lbs	Average Count (hanks per lb)	Labour Cost per lb (pence)
1801	514,750	24.5	5.5
1802	584,325	24	5.4
1803	510,175	24.4	5.4
1805	736,925	23.4	6.1
1809	1,146,842	18	9.5
1810	1,440,895	18	9.1
1811	1,620,373	18.5	8.9
1812	1,622,070	19.25	7.5
1814	1,385,390	25	4.7
1815	1,451,947	24.5	4
1816	1,339,434	26.5	5.4
1817	1,424,513	25.8	5.2
1818	1,457,096	24.2	4.9
1819	1,465,445	24.8	5.1
1820	1,459,094	27.2	5.3
1821	1,377,580	27	5.2

Sources: Gourock Ropework Company MSS, Owen Correspondence, Manchester, 129.

Table A2a:　*Profits at New Lanark 1810–14, New Lanark Twist Company.*

Year	Profit/Loss £　s d	'Interest' £	Gross Profit £　s d
1811	8,817 16 9	3,000	11,817 16 9
1812	8,000　0 0	3,000	11,000　0 0
1813	49,953 15 6	3,000	52,953 15 6
Totals	66,771 12 3	9,000	75,771 12 3
Capital gain from sale of mills			34,100　0 0
Total gross gain from partnership 1810–14			109,871 12 3

Table A2b:　*Profits at New Lanark 1814–25, Robert Owen & Company.*

Year ending Dec 31	Profit/Loss £　s d	'Interest' £　s d	Gross Profit/Loss £　s d
1814*	−9,831 11 1	3,827　8 5	−6,004　2 8
1815	21,100 16 0	4,548 17 3	25,649 13 3
1816	12,984 12 8	6,500　0 0	19,484 12 8
1817	9,000　0 0	6,500　0 0	15,500　0 0
1818	9,000　0 0	6,500　0 0	15,500　0 0
1819	15,500　0 0	6,500　0 0	22,000　0 0
1820	−2,162 19 5	6,500　0 0	4,337　0 7
1821	−6,666 11 6	6,500　0 0	−166 11 6
1822	13,000　0 0	6,500　0 0	19,500　0 0
1823	22,432　0 0	6,500　0 0	28,932　0 0
1824	15,015　0 0	6,500　0 0	21,515　0 0
Totals	99,371　6 8	66,876　5 8	166,247 12 4
Capital depreciation allowed			20,667 19 0
*Loss made at Stanley in 1814			6,000　0 0
Total gross gain at New Lanark			192,915 11 4

Table A2c: *Profits at New Lanark 1814–25, Robert Owen & Company.*

Year ending 31 Dec	Profit/Loss £	'Interest' £	Gross Profit £ s d
1825	—	6,500	6,500 0 0
1826	−4,000	6,500	2,500 0 0
1827	−13,000	6,500	−6,500 0 0
Totals	−17,000	19,500	2,500 0 0
Fund for insuring debts			4,058 16 0
Total gross gain			6,558 16 0

Table A2d: *General Abstract of Gross Gain.*

	Profit £	'Interest' £		Gross Gain £ s d
1799–1819	60,000	30,000		90,000 0 0
1810–1814				109,871 12 3
1814–1825				192,915 11 4
1825–1828				6,558 16 0
			Total	399,345 19 7

Source: Owen Correspondence, Manchester, OC 2100, J. Wright to R. Owen 10 January 1853.

Table A3:   *Workforce, 1885*

BLOWING ROOM		
Master/Asst. Master	1	
Operatives	9	10
NOS. 1 and 3		
PREPARATORY MILLS		
Master	2	
Operatives	40	42
NOS. 1 and 2 TWIST MILLS		
Masters	3	
Cleaners/Carriers	9	
Doffers/Learners	13	
Half Timers	4	
Winders	43	
Reelers	2	
Spinners	9	
Warpers/Beamers	21	104
NO. 3 MULE SPINNING MILL		
Master	1	
Cleaners/Carriers	4	
Piecers etc	18	
Half Timers	3	26
WATERHOUSE		
Master	1	
Operatives	12	13
MECHANICS' WORKSHOP		
Engineers, Joiners,	13	
Masons etc.		
Others	15	28
TOTAL WORKFORCE		223

Source: Gourock Ropework Company mss.

REFERENCES

CHAPTER ONE

1. For the history of the linen industry see Durie; and on the development of the Scottish cotton industry see Hamilton, chs. V and VI; Campbell, ch. VI; Slaven, ch. 4; Donnachie, ch. 3.

CHAPTER TWO

1. See Reid (Senex), *Glasgow Past and Present*, III, 180, 371; Mitchell, *Old Glasgow Essays*, 41; Chambers (ed.), *Biographical Dictionary of Eminent Scotsmen*; McLaren, *David Dale of New Lanark*, ch 6; *Jone's Directory*, 47.
2. See J. R. Anderson (ed.), *Burgess and Guild Brethren of Glasgow*, 67; Glasgow Chamber of Commerce Papers (1783–4); Hamilton, 167; Mitchell, 41; Reid (Senex), 283; Butt (ed.), 173; Indiana State Library, Robert Dale Owen mss.
3. Reid (Senex), 372; Checkland, *Scottish Banking: A History, 1695-1973*, 146–7; Butt (ed.), 173.
4. *Glasgow Mercury*, Jan. 1783, Oct. 1784; Glasgow Chamber of Commerce Minutes, I, 7; Glasgow Chamber of Commerce Papers (1783–4).
5. Fitton, *The Arkwrights, Spinners of Fortune*, ch. VIII; Hills, *Power in the Industrial Revolution*, 60–71.
6. *Glasgow Mercury*, Oct. 1784; Fitton, 72–3; Reid (Senex), II, 53.
7. *The Correspondence of Sir John Sinclair, I*, 361–2; Fitton, 72–3; Cooke, 'Richard Arkwright and the Scottish Cotton Industry', *Textile History*, vol. 10, 197–202.

8. *The Correspondence of Sir John Sinclair, I,* 360; Baines, *History of the Cotton Manufacture in Great Britain,* 193; Fitton and Wadsworth, *The Strutts and the Arkwrights, 1758–1830,* 87.

9. Brown, *History of Glasgow,* 225; Reid (Senex), 53; Sir J. Sinclair (ed.) *The Old Statistical Account of Scotland,* XV, 46 (hereafter OSA); *The Correspondence of Sir John Sinclair I,* 361; Cooke, 196–201.

10. OSA, XV, 38–48; T. Garnett, *Observations on a Tour Through the Highlands,* II, 232; A.D. Robertson, *Lanark: the Burgh and Councils,* 229, 254, 281; Hills, 234, 236; R. Renwick (ed.), *Extracts from the Records of the Royal Burgh of Glasgow,* IX, 66.

11. OSA, V, 40–1; Chambers (ed.); *Register of Seisins (Lanark),* 1011, 1026; Butt (ed.), 216–17; Gourock mss, Legal Papers.

12. OSA, XV, 40–1; Butt (ed.), 218–20.

13. OSA, XV, 41–2; Butt (ed.), 218–25.

14. OSA, XV, 41–3; Butt (ed.), 225–30; Garnett, 232; Owen, *Life,* 59–60.

15. *The Correspondence of Sir John Sinclair, I,* 361–2; R. Dale Owen, *Threading My Way,* 8–10; Fitton, 74; *Glasgow Mercury,* Nov. 1785; Baines, 193–4; Cooke, 196–201.

16. S. G. E. Lythe and J. Butt, *An Economic History of Scotland, 1100–1939,* 186; Mitchell Library mss, 63; Fitton, 79; Cooke, 196–201.

17. McLaren, ch. 3; *Report of the Select Committee on the State of Children* (1816), 25; Mitchell Library mss, 63, Owen, *Life,* 59.

18. OSA, XX, 177; Mitchell Library mss, 63.

19. *James Finlay and Company Ltd (1750–1950),* 60; Renwick (ed.), VIII, 625; Owen, *Life,* 59; Mitchell, 42; D. Bremner, *The Industries of Scotland,* 279; I. Donnachie, *The Industrial Archaeology of Galloway,* 91–2; Edinburgh University mss, 14298; J. Cleland, *Annals,* II, 373; *The Three Banks Review* (1960), 38–9; Cooke, 'The Early Development of Stanley', *Stanley, Its History and Development,* 11–18.

20. Mitchell Library mss, 63; Glasgow Chamber of Commerce Minutes, I–III.

21. Checkland, 146–7; Reid (Senex), *Old Glasgow and Its Environs,* 119–21.

22. Checkland, 219, 230, 297; *The Three Banks Review* (1960), 36; Reid, *Glasgow Past and Present,* III, 232.

23. Signet mss, 415/19,52; 173/10,14; 455/39; 421/12; Alison, 189; Renwick, VIII, 438, 465, 495, 538, 625; IX, 29, 162: Reid, III, 206; Mitchell, 43; McLaren, ch. 6.

24. Chambers (ed.); Renwick (ed.), IX, 162; G. Eyre–Todd, *History of Glasgow,* III, 318; *Glasgow Courier,* March 1783, Dec. 1791.

CHAPTER THREE

1. OSA, XV, 39; Fitton, 77; W. Davidson, 164; Hamilton, 12; Hills, 234; Robertson, *Lanark,* 229, 254; H. Davidson, x–xi.

2. OSA, XV, 41; S. D. Chapman, *The Cotton Industry in the Industrial Revolution*, 45–6; T. C. Smout, *A History of the Scottish People*, 406–7.
3. OSA, XV, 44; Cullen, 14; Murray, 31; J. Butt and K. Ponting (eds), *Scottish Textile History*, 142; J. Bumstead, *The People's Clearance*, 49.
4. OSA, XV, 44; Bumsted, 76–7; *Scots Magazine*, 1791, 513–14.
5. PP 1816 III, Report from Select Committee on the State of Children Employed in Manufactories, 20; Butt and Ponting (eds), 141, 145; OSA, XV, 42; Fitton and Wadsworth, 97–8; Owen, *Life*, 60.
6. OSA, XV, 41.
7. *Ibid.*, 41–2; Glasgow Chamber of Commerce Papers 1784–5.
8. PP 1816 III, 377.
9. Brown, *History of Glasgow*, III, 230–9.
10. Garnett, II, 236; Sir T. Bernard, *Society for Bettering the Condition and Increasing the Comfort of the Poor*, passim; Heron, II, 16; Raistrick (ed.), *The Hatchett Diary*, 100; PP 1816 III, 20–1.
11. Gourock mss, Visitors Book, 1795–9.
12. Smout, 409; Acts of Parliament, vol. 42, 87.
13. PP 1816 III, 20; Owen, *New View*, 28.
14. *Glasgow Mercury*, 13 Jan. 1795.
15. OSA, XV, 45; Owen, *Life*, 57; *New View*, 27.
16. H. Davidson, 168; Minutes of the Commissioners of Supply for the County of Lanark, 1793; M'Gavin, 51; Aiton, passim.
17. PP 1833 XX, First Report on the Employment of Children in Factories, 96–7; Butt (ed.), 228, 240; Mitchell Library mss. 63; Gourock mss.
18. Owen, *Life*, 57–9; Butt (ed.), 240–1; Baines, 202, 205–7; Hills, 126–7; J. Montgomery, *The Theory and Practice of Cotton Spinning*, 291; OSA, XV, 39.
19. *Ibid.*, 42; Butt (ed.), 234–5, 240–1.
20. Owen, *Life*, 59; Anderson (ed.), 240; Reid (Senex), I, 522; III, 285; J. Malden, *John Henning 1771–1851*, passim; G. Stewart, *Curiosities of Glasgow Citizenship*, 52; J. Butt, *The Industrial Archaeology of Scotland*, 65.
21. Anon. *A Walk from the Town of Lanark*.
22. *Scots Magazine*, Jan. 1806.

CHAPTER FOUR

1. Owen *Life*, viii; Podmore, ch. 1.
2. Butt (ed.), 169; Owen *Life*, ix; Podmore, 45–6; W.H. Chaloner, 'Robert Owen, Peter Drinkwater and the Early Factory System', *Bulletin of John Rylands Library*, 37, 78–102.
3. Butt (ed.), 170; Owen, *Life*, 54–5; Podmore, 48, 55–60.

4. Owen, *Life*, 47–50, 55; Butt (ed.), 171.
5. Owen, *Life*, 53; Gourock Ropework mss, Visitors Book 1795–9.
6. Owen, *Life*, 56–7; Butt (ed.), 171.
7. Anon., *Three Banks Review*, 1960, 38; Butt (ed.), 173; Owen, *Life*, 59; Anderson (ed.), *Burgess and Guild Brethren of Glasgow*, II, 238.
8. Owen *Life*, 72–5.
9. Owen, *A Statement Regarding the New Lanark Establishment*, 4; *Life*, 57, 59.
10. *Ibid.*, 80–1; Podmore, 91; Pollard and Salt (eds), *Robert Owen, Prophet of the Poor*, 153.
11. PP 1833 XX, First Report on the Employment of Children in Factories, 74; Gourock mss, Notebook, 1813–20.
12. Gourock mss, Produce Book, 1803–5; Report Book, 1803–8.
13. *Ibid.*, General Ledger, 1804–8.
14. *Ibid.*, Sales Book, 1814–15; SRO, GD 134/1/147.
15. Gourock mss, Census 1811, 1815; Owen, *Life*, 61; Butt (ed.), 188, 191; Davidson, *History of Lanark*, 166–7.
16. Owen *Life*, 57, 63; Podmore, 82, 84–6, 166–8; R.D. Owen, *Threading My Way*, 70; PP 1816 III, Report from the Select Committee on the State of Children Employed in the Manufactures, 22–3; Aiton, *Mr Owen's Objections to Christianity*, 42–3.
17. Podmore, 87–8, 169; Baines, *Mr Owen's Establishment at New Lanark a Failure*, 7; One Formerly a Teacher at New Lanark, 4–5.
18. *Ibid.*, 5; Taylor, *Visions of Harmony*, 66.
19. Owen, *Life*, 63; R. D. Owen, *Threading My Way*, 15.
20. SRO, Court of Session, UP Innes Mack L 14/9, Lanark Twist Co. vs Edmonstoun, 1810.
21. Gourock mss, General Ledger 1808–12; One Formerly a Teacher at New Lanark, 6–7.
22. R. D. Owen, *Threading My Way*, 115; D. Wordsworth, *Recollections of a Tour in Scotland*, 32–3.
23. J. Schopenhauer, *A Lady Travels*, 87.
24. E. T. Svedenstierna, *Svedenstierna's Tour of Great Britain*, 802–3, xiii, 148–9.
25. Owen, *Life*, 85–6.
26. *Ibid*, 87.
27. *Ibid.*, 87; Butt (ed.), 173–9; A. J. Robertson, 'Robert Owen and the Campbell Debt 1810–22', *Business History*, 11, 23–30.
28. Butt (ed.), 179–82.
29. *Ibid.*, 182–6; Owen, *A Statement*.
30. Owen, *Life*, 88–9.
31. *Ibid.*, xv, 94–6; *Bentham Correspondence*, 361–2; Podmore, 96–7.
32. Owen, *Life*, 90–2; *Glasgow Herald*, 24 Dec. 1813.
33. *Ibid.*, 10 Jan. 1814; Owen, *Life*, 92–3, 97–8.

CHAPTER FIVE

1. On education see Owen, *A Statement*, 4–55, 15–18. His many absences from New Lanark are catalogued in his *Life*.
2. Flinn (ed.), *Svedenstierna's Tour*, 146, with reference to the nearby Wilsontown Ironworks.
3. Owen, *A Statement*, 11; Butt in Butt (ed.), 195–9.
4. Gourock mss, New Lanark Population Statistics 1806–61; Census of Scotland.
5. Gourock mss, Notebook ('Robert Owen's Diary') 1813–22; Owen, *Life*, 80–1.
6. Gourock mss, Notebook 1813–22.
7. *Ibid.*; SRO, Court of Session, UP Innes Mack L 14/9, Lanark Twist Company vs Edmonstoun, 1810; Macnab, 126; Griscom, II, 376.
8. Gourock mss, Legal Papers of the New Lanark Co., Copy of Agreement between Miss Ann Edmonstoun and the New Lanark Co., 1813; Notebook 1813–22.
9. Bentham Corr. Owen to Bentham, 1 Dec. 1819; Gourock mss, Notebook 1813–22.
10. Butt in Butt (ed.), 195–9, 209–10.
11. Baines, *New Lanark*, 8; Co–operative Union, Owen Corr. 2100, Wright to Owen, 10 Jan. 1853; Butt in Butt (ed.), 199–200, 212.
12. Gourock mss, New Lanark Population Statistics; on birth control see A. McLaren, 182–9, 195.
13. Owen, *A Statement*, 12–18; *Glasgow Herald*, 24 Dec. 1813; Signet Library, SP, Lanark Twist Co. vs Miss Ann Edmonstoun, 1809; Griscom, II, 383–4; Davidson, 181–2.
14. Owen, *Address*, in *New View* (Everyman's ed. 1972), 93–119; *Ibid.*, Third Essay, 40.
15. Dale Owen, *Outline*, 28.
16. Owen *Life*, 138–42.
17. Griscom, II, 385–6.
18. PP 1816 IV, 238–42. See also PP 1816 III, 91–2 on Owen's evidence. PP 1819 IX, Report from the SC on the Education of the Poor (1818), 1389, mentions a Sunday school paid for by the New Lanark Co.
19. Dale Owen, *Outline*, 30; Edinburgh University Library, Cash Book of the New Lanark Institution 1816–25. On Miss Whitwell see Donnachie in Butt (ed.), 154 and Taylor, 122. Podmore refers to his visit in his life of Owen, 158–9.
20. Owen, *Life*, 144.
21. For Owen on dancing see *Life*, 141–2; Griscom, II, 378; at New Harmony see *New Harmony Gazette* and C.K. Sluder, 'Music in the Owenite Experiment at New Harmony', Proceedings of the International

Communal Studies Association, 1988, which contains a list of music brought from New Lanark.

22. Macnab, 136–7.
23. PP 1816 III, 17–18. This was later taken up by both M'Gavin and Aiton.
24. J. R. Hume, 'The Industrial Archaeology of New Lanark', in Butt (ed.), 233; Macnab, 132–4.
25. Southey, *Journal*, 259–65.

CHAPTER SIX

1. Owen, *Life*, 3; Taylor, 61.
2. Owen, *Statement*, 4, 10–12, 20–1.
3. Taylor, 64–5.
4. Owen, *New View*, 5–6, 14.
5. Butt in Introduction to Owen's *Life* (reprinted 1971), xxiv.
6. Owen, *New View*, 18–19.
7. *Ibid.*, on improvements at New Lanark, 29–35.
8. *Ibid.*, 42–3.
9. See Owen, *A New View of Society*, 2nd ed., London, 1816 – the first printed for sale. On religion and church-going see many references in Macnab and W. Davidson. See also H. Davidson, 228–9.
10. On Owen's proposals for a national system of education see *New View*, 74–7.
11. Owen in his *Life* lists many such people, see, for example, 103, 211–2.
12. J. T. Ward, 'Owen as Factory Reformer' in Butt (ed.), 99–134.
13. Owen, *Life*, 115–26.
14. Owen, *Observations*, in *New View*, 120–9.
15. Owen, *Address*, in *New View*, 105–6; Dale Owen, *Threading My Way*, 101.
16. PP 1816 III provides many instances of such evidence by mill masters, though others from Scotland seemed to be relatively humane.
17. Owen, *On the Employment of Children in Manufactories* and *To the British Master Manufacturers*, both in *New View*, 130–47.
18. See, for example, PP 1833 XX and 1837–38 XXVIII on Factory Inspection.
19. Owen, *Relief of the Manufacturing Poor*, in *New View*, 156–69.
20. *Political Register*, 2 Aug. 1817.
21. Owen, *Life*, 110–11; Taylor, 75.
22. M. Cole, 126.
23. Owen, *Further Development of the Plan for the Relief of the Poor and the Emancipation of Mankind*, in *New View*, 224–44.
24. Quoted in Taylor, 66.

25. Griscom was on good terms with many English Quakers, including Allen. For his itinerary see *A Year in Europe*, 2 vols, and on his life, *Dictionary of American Biography*, vol. VIII, 7.

26. Hazlitt, *Works*, VI, 66.

27. Harrison, 26–42 on prominent Owenites; Owen, *Address to the Working Classes*, in *New View*, 148–55.

28. Macnab made a thorough survey, and, like Griscom and Southey, placed considerable emphasis on the rigid discipline imposed by Owen.

29. G. Courtauld, *Address to those who may be disposed to remove to the United States of America*, 1820; J. Melish, *Travels in the United States of America*, 1818.

30. See Owen, *Mr Owen's Proposed Arrangement for the Distressed Working Classes . . . in three letters addressed to David Ricardo, MP*, 1819.

31. Owen, *Report to the County of Lanark*, Glasgow, 1821, Appendix, 63. Modern ed. in *New View*, 245–98 does not include Appendix.

32. On Orbiston Community see I. Donnachie, 'Orbiston: A Scottish Owenite Community 1825–28' in Butt (ed.), 135–67.

33. Thorne, II, 609–13; *Ibid.*, V, 18–19; SRO, Melville Castle Muns, GD 51/1/27/9 and 10, Owen to Melville, 8 and 13 Feb. 1820; Owen, *Life*, 225–6, 230.

34. *Hansard*, New Series, V, 1316–25, 26 June 1821.

35. *Proceedings of the First General Meeting*, 17–20, 44.

36. Owen, *Report of the Proceedings . . . in Dublin*, which also contains an interesting account of New Lanark.

37. PP 1823 VI, 90–102 contains the bulk of Owen's evidence.

38. Owen, *Life*, 117–20; Macnab, 115–16.

39. Owen, *Life*, vol. IA, Appendix W, 'Address of the Inhabitants of New Lanark to the London Proprietors. With Reply. 7 May 1818'.

40. 'One Formerly a Teacher', 9–12; SRO, Register of the Presbytery of Lanark, 14 Aug. 1823; M. Browning, 'Owen as an Educator', in Butt (ed.), 52–75.

41. Butt in Butt (ed.), 199–201, 212–14; Co–operative Union, Owen Corr., 2100, Wright to Owen, 10 Jan. 1853.

42. M'Gavin, 51–2; Aiton, 36–40; *Glasgow Chronicle*, 17 Jan. 1824.

43. *Hansard*, New Series, XI, 900, 26 May 1824.

44. See Jeremy on the use of British machinery in the USA; on espionage see J.R. Harris, 'Industrial Espionage in the Eighteenth Century', *Industrial Archaeology Review*, vol. VII, no. 2, 1985, 127–38; Flinn (ed.) *Svedenstierna's Tour*, introduction; Macdonald Diaries, 187.

45. For Maclure see *Dictionary of American Biography*, vol. XII, 135–7.

46. New Harmony Working Men's Institute (NHWMI), Maclure Journals, 22 Nov. 1809, 30 July–1 Aug. 1824.

47. Owen's letter to Rapp quoted in G. Flower, *History of the English Settlement in Edwards County, Illinois*, Chicago, 1882; Taylor, 50–1.

48. On the purchase price of New Harmony see Carmony and Elliott, 165; Taylor, 73–5.

CHAPTER SEVEN

1. Dawson, *Abridged Statistical History of Scotland*, 686.
2. NHWMI, Branigin–Owen Coll., Papers re David Dale Trust; Indiana State Library, Indiana Division mss, Robert Dale Owen Papers.
3. Co–operative Union, Owen Corr., 80, Wright to Owen, 10 Dec. 1825; SRO, Register of Sasines, Lanark, 5 Jan. 1838.
4. *Glasgow Herald*, 10 Mar. 1851.
5. See the generally favourable reports of the Factory Inspectorate for this period listed in the Bibliography.
6. Blake, 106; Morgan in Checkland and Slaven, 313–16.
7. Bremner, 280–1.
8. Census of Scotland; PP 1833 XXI, Second Report on the Employment of Children in Factories, 70; Gourock mss, New Lanark Population Statistics, 1806–61.
9. PP 1834 X, Report from SC on Handloom Weavers, 195, 200, 208, 213.
10. PP 1833 XX, First Report on the Employment of Children in Factories, 18.
11. *Ibid.*, 92–3.
12. *Ibid.*, 96–7.
13. *Ibid.*; PP 1833 XXI, Second Report, 54–5.
14. *Ibid.*, 53; see also First Report, 93.
15. NSA, IV, 22, 27.
16. PP 1851 XXIII, Report of the Inspectors of Factories for 1851, 37; Gourock mss, School Certificate Book, 1852.
17. *Slater's Directory of Scotland*, 1000–1003.
18. PP 1867 XXVI, Statistics Relative to Schools in Scotland; Podmore, 158–9.
19. PP 1843 XXVII, Report of Inspectors of Factories for 1842, 24–5.
20. NSA IV, 20; I. Levitt and T. C. Smout, *The State of the Scottish Working–Class in 1843*, Edinburgh, 1979, 22–53.
21. PP 1833 XX, First Report, 97–8; XXI, Second Report, 54–5.
22. *Ibid.*, 53.
23. NSA IV, 20–22, 23–4.
24. Gourock mss, Extras Wages Book 1855–70.
25. Hume in Butt (ed.), 215–53.
26. *Glasgow Herald*, 10 Mar. 1851. Gourock mss, Account Book 1875–84; Hume, 242–3.
27. Gourock mss, Works Manager's Report Book, 1879–1904.
28. *Ibid.*

29. *Glasgow Herald*, 10 Mar. 1851.
30. Gourock mss, Plan of Works and Village of New Lanark, Sept. 1851 (copy 1881).
31. *Ibid.*, Lanark Spinning Co. Letter Book, 12 Mar. 1881.
32. *Ibid.*, 13, 14 and 25 Apr. 1881; Legal Papers, Guarantee of Sommerville and Co. 1881; SRO, Register of Sasines, Lanark, 17 May 1881.

CHAPTER EIGHT

1. Morgan, in Slaven and Checkland, 313–16; Blake, 106.
2. Gourock mss, Files on Research for 'Gourock' History, letter of J. Howe, 21 Feb. 1955; Blake, 110.
3. *Ibid.*, Works Manager's Report Book, 1879–1904.
4. *Ibid.*, Papers re Hydro–Power on the River Clyde, 1922–4.
5. *Ibid.*, Valuation Papers, 1903–4.
6. *Ibid.*, Corr. re Church Affairs; *Hamilton Advertiser*, 7 Nov. 1914.
7. *Ibid.*, Valuation Papers, 1903–4.
8. *Ibid.*, Valuation of Machinery etc. at New Lanark by Stott and Sons, 1903.
9. *Ibid.*, Works Manager's Report Book, 1879–1904.
10. *Ibid.*, Valuation by James Barr, 1903.
11. *Ibid.*, Excursion of Lanark Spinning Co.s' Employees Handbill, 9 Aug. 1884.
12. T. Reid, *Lanimer Day, Lanark 1570–1913, with Appendix 1921*, Edinburgh, *c.* 1921.
13. Gourock mss, Valuation by James Barr, 1903.
14. *Ibid.*, Rent Roll, 1901.
15. *Ibid.*, New Lanark Medical Report 1903–4; Glen to Lanark Spinning Co., 12 Dec. 1902.
16. *Ibid.*, Lecture Notes of J. Nicol, n.d.; Letter and Notes from Nicol to Dunsmore, 4 Jan. 1955.
17. See, for example, Sargant and Jones, cited in Bibliography.
18. See the various editions of Podmore.
19. Cullen contains good accounts of both New Lanark and Orbiston.
20. Lindsay Institute, Lanark, Scrap Books, 1914–18, 1922.
21. Gourock mss, Lanark Works Yearly Accounts, 1920–4.
22. *Ibid.*, Report by National Institute of Industrial Psychology, May – Dec. 1935.
23. *Ibid.*, Papers re Bedaux System of Labour Measurement and Payment, 1932–3; Nicol's Notes.
24. *Ibid.*, Papers re Hydro–Power, 1922–4.
25. *Ibid.*, Nicol's Lecture Notes.
26. *Ibid.*, Papers re Modernisation of Cotton Industry, 1946–8.
27. *Ibid.*, Production Standards for New Lanark Mills, Sept. 1942.

28. *Ibid.*, Files on Research for 'Gourock' history, Inglis to Dunsmore, 22 Dec. 1955.
29. *Ibid.*, Papers re Modernisation; Robson, 57–62.
30. *Ibid.*, Papers re Cotton Board, 1947–8.
31. *Third Statistical Account of Scotland. The County of Lanark*, 1960, 525; Oakley, 23–4.
32. Gourock mss, Lanark Mills – File, 1950–5, Inglis to HQ, 12 July 1953.
33. *Ibid., The Gourock*, 1954, 17–18.
34. *Ibid.*, New Lanark House Property File, Inglis to Campbell, 13 July 1960.
35. *Hamilton Advertiser*, 7 July 1961.
36. Gourock mss, General File – Lanark, 1963; Papers re Modernisation.
37. *Ibid.*, 26 Mar. 1963.
38. Lanark Lanimer Day Brochure, 1965.

CHAPTER NINE

1. Gourock mss, Files on 'Gourock' history contain much correspondence on New Lanark's future as seen at the time.
2. *Ibid.*, New Lanark House Property, Inglis to Campbell, 21 June, 23 June and 13 July 1960.
3. New Lanark Association (NLA), *New Lanark*.
4. Gourock mss, New Lanark House Property file contains extensive correspondence.
5. *Ibid.*, A. Mitchell to Gourock Ropework Co., 27 Feb. 1963.; *Scotsman*, 24 Dec. 1962.
6. *Ibid.*, Wolfson and Co. to Gourock Ropework Co., 1 Feb. 1963.
7. *Ibid.*, Dunhill to Campbell, 20 June 1963.
8. *Ibid., Daily Mail*, cutting, n.d.
9. *Ibid.*, Files on Research Background, Inglis to Campbell, 20 Nov. 1963.
10. *Ibid.*, Report of Meeting, 21 Nov. 1963.
11. NLA, *New Lanark*.
12. *Ibid.*
13. *Guardian*, 21 Apr. 1966; Gourock mss, Valuation of Company's Property, Report and Capital Valuation of the Land and Buildings at New Lanark Mills, 1967.
14. NLA, *New Lanark*.
15. Hume in Butt (ed.), 248–9; personal memory.
16. Arnold, *Reviving an Historic Village*.
17. *Ibid.*
18. Scottish Office Press Release, 10 Jan. 1983.

19. N. Allen describes the restoration project in a well-illustrated book-let cited in the bibliography; information from New Lanark Conservation Trust (NLCT).
20. *Glasgow Herald*, 3 May 1990.
21. Information from NLCT.
22. *Ibid.*
23. *Ibid.*
24. Information from Lorna Davidson.
25. *Lanark Gazette*, 30 Nov. 1990.

BIBLIOGRAPHY

MANUSCRIPT SOURCES

Co-operative Union Ltd, Manchester
Robert Owen Correspondence.

Edinburgh University Library
Cash Book of the New Lanark Institution, 1816–25.
Letters of Dale and Owen.

Glasgow University Archives
Gourock Ropework Company mss.

Indiana State Library, Indianapolis
Robert Dale Owen Papers.

Library of Congress, Washington D.C.
Department of Prints and Photographs Collection.

Lindsay Institute, Lanark
Miscellaneous Records.
Newspaper Cuttings Books.

Mitchell Library, Glasgow
Burgesses and Guild Brethren of Glasgow.
Dale–Alexander Correspondence, 1787–97.
Patent Records.

Motherwell District Libraries
Hamilton of Dalzell Collection.

National Library of Scotland
Combe Papers.
Dale–Moncrieff Letters.
Liston Papers.
Owen Letters.
Advocates' Manuscripts.

National Libary of Wales
Letters of Robert Owen.

Robert Owen Memorial Museum, Newtown
Robert Owen Collection

Scottish Record Office
Abercromby of Forglen Muniments.
Campbell of Jura Papers.
Court of Session Records.
Melville Castle Muniments.
Register House Plans.

Signet Library
Session Papers.

Strathclyde Regional Archives
Commissioners of Supply for the County of Lanark Minutes.
New Lanark School Books and Records.
Plans, drawing and maps of New Lanark.

University of Southern Indiana, Evansville
Centre for Communal Studies Collection.

Workingmen's Institute and Library, New Harmony, Indiana
New Harmony Papers.
Branigin–Owen Papers.
Robert Owen Papers.
Robert Dale Owen Papers.

NEWSPAPERS AND PERIODICALS

Blackwood's Magazine
Caledonian Mercury

Clydesdale Journal
Clydesdale Journal and *Upper Ward Weekly Advertiser*
The Crisis
Glasgow Chronicle
Glasgow Courier
Glasgow Herald and *Glasgow Herald Weekly*
Glasgow Mercury
Hamilton Advertiser
The Mirror of Literature, Amusement and Instruction
Lanark Gazette
Lanarkshire Examiner and *Upper Ward Advertiser*
Lanarkshire Monthly Advertiser and *Clydesdale Journal*
Lanarkshire Upper Ward Examiner
New Harmony Gazette
Orbiston Register
The Scotsman
Scots Magazine

PARLIAMENTARY PAPERS

1816 III Report from the Select Committee on the State of Children Employed in the Manufactories of the United Kingdom.

1816 IV Reports from the Select Committee on the Education of the Lower Orders of the Metropolis.

1819 IV Digest of Parochial Returns made to the Select Committee on the Education of the Poor. Part III.

1824 V Reports of the Select Committee on Artisans and Machinery.

1833 XX First Report . . . on the Employment of Children in Factories.

1833 XXI Second Report . . . on the Employment of Children in Factories.

1834 X Report from the Select Committee on Handloom Weavers' Petitions.

1834 XIX Supplementary Report . . . on Children.

1835 VII Report from the Select Commitee on Education in England and Wales.

1836 XXIII Report from the Committee on the Municipal Corporations of Scotland. Local Reports, Part II.

1837–8 XXVIII Reports of Inspectors of Factories (and subsequent years).

1839 XLII Reports of the Assistant Commissioners on Handloom Weavers.

1840 X Reports from the Select Committee on the Act for the Regulation of Mills and Factories.

PP 1867 XXVI Statistics Relative to Schools in Scotland. Education Commission (Scotland).

BOOKS

Early Works

Aiton, Revd J., *Mr Owen's Objections to Christianity and a New View of Society, refuted by a plain statement of facts. With a hint to Archibald Hamilton Esq. of Dalziel*, Edinburgh, 1824.

Allen, W., *Reply on Behalf of the London Proprietors to the Address to the Inhabitants of New Lanark*, London, 1819.

Anderson, J. R., *Burgess and Guild Brethren of Glasgow*, Edinburgh, 1935.

Baines, E., *Mr Owen's Establishment at New Lanark, a Failure!*, Leeds, 1838.

History of the Cotton Manufacture in Great Britain, London, 1835

Biographical Dictionary of Eminent Scotsmen, Glasgow, 1875.

Brown, A., *History of Glasgow*, Glasgow, 1797.

Brown, J., *Remarks on the Plans and Publications of Robert Owen Esq. of New Lanark*, Edinburgh, 1817.

Brown, P., *Twelve Months in New Harmony*, Cincinnati, 1827.

Buchanan, C., *A Walk from the Town of Lanark to the Falls of Clyde*, Glasgow, 1816.

Chambers, R. (ed.), *Biographical Dictionary of Eminent Scotsmen*, London, 1874.

Clayton, J., *Robert Owen. Pioneer of Social Reforms*, London, 1908.

Cole, G. D. H., *Robert Owen*, London, 1925.

Constable and Murray's Gazetteer of Scotland, Edinburgh, 1806.

Cullen, A., *Adventures in Socialism: New Lanark Establishment and Orbiston Community*, Glasgow, 1910.

Davidson, H., *Lanark. A Series of Papers*, Edinburgh, 1910.

Davidson, W., *History of Lanark and Guide to the Scenery*, Lanark, 1828.

Dawson, J. H., *Abridged Statistical History of Scotland*, new ed., Edinburgh, 1855.

Fleming, G. A., *A Day at New Lanark by the Editor of the New Moral World*, Birmingham, 1839.

Flower, G., *History of the English Settlement in Edwards County, Illinois, founded in 1817 and 1818 by Morris Birkbeck and George Flower*, Chicago, 1882.

Garnett, T., *Observations on a Tour Thro' the Highlands and part of the Western Islands of Scotland . . . to which are added . . . A Description of the Falls of Clyde etc*, new ed., London, 1811.

Griscom, J., *A Year in Europe. Comprising a Journal of Observations in England, Scotland, etc in 1818 and 1819*, 2 vols, New York, 1823.

Groome, F. H. (ed.), *Ordnance Gazetteer of Scotland*, new ed., c. 1893.

Hebert, W., *A Visit to the Colony of Harmony in Indiana, in the USA recently purchased by Mr Owen*, London, 1825.

Heron, R., *Observations made in a Journey through the Western Counties of Scotland in the Autumn of 1792*, 2 vols, Perth, 1793.

Jones' Directory or Useful Pocket Companion, Glasgow, 1787.

Jones, L., *The Life, Times and Labours of Robert Owen*, London, 1890.

Leopold, R. W., *Robert Dale Owen. A Biography*, London, 1940.

Lewis, S. *A Topographical Dictionary of Scotland*, London, 1846.

Lockwood, G. B., *The New Harmony Movement*, New York, 1905 (reprinted with new introduction by Mark Holloway, 1971).

Macdonald, D., *The Diaries of Donald Macdonald 1824–6* (ed. C.D. Snedeker), Indiana Historical Society, 1942 (reprinted, 1973).

M'Gavin, W., *The Fundamental Priciples of the New Lanark System Exposed*, Glasgow, 1824.

Macnab, H. G., *The New Views of Mr Owen of Lanark Impartially Examined*, London, 1819.

Mitchell, J., *Old Glasgow Essays*, Glasgow, 1905.

'One Formerly a Teacher at New Lanark', *Robert Owen at New Lanark*, Manchester, 1839.

Owen, R., *A Statement Regarding the New Lanark Establishment*, Edinburgh, 1812.

A New View of Society, London, 1813–16.

An Address Delivered to the Inhabitants of New Lanark, London, 1816.

Observations on the Effect of the Manufacturing System, London, 1817.

New View of Society. Tracts relative to this subject; viz a College of Industry ... a Brief Sketch of the Religious Society of People called Shakers. With an Account of the Public Proceedings, London, 1818.

Two Memorials on Behalf of the Working Class, London, 1818.

Mr Owen's Proposed Arrangements for the Distressed Working Classes Shown to be Consistent with Sound Principles of Political Economy, in three Letters to David Ricardo, MP, London, 1819.

Report to the County of Lanark, Glasgow, 1821.

Report of the Proceedings ... in Dublin and an Introductory Statement of his Opinions and Arrangements at New Lanark, Dublin, 1823.

Two Discourses on a New System of Society, Philadelphia, 1825.

Address to the Agriculturists, Mechanics and Manufacturers of Great Britain and Ireland, London, 1827.

Six Lectures on Charity delivered at the Institution of New Lanark, London, 1834.

The Revolution in the Mind and Practice of the Human Race, London, 1849.

Life of Robert Owen by Himself, London, 1857 (reprinted 1971 with introduction by John Butt).

A Supplementary Appendix to the First Volume of the Life of Robert Owen Containing a Series of Reports, Addresses, Memorials etc, vol. 1A, (1803–20), London, 1858.

Owen, R. D., *An Outline of the System of Education at New Lanark,* Glasgow, 1824.

Threading My Way: Twenty-Seven Years of Autobiography, London, 1874.

Podmore, F., *Robert Owen: A Biography,* London, 1906.

Proceedings of the First General Meeting of the British and Foreign Philanthropic Society for the Permanent Relief of the Labouring Classes, London, 1822.

Reid, R. (Senex), *Glasgow Past and Present,* Glasgow, 1884.

Reid, R. (Senex), *Old Glasgow and Its Environs,* Glasgow, 1864.

Sargant, W. L., *Robert Owen and His Social Philosophy,* London, 1860.

Slater's Commercial Directory of Scotland, London, 1860.

Southey, R., *Journal of a Tour in Scotland in 1819,* John Murray, London, 1929.

(Old) *Statistical Account of Scotland.*

(New) *Statistical Account of Scotland.*

Svedenstierna, E. T., *Tour through part of England and Scotland in the years 1802 and 1803,* Stockholm, 1804 (English ed. with introduction by M. W. Flinn, Newton Abbott, 1973).

Wordsworth, D., *Recollections of a Tour Made in Scotland A.D. 1803*, 3rd ed., Edinburgh, 1894.

Modern Works

Aldrich, R. and Gordon, P., *Dictionary of British Educationists*, London, 1989.

Allan, J. M., *New Lanark Village*, Glasgow (Jordanhill College), 1979.

Allen, N., *David Dale, Robert Owen and the Story of New Lanark*, Edinburgh, 1986.

Arndt, K. J. R. (ed.), *Harmony on the Wabash in Transition 1824–1826. A Documentary History*, Worcester, Mass., 1982.

Bestor, A. E. (ed.), *Education and Reform at New Harmony. Correspondence of William Maclure and Marie Duclos Fretageot 1820–1833*, Indiana Historical Society, Indianapolis, 1948.

Blake, G., *'The Gourock'. The Gourock Ropework Company Ltd*, Glasgow, 1963.

Board of Trade Working Party Reports, *Cotton*, HMSO, 1946.

Brogan, C., *James Finlay and Company Ltd. Manufacturers and East India Merchants 1750–1950*, Glasgow, 1951.

Bumsted, J., *The People's Clearance*, Edinburgh, 1982.

Butt, J., *The Industrial Archaeology of Scotland*, Newton Abbot, 1967.

Butt, J. (ed.), *Robert Owen: Prince of Cotton Spinners*, Newton Abbot, 1971.

Campbell, R. H., *Scotland since 1707. The Rise of an Industrial Society*, Oxford, 1975.

Carnegie United Kingdom Trust, *New Lanark. A scheme for its interpretation to the public*, Dunfermline, 1981.

Chapman, S. D., *The Early Factory Masters*, Newton Abbot, 1967.

The Cotton Industry in the Industrial Revolution, 2nd ed. London, 1987.

Checkland, S. G., *Scottish Banking: A History, 1695–1973*, Glasgow, 1975.

Claeys, G., *Machinery, Money and the Millenium. From Moral Economy to Socialism, 1815–1860*, London, 1987.

Cole, G. D. H., *The Life of Robert Owen*, with new introduction by Margaret Cole, London, 1965.

Cole, Margaret, *Robert Owen of New Lanark*, London, 1953.

Conway, S. (ed.), *The Correspondence of Jeremy Bentham*, vols 8 and 9, Oxford, 1988–9.

Cooke, A. J., *Stanley. Its History and Development*, Dundee, 1977.

Donnachie, I., *The Industrial Archaeology of Galloway*, Newton Abbott, 1971.

Doskey, J. S. (ed.), *The European Journals of William Maclure*, American Philosophical Society, Philadelphia, 1988.

Durie, A. J., *The Scottish Linen Industry in the Eighteenth Century*, Edinburgh, 1979.

Edwards, M. M., *The Growth of the British Cotton Trade 1780–1815*, Manchester, 1967.

English, W., *The Textile Industry*, London, 1969.

Farnie, D. A., *The English Cotton Industry and the World Market 1815–1896*, Oxford, 1979.

Fitton, R. S., *The Arkwrights. Spinners of Fortune*, Manchester, 1989.

Fitton, R. S. and Wadsworth, A. P., *The Strutts and the Arkwrights*, Manchester, 1958.

French, G. F., *Life and Times of Samuel Crompton* (1859) with an introduction by Stanley D. Chapman, Adams & Dart, 1970.

Hamilton, H., *An Economic History of Scotland in the Eighteenth Century*, Oxford, 1963.

Hardy, D. and Davidson, L. (eds), *Utopian Thought and Communal Experience*, Middlesex Polytechnic, 1989.

Harrison, J. F. C., *Robert Owen and the Owenites in Britain and America*, London, 1969.

Henderson, W. O., *The Lancashire Cotton Famine 1861–1865*, Manchester, 2nd ed. 1969.

Hills R. L., *Power in the Industrial Revolution*, Manchester, 1970.

Howe, A., *The Cotton Masters 1830–1860*, Oxford, 1984.

Hoppit, J., *Risk and Failure in English Business 1700–1800*, Cambridge, 1987.

Indiana Historical Commission, *New Harmony As Seen by Participants and Travellers*, Philadelphia, 1975.

James, Patricia, *Population Malthus. His Life and Times*, London, 1979.

Jeremy, D. J., *Transatlantic Industrial Revolution: The Diffusion of Textile Technologies Between Britain and America, 1790s–1830s*, Oxford, 1981.

Jowitt, J. A. and McIvor, A. J. (eds), *Employers and Labour in the English Textile Industries, 1850–1939*, London, 1988.

Levitt, I. and Smout, T. C., *The State of the Scottish Working Class in 1843*, Edinburgh, 1979.

MacLaren, D., *David Dale. A Bright Luminary to Scotland*, Glasgow, 1983.

McLaren, Angus, *A History of Contraception*, Oxford, 1990.

Michaelis–Jena, R. and Merson, W. (eds), *A Lady Travels. Journeys in England and Scotland from the Diaries of Johanna Schopenhaur*, London, 1988.

Morton, A. L., *The Life and Ideas of Robert Owen*, London, 1962.

Murray, N., *The Scottish Handloom Weavers 1790–1850: A Social History*, Edinburgh, 1978.

New, Chester, W., *The Life of Henry Brougham to 1830*, Oxford, 1961.

New Lanark Association, *New Lanark*, Edinburgh, *c*. 1967.

Oakley, C. A. (ed.), *Scottish Industry*, Scottish Council (Development and Industry), 1953.

Pankhurst, R. K. P., *William Thompson (1775–1833). Britain's Pioneer Socialist, Feminist and Co–operator*, London, 1954.

Pollard, S. and Salt, J. (eds), *Robert Owen. Prophet of the Poor*, London, 1971.

Pollock, J., *Wilberforce*, London, 1977.

Raistrick, A. (ed.), *The Hatchett Diary. A tour through the counties of England and Scotland in 1796 visiting their mines and manufactories*, Truro, 1967.

Renwick, R. (ed.), *Extracts from the Records of the Burgh of Glasgow*, vol. IX, 1796–1808, Glasgow, 1914.

Robert Owen Bicentennial Conference, *Robert Owen's American Legacy*, Indiana Historical Society, Indianapolis, 1972.

Robertson, A. D., *Lanark: the Burgh and its Councils*, Lanark Town Council, 1974.

Robson, R., *The Cotton Industry in Britain*, London, 1957.

Roger, T., *A Short History of New Lanark*, Lanark, *c*. 1960.

Scottish Development Department, *New Deal for New Lanark*, Scottish Information Office, 1983.

Silver, H. (ed.), *Robert Owen On Education*, Cambridge, 1969.

Slaven, A., *The Development of the West of Scotland 1750–1960*, London, 1975.

Slaven, A. and Checkland, S.G. (eds), *Dictionary of Scottish Business Biography 1860–1960. Vol. I, The Staple Industries*, Aberdeen, 1986.

Smout, T. C., *A History of the Scottish People 1560–1830*, London, 1969.

Taylor, Anne, *Visions of Harmony. A Study of Nineteenth–Century Millenarianism*, Oxford, 1987.

Thorne, R. G. (ed.), *The History of Parliament. The House of*

Commons 1790–1820. Vol. II, Constituencies; and Vol. V, Members Q–Y, London, 1986.

Ward, J. T., *The Factory Movement 1830–1855*, London, 1962.

Ziegler, P., *Addington. A Life of Henry Addington, First Viscount Sidmouth*, London, 1985.

ARTICLES

Arnold, J., 'Reviving an Historic Village', *Heritage Outlook*, vol. 1, no 3, 1981.

Butt, J., Donnachie, I. and Hume, J. R., 'Robert Owen of New Lanark (1771–1858)', *Industrial Archaeology*, vol. 8., 1971, 186–93.

Carmony, D. F. and Elliott, Josephine M., 'New Harmony, Indiana: Robert Owen's Seedbed for Utopia', *Indiana Magazine of History*, vol. LXXVI, 1980, 161–261.

Chaloner, W. H., 'Robert Owen, Peter Drinkwater and the Early Factory System in Manchester, 1788–1800', *Bulletin of the John Rylands Library*, 37, 1954, 78–102.

Cooke, A. J., 'Richard Arkwright and the Scottish Cotton Industry', *Textile History*, vol. 10, 1979, pp 196–202.

Donnachie, I., 'Restoring New Lanark', *Glasgow Illustrated*, June 1967.

Dunhill, N., 'An Experiment in Preservation', *Ontario Housing*, 1964.

Hume, J. R., 'The Water Supply of New Lanark', *Industrial Archaeology*, vol. 5, 1968, 384–7.

Pitzer, D. E. and Elliott, Josephine M., 'New Harmony's First Utopians', *Indiana Magazine of History*, vol. LXXV, 1979, 224–300.

Robertson, A. J., 'Robert Owen and the Campbell Debt 1810–22', *Business History*, 11, 1969, 23–30.

INDEX

239